Born in Kansas but Made in Africa

An American man's recollections of 50 years in Africa

By Mark G. Wentling

Table of Contents

Dedication

Dedicated to all the unsung heroes in Africa

More About the Author

Mark Gregory Wentling was born on July 3, 1945, in Wesley Hospital in Wichita, Kansas, and grew up in the nearby rural communities of Eldorado and Udall. He has a wealth of international development experience, working mostly in Africa for the Peace Corps and the United States Agency for International Development (USAID). He began his career at the age of 21 as a Peace Corps Volunteer in Honduras in the 1967-69 period and, in September 1970, he continued working with the Peace Corps in Togo, where he served three years as a volunteer in village construction and agricultural education programs in the Agu District. In 1973, he served as a volunteer leader for these programs. In 1974, he became Associate Peace Corps Director responsible for rural development programs in Togo. In February 1975, he was assigned to Gabon as Peace Corps Director, and in 1976 he started the same position in Niger.

In 1977, Mr. Wentling accepted an appointment as a Foreign Service Officer with USAID.

During the 1977-1981 period, he managed one of the most complex integrated rural development projects in West Africa, the Niamey Department Project. For his work in Niger, he received a Superior

Honor Award from USAID and an award from the Government of Niger.

Following his work in Niger, Mr. Wentling managed regional projects in the areas of agricultural research, rural credit, and private sector development from USAID's headquarters in Washington.

In 1983, he was assigned to Guinea and served as USAID Representative until June 1987. For his work in Guinea with private investment promotion, agribusiness, local farmers, and food aid, Mr. Wentling received recognition from USAID, the State Department, and the Government of Guinea.

From June 1987 to July 1991, Mr. Wentling was USAID's Representative to Togo and Benin. For sustained outstanding work during this four-year period with population, child survival, export promotion and agricultural policy reform activities, he was awarded Meritorious Awards by USAID and the U.S. Ambassador. In April 1989, in recognition of performance through March 31, 1988, Mr. Wentling received the honor of being promoted to the U.S. Senior Foreign Service.

In August 1992, Mr. Wentling was named the first USAID Director to Angola, but insecurity in that country prevented him from pursuing this assignment, and he was assigned in November 1992 to Washington as the Director of the Southern Africa Drought Emergency and African Disaster Assistance Task force, including the Somalia working group. In March 1993, Mr. Wentling was assigned as the Director of USAID/Somalia. Mr. Wentling left this position in April 1994 to serve as Director of USAID/Tanzania until September 1996. Following his retirement as a USAID Senior Foreign Service Officer on September 30, 1996,

Mr. Wentling was hired as USAID's Senior Advisor for the Great Lakes Region of Africa until November 1997. Beginning in late 1997, Mr. Wentling worked as a specialist consultant for USAID missions in Zambia, Guinea, Senegal, and Malawi.

In the 1999 – 2006 period, Mr. Wentling worked for CARE in Niger and Mozambique and for World Vision in a regional position that covered all of Africa. From August 2006 to December 2010, he worked for USAID's West Africa Mission as its Country Program Manager for Niger and Burkina Faso. He was Plan International's Country Director in Burkina Faso from July 2011 to June 2015. From June 2015 to October 2016, he worked as a Senior Consultant for Breedlove Foods in Lubbock, Texas. In January 2016, he taught for one semester an honors course in

International Development at Texas Tech University. (The syllabus is in the annexes.)

He worked for USAID/West Africa in Accra, Ghana, from October 2016 to May 2017 as a Senior Agriculture Advisor and held a similar six-month position with USAID/Mali in Bamako from July until the end of December 2017. He was the interim Presidential Malaria Initiative advisor for USAID/Angola in Luanda from June to November 2018. He was a consultant for a month in early 2019 to assist USAID/West Africa, Accra, Ghana to revise in Ouagadougou, Burkina Faso, a cooperative agreement with the West Africa Monetary Union (UMEOA). Also, in 2019/20, he worked remotely for USAID/Guinea, designing a five-year health systems project and consulted with USAID/Côte d'Ivoire on countering violent extremism.

In July 2022, he went to Cambodia for six months to design for USAID, a five-year environmental project, and he went to Nepal for five months in 2023 to assist the USAID Mission's sustainable Economic Growth Office.

Mr. Wentling holds a bachelor's degree from Wichita State University (WSU) and a master's degree in international agricultural development from Cornell University. WSU Alumni

Association awarded him its annual achievement award for 2014, and he was inducted into WSU's Liberal Arts College's Hall of Fame on February 4, 2025. He was also honored to be among a select group of senior civilian and military officials to complete an intensive ten-month master's course of study on national security and international strategic issues at the prestigious National War College (NWC) in June 1992. While at NWC, he received an annual award for his paper, "Redesigning U.S. Assistance to Africa in the Post-Cold War Era."

He speaks six languages. He is the author of numerous professional articles and thirteen novels. He was awarded the Maria Thomas Award by the Peace Corps Writer's Association. He resides in Lubbock, Texas, with his Ethiopian spouse. He has seven adult children and six grandchildren residing in the US.

He considers this biographical sketch to be part of his last testament. He has requested that he be buried next to his mother's remains in the Belle Vista Cemetery in El Dorado, Kansas. He has also requested that the inscription on his gravestone include the following: "Here Lies the White Baobab, Son of Georgia, Husband of Almaz, Born in Kansas but Made in Africa."

Map of Africa

PREFACE

The following random vignettes are snapshots of a lifetime in Africa. These brief segments should convey a good idea of my experiences in Africa since 1970. I tried to wean myself off Africa by taking a couple of work stints in Asia, but there is no getting away from Africa, and the tight grip this vast and diverse continent continues to have on me.

Doing nothing but Africa for a half-century is a burden and a joy with which I must deal. Maybe sharing with you this assortment of bullets of what I did or overheard in Africa is one way of doing this. And maybe there are some lessons learned that need to be shared and some pearls of wisdom that can be gleaned from these brief remembrances.

I try to note what I can remember, but I refrain from naming people and limit the expression of my opinions. I do hope that some of what I write sparks the reader's interest and encourages deeper research into some of the many topics I touch upon.

This is not all that happened to me while I was in Africa. There are a few more musings, experiences, and views I could cite, but the highlights I have jotted down are probably more than you want to read. But I am hoping that what I have written is enjoyable, educational, and easy to read. And the biographical information about myself is not too boring.

I did not learn much more after my first decade in Africa. However, I realized increasingly with each passing year that I had much more to learn about Africa. Now, I feel I know less about Africa than I did in the early 1970s, especially as the Africa of today is not in many respects the same as the Africa I previously knew.

I offer the following true-life experiences for those who care about Africa and its future. I hope much of what I write is relevant and contributes to expanding knowledge about Africans and their continent. At the very least, I hope these snippets will fill some knowledge gaps and motivate the reader to dig deeper into a given subject. I cannot help but wonder about what Africa will be like after the passage of another fifty years.

Although I have been constantly searching for decades for the answers to Africa's development predicament, I have not found them. I do know that these answers must be provided and guided by genuine African leaders. The question I often ask myself is: "Where are those Renaissance leaders who have the will and foresight to trace intelligently and unselfishly a path to Africa's progressive betterment?"

For me, these leaders must have the power they need to make changes in their society while putting the best interests of their fellow citizens before their own. After a half-century, I am still waiting for such leaders to appear on national scenes to advance the development of their respective African countries and regions.

I mourn that advanced age and poor health will prevent me from going to Africa again. If I am able to make the trip, it will have to be to a city where there is good healthcare and top-notch security. In this, I find myself like many Africans who seek peace and stability in their societies. These fundamental conditions serve as prerequisites for developmental progress.

I am amazed by my long African saga. I am stunned by the fact that I was able to visit all fifty-four African countries. One thing led to another, and it was hard to know in advance what the next thing would be. Before I knew it, a half-century of living, eating, and dreaming about Africa had passed.

Sadly, I consider what I have written in the following to be my final testament on Africa.

Part I: The First Decade (1970 - 1980)

Togo - Gabon - Niger

Togo

1. Thanks to the Peace Corps, I was given the opportunity to go to Africa. I trained in 1970 as a Peace Corps Volunteer (PCV) for Togo in the US Virgin Islands. The first part of the three-month training program was on St. Thomas Island, and the last few weeks were on St. Croix Island.

A jovial, average middle-aged Togolese man, Clément Hihétah, headed the program on St. Croix Island. This part of the training was designed to give me and my fellow trainees an opportunity to associate with and learn about Togo from a genuine Togolese. An important segment of this training consisted of drinking beer with this man and listening to him expound on Togo. It also gave us an opportunity to practice our French and to become accustomed to the Togolese French accent.

It also involved an important Q&A session. After a few sessions, one of my fellow trainees asked, "Tell us about the Togolese women?"

Without hesitation and with some hearty laughter, our Togolese trainer said, "In the whole world, woman is woman."

(I did not know then that this Togolese man would become a close personal friend and that he would play a decisive role in determining my PCV posting in Togo.)

2. I arrived in Togo with a handful of my fellow Peace Corps trainees by taking a PanAm flight from New York to Dakar, Senegal, and on to the Lomé Airport. We made a brief nocturnal stop at the Dakar airport to allow ground workers to paste a large decal over the Pan American letters, indicating that this was henceforth an Air Afrique flight to Lomé. (Later, we affectionately baptized the popular Air Afrique airline with the epithet Air Peut-Être—"maybe"—because its scheduled flights were frequently cancelled or delayed. This multi-African-country airline ceased operations in early 2002.)

3. When I first arrived in Togo in September 1970, there was an attractive poster pinned on the wall of the warehouse-type building used for processing passengers at the Lomé international airport. This poster proclaimed in French, "You can't know Africa

without knowing Togo" (Vous ne pouvez pas connaître l'Afrique sans connaître le Togo.)

I have often thought about these words and how they proved, for me, to be mostly true. However, I did not plan to be in Africa for so long, but one thing led to another, and before I knew it, my entire adult life had passed on the continent.

4. In Lomé, Togo, in 1970, I stayed in the Peace Corps hostel for a month before being assigned upcountry to my PCV village. I walked along the seacoast, which bordered southern Lomé, and admired the old German wharf that had been abandoned for decades. I was intrigued by the Togolese men fishing off the dilapidated wharf.

There were signs posted declaring the wharf to be dangerous and warning that no one should dare go out on it. Yet it was cluttered with local fishermen, especially at night, because the darkness offered the best time to fish. But a pitch-black night was also when going out on the wharf was the most dangerous. I heard stories of local men who had fallen to their deaths through the gaps in the old boards covering a wharf that was originally built in 1905 when all of Togo was a model German colony.

The old wharf was so scary that I enlisted the support of another PCV, Walter Lehle, who was staying in the hostel with me. Against all advice, we befriended a local fisherman and ventured onto the wharf at night with him. He showed us how to navigate the rough and irregular surface of the wharf and how to fish in the sea waters, which flowed eastward fifty feet below the wharf.

We came prepared with the items he had told me the day before to bring. These included chunks of fish meat bait, fishing line, old metal washers and bolts, and a small empty can of condensed milk filled with small pebbles. He showed us how to bait our hooks and throw our fishing lines into the water on the east side of the wharf.

He also showed us how to add weight to our lines with washers and wheel nuts. He then backed up and wrapped our lines around our small cans after inserting several more pebbles in them. After tying our lines tightly around a rusty rail in the middle of the wharf, I asked him, "What should we do now?"

He replied, "Nothing. Lay down and study the stars. But when your can rattles, get up and be ready to pull in your catch."

He smiled as he said that. I stared at the wide gap between his two front teeth. He noticed my stare and exclaimed, "Aren't I beautiful?"

I learned later that a wide gap between your two upper front teeth is a sign of beauty in local culture.

(We did catch a big red snapper that night and took it to a local café—Café Tabac—to cook and make us a sumptuous meal.)

5. During my first week in Lomé, Togo, I met an older PCV, Phil DeBarros who worked in a teaching position at an all-girls' Catholic secondary school. I was honored to spend time with him, as he had already been a PCV in Togo for five years. He invited me for a meal at Café Nasser, which was located near Lomé's Grand Marché.

I am still in touch with this amazing man. He married a Togolese woman and went on to become a university professor. He has made many trips to northern Togo to study the ancient iron-making furnaces in the area of Bassar, Togo. He is one of two former Togo PCVs I remain in contact with who make regular trips to Togo.

6. When I first arrived in Africa in 1970, the most popular music played was that of the colossus of Congolese rhumba music, Franco and his OK Jazz Band, the Jamaican reggae singer Bob Marley, and the Black American singer James Brown. These musicians competed with local highlife music and the home-grown Togolese singer, Bella Bellow.

In the early 1970s, there were weekly open-air dances in front of one of Lomé's major hotels, and the Melo Togo brass orchestra held forth with its music. I recall dancing to it—two steps to the right and two steps to the left. Once, I was delighted by a singing performance by Bella Bellow herself.

7. I was delighted to have my clothes tailor-made for the first time in my life. Soon after my arrival in my PCV village in September 1970, I was advised to buy khaki cloth material in the local open market and go to one of the many tailors to be measured and have my clothes made by hand. My first purchase was knee-length shorts that I needed for my work.

I was also delighted to engage a local carpenter to build my home desk and other furniture.

8. While residing in my Togo PCV village (1970–73), I tried to adopt the local diet and eat everything at least once. I ate, at least once, the meat of bats, rats, mice, snakes, grubs, and the cooked,

hairy meat of a warthog. I also sampled termites and enjoyed eating the seasonal large land snails. I drank whatever alcoholic or fermented drink was served to me.

9. I laughed when the leader of a fierce group from the local hunters' association said, "We adorn ourselves with the same protective amulets that our ancestors did when hunting elephants, but now we're reduced to hunting mice."

10. I wanted to help construct a primary school in my PCV village, but I needed laborers to do so. There were groups of young men sitting much of the time under the shade of a big tree in the center of the village. I asked them if they could help with the building of the school. The response I got back was loud and clear: "We've been to school, so we can't work."

I later learned that local culture dictated that if you had been to school, you should not get your hands dirty by doing menial labor. A person with any education or money should not work. This explained why most of the common laborers at my school construction sites were women.

I also noted that a wealthy man could allow one fingernail on his left hand to grow exceptionally long to indicate that he does not work with his hands.

11. In those days, the big goal was to receive a primary school diploma and go to the capital city, Lomé, to find a paying job that would allow you to send money back to your family in the village. Nowadays, you can have a master's degree from Togo's top university and still not find a job that pays a decent wage.

12. There were other men in the village who had earned high status by going to good schools, even up to the university level. One such man in my PCV village had outclassed everyone by graduating in the 1950s from the special Ponty School for elite students from Francophone Africa, which the French colonists operated on Gorée Island, Senegal.

Usually, the most respected people in a village—besides the chief and his council of elders—were teachers and military veterans of foreign wars. The status of the latter was elevated because they received a pension from a foreign government.

13. In my early years in Togo, there was a high level of euphoria in the village. After all, the country had been independent for ten years, and full development seemed just around the corner. Many believed that the day was near when Togo could end its dependence on external funding.

Furthermore, the two small countries of Benin and Togo had announced at the time of their independence in 1960 that they would collaborate closely—even establishing a joint university, since neither country could afford one on its own. Sadly, disagreements between the heads of the two governments killed this good idea. A united Africa and regionalization remained a dream.

14. There were only two old men remaining in my PCV village in Togo who understood the language of the talking drum (atupani). I knew that when they died, much knowledge of the old ways would die with them.

15. In 1971, my PCV village chief counseled me to get a new wife every five years. He sincerely believed that getting a young wife every five years was necessary to keep a man young.

The thing that prompted him to say this was that when I entered his compound, I congratulated him on having such a beautiful daughter. He replied by saying, "She's not my daughter... she's my new wife."

16. This same chief had numerous wives sitting around his compound with lots of children playing nearby. I asked him, "How many children do you have?"

He replied, "Ten."

I counted the kids in the compound, and there were clearly more than ten. He noticed me counting and said, "So many children die in their early years that we don't start counting them until they have attained around five years of age."

17. When I was a PCV in Togo in 1971, I built a model elevated bamboo chicken house. It was designed so that everything could be managed from the outside: the chickens fed and drank from bamboo troughs by poking their heads through the slats, hens laid eggs in side compartments accessible from outside, and the manure fell through the floor gaps and could be collected from the ground a meter below.

People came by to admire the structure, but no one replicated it. It simply took too much time and money.

My real challenge, however, was getting the feed right. The hens weren't laying because the ration lacked protein. A local woman showed me how to trap protein-rich termites by stuffing large clay pots with decaying wood. Another taught me how to catch flying termites during their swarms.

On swarm nights, I would place a kerosene lamp on a stone in the middle of a water-filled wash tub. The termites, drawn to the light, would fall into the water and be scooped up by the handful. (The villagers were baffled—these highly nutritious insects were normally eaten by people, not fed to chickens.)

Still, the feed was incomplete. I needed calcium to strengthen the eggshells. This problem was solved by hiring women to collect mussel shells from local streams. After crushing them, I mixed them into the ration.

The last step was grinding it all. The operator of the local white maize mill agreed to help with a small payment on one condition: I had to come after dark when his usual customers were gone. He'd then clean the blades to prevent any off-taste in the maize flour.

Finally, I had the perfect feed. But as I lay awake that night, I realized just how much effort I had spent on these chickens. Certainly, no Togolese villager would go to such lengths to keep chickens alive and productive.

The next morning, I opened the coop and let them go. The chickens eagerly scratched the earth, finally free of their bamboo prison. An elderly Togolese man watched them and smiled.

"That is how God intended it to be," he said.

18. My Togolese village is named Agu-Nyogbo. I decided in 1971 to legally marry my local village girlfriend. The first step was to

ask her very traditional African father for her hand in marriage. He accepted and showed me a large trunk and said, "First, you must fill this trunk with a collection of real Dutch wax cloth. You also must also give a golden necklace and pay for a feast to be given to the village. Our family will give your bride an ancestral bracelet made with antique 'dzonu' beads."

I gulped and said, "It'll take me some time to do all this."

He replied, "That's all right. You can live together until you have satisfied all these traditional requirements. All we got is time."

19. It took me a full year to fulfill all the traditional marriage requirements. By 1972, we were finally ready to visit the local administrative official and complete our legal marriage certificate. Before we did, my soon-to-be legally married wife insisted on changing her birthdate to make herself appear two years older. The official looked puzzled and asked, "Why do that? Age is just a number, and we all get old fast enough."

20. That same year, we were preparing for my first trip back to the U.S. since my Peace Corps assignment began. Word of the trip reached a well-known village fetisher, who summoned me and made a curious demand: she wanted a small pebble and a vial of water from a U.S. river.

I found the request strange but didn't dare question it.

Since I was traveling to Washington, D.C., I picked up a small rock along the Potomac River and filled a tiny glass vial with its water. When I returned to Agu-Nyogbo and presented her with the items, she was visibly elated.

A bystander leaned over and whispered, "You have just enlarged her powers."

21. I traveled to the U.S. with my new Togolese village bride. Before our departure, we had to visit the ancestors' house to offer libations and ask for their blessing.

I was told that some of the ancestors' flesh was still stored in this house and that in earlier days, elders would sometimes take bites of the body before burial.

My bride remained outside the small earthen hut—entry was forbidden to menstruating women.

22. My Togolese wife was sworn in as a U.S. citizen in 1972 in Washington, D.C. At the conclusion of the ceremony, Judge Sirica addressed the new citizens.

"You are no longer Irish, Italian, German, Togolese, etc. You are all Americans," he declared.

As he spoke, he looked directly at my wife, a new American who had been in the country for less than six weeks.

Maybe this isn't the place to say it, but I will: marrying into an African family is one of the greatest teachers of local culture. It also comes with many hidden responsibilities.

23. When we returned to Togo six weeks later, my wife carried a U.S. passport. The immigration official at the border was baffled—he couldn't comprehend how she had left as a Togolese citizen and returned as an American.

Fortunately, the U.S. Ambassador, Dwight Dickerson, happened to be there and ensured this newly minted American citizen had no trouble re-entering the country where she was born and raised.

Even the Peace Corps seemed confused, insisting she now had to be a PCV. With her living allowance and my double allowance for a staff job, we were—quite unexpectedly—the wealthiest I had ever been.

There were many highlights from that first trip together to the U.S., but not all were joyful. I quickly discovered that a Black-and-white couple wasn't welcomed by everyone. During a cross-country bus ride, the driver told us to sit in the back.

Perhaps the most memorable moment came when my wife returned from the store carrying a sack of groceries balanced on her head, a sight perfectly normal in Togo but astonishing in a small town in the American Midwest.

24. No West African travels without packing a plastic bag filled with cassava (manioc) flour—gari. During all my years in Togo (1970–75 and 1987–91), I made sure to carry a bag of this flour to snack on during trips. It became as essential to my travel routine as a passport.

25. I always kept a copy of René Dumont's seminal book, False Start in Africa (originally published in 1962 in French as L'Afrique Noire est Mal Partie). His central thesis was that many African countries got off to a poor start in the post-colonial era under radical national leadership.

That book reminded me of one man from my PCV village who had belonged to a political party that advocated for Togo's independence to be granted in stages. His house was eventually torn apart by rival groups demanding immediate independence.

I thought about this many times over the years, and I concluded that some African countries should not have been granted independence until after they were able to ensure they had the competency to run a country. In particular, I thought of the DRC (larger than Western Europe), which had only one college graduate when it was granted independence by Belgium in 1960.

26. Of course, Togo is no model because a father and son have occupied the presidency since 1963. (Maybe the presidency is like a traditional village chief who is named for life.) Yet, Togo's family presidential dynasty (the longest in Africa) lays many of its problems at the doorstep of the French colonialists, who granted Togo independence in 1960. After more than 60 years, is it not time to stop blaming the colonialists?

I know that after more than 50 years, I am still waiting for competent and honest national leadership that puts the best interests of the people first. For me, such leaders will not have any blood on their hands or fortunes stashed away in offshore banks.

I hope not to be like a trusted Togolese friend who told me as he waited for their long-serving president to die. He would say in a whisper, "We're waiting."

It was clear to me that he was waiting for their president to die. After thirty-eight years in power, he did die, but one of his many sons replaced him and continued in power. I asked my Togolese friend for his updated comment on the current state of the political affairs of his country, and he said simply, with much sadness in his voice, "Lost cause."

He had no choice after many years of waiting for change and thus, he was resigned to living with a benevolent (hopefully) dictator and putting aside all hopes for the kind of freedom and social justice offered by a fairly elected representative government. There was not a word for 'democracy' in his local language, but there was a word for 'justice." He wanted justice for himself and all the people in his country.

27. In 1972, I hired a group of Togolese women to break large rocks into hard, jagged gravel that could be used to make concrete for the building of their local three-classroom primary school. I paid an agreed-upon amount for each washtub they filled with broken rocks. I provided them with heavy hammers and protective glasses, but they had to bring their own washtubs and collect their own rocks. Without the hard and good work of local women, none of my construction projects would have been possible.

28. The prevailing attitude among young men with even a basic primary school education—to avoid menial labor—was underscored for me one day as I painted my modest house in the

village. Many locals believed that because I was white, I must be wealthy. Therefore, I should hire a Togolese worker to do the job.

To them, my few possessions were enough to place me among the village's elite.

That belief was reinforced during a walk through the village when someone asked, "Where is your motorbike?"

"At home," I replied, "parked in my living room."

The man frowned. "If you have a motorbike, why do you walk?"

"I enjoy walking," I said.

My answer left villagers scratching their heads. In their eyes, anyone who owned a motorbike should use it.

The truth was, part of my reasoning came down to Peace Corps rules: volunteers were not allowed to take passengers. Walking was easier than constantly having to explain—or refuse—when someone asked for a lift.

29. Incidentally, the house I was painting was the same one I had constructed for my own use, on land granted to me by the village chief and his council of elders. One small novelty I built into the house was a sit-down white porcelain toilet connected by large PVC pipes to an underground septic tank I had dug and constructed myself.

The toilet installation was a personal triumph. But soon, I encountered an unexpected challenge: my Togolese friends wanted to use it.

I didn't mind sharing the facility. The problem was that most of them had never used a sit-down toilet before. Accustomed to squatting, they would climb onto the toilet seat with both feet and attempt to squat over it.

In hindsight, I regretted not installing a Turkish flat toilet. It would have made far more sense in that context.

30. Living like an African was not easy for me. They usually had small houses built of earthen blocks that were usually used only for sleeping at night. The rest of the time, they were sitting outside their houses in the shade. They also did their cooking in outside kitchens, and they consumed their food outside.

31. As a PCV, my core responsibility was to help implement a new primary school reform program. The idea behind the reform was to adapt the curriculum to the realities of Togo rather than continue replicating the French model.

For me, that meant setting up vegetable gardens at twenty different village primary schools in the Agu district. On paper, the concept was simple. In practice, it was anything but. A functional school garden required far more than a plot of land; it needed quality seeds, water, fertile soil, fencing, tools, prepared beds, and, most importantly, the willing labor of students.

Coordinating all of those elements at the right time and in the right place proved nearly impossible.

Despite the best efforts, the reform program failed. In my view, the reasons were many, but the biggest was this: the students didn't want to learn about agriculture. For them, school was a way to escape their rural roots, not return to them.

Other factors played a role as well. Vegetables grown in the gardens were often sold for profit by the teachers in local markets rather than consumed by the students. Worse still, teachers frequently used gardening as a form of punishment, further undermining the program's goals.

32. In Lomé, I ran into a hard-working man from my PCV village. He greeted me with the usual snap of our middle fingers in a quick, practiced handshake. Then, almost immediately, he pulled me aside and begged me not to tell anyone in the village that I had seen him—or where he lived.

He explained that if people back home knew he had a job and was earning money, many would come to live with him and bleed him dry.

I reassured him, saying, "Don't worry—I'm familiar with the crab-barrel effect."

33. Also in Lomé, around late 1972, I knew a Togolese woman who worked for an African-American woman. One day, I asked her how she liked the job.

She replied, "My boss is Black like me, but she confuses me. She acts like a white foreigner."

34. That same year, one of my good Togolese friends was always cheerful—no matter how difficult life was. Curious, I asked him at his home in Lomé, "Why are you happy all the time?"

He laughed and said simply, "I don't sweat the small things."

35. In 1972, a village fetish woman offered to show me medicinal plants during a slow walk through the woods. We came upon two narrow paths. I asked where they led.

She pointed. "That one leads to where people defecate—you can tell by the broken twigs on the bushes. The other leads to a holy shrine."

"Let's see the shrine," I said.

She agreed and led me to a circular space marked by half-buried bottles forming an inner border, glass bottoms facing upward like eyes in the soil. In the center stood a three-pronged wooden post, upright, with a calabash full of a magical liquid delicately balanced on its forked top.

As we stood observing it, I asked, "What if I went in and broke everything? What would happen?"

Without hesitation, she replied, "The spirits would kill you."

"Right away?"

"No. But they will follow you and kill you when you least expect it."

After that, I made a point to give every fetish shrine a wide berth. And as I later came to understand: in the village, no one ever died of "natural causes."

Incidentally, I used to carry a pocket notebook and phonetically record the names of each plant she showed me, along with its purpose. I lost that notebook long ago, but I still wonder how I would have translated those local names into English.

36. In the 1970s, I was always intrigued by the West African market women. Despite their size, they were energetic, driven, and impressively active. I mentioned this to a Togolese colleague,

who replied, "Yes, they're fat, but that's their form. They make a lot of money in the markets."

We continued talking, and I asked, "Do they have husbands?"

"Yes," he said, "but they only want a man to have children. They're only interested in making money."

"Given their wealth," I suggested, "they could band together and create a political force."

He shook his head. "They think politics is folly. They're happy to let the men waste their time with that."

37. I was also fascinated by the topless teenage girls working in Lomé's main markets. They wore simple white cloth skirts wrapped around their waists and helped customers carry their purchases, balancing goods effortlessly on their heads.

They never spoke a word.

I later learned they had taken vows of silence at their residence under the authority of a chief fetish woman. These girls were undergoing spiritual initiation into a fetish cult and took their vow very seriously.

38. In my PCV village in 1972, too many children were dying. I asked why, and the response I received was, "The bad spirits from

the East are taking our children. We need to do more ceremonies, call upon the good spirits and the ancestors to protect us."

I did some research and discovered that nearly half the villagers were carriers of sickle cell anemia. It was this genetic condition that was killing many of the children—especially around puberty.

But no one believed me. They continued relying on their traditional ceremonies and spiritual explanations.

Their worldview revolved around a supreme deity, Mawu, and a vast pantheon of lesser gods and spirits beneath her. Then, of course, there were the ancestors—reverently called togbuis, or "grandfathers"—whose influence loomed large in village life.

39. The village looked simple, but living there was complicated by the belief in so many deities, spirits, and ancestors. I was convinced that there was mass psychic power at play when everybody deeply believed strongly in the same thing.

40. The local language, Ewe, also appeared simple, but it was not. This language had less than 2,000 distinct words but was complicated and hard to learn because it was tonal. Some words were spelled the same but could have different meanings by changing the tone with which they were spoken and varied according to the context.

When a pure Ewe-speaker went to the coast and heard Mina, they could understand it, but the quasi-absence of any tones made it hurt their ears. In effect, the Mina had simplified the Ewe language by eliminating many of its tones.

41. While I was in my PCV village in Togo in 1972, I decided to climb the steep footpath up Mt. Agu (at 983 meters, it represented the tallest point in Togo) to visit the old village of Dogbadzi which was built on terraces made by the villagers' ancestors. The chief of the village received me well, taking me to his house. There he regaled me with stories on how his village had repelled in olden days slave traders and Ashanti warriors by pushing boulders down upon them as they scaled the mountain.

He also shared with me a couple of keepsakes from German times. He possessed a well-polished metal helmet (pickelhaube) that was used for ceremonial purposes and a large wall map of Togo in German. I found this map of interest. The spelling in German of commonplace names is known today from their French titles or local language words. For example, I noted that 'Bismarckburg' stood out because it was in larger bold type.

Moreover, the chief's first name, Adolf, struck me with how powerful Germany's rule of Togo as its model colony was. There were some elderly Togolese who could still speak German, and they stated, "The Germans worked hard, and if Germany had remained our colonizer, Togo would be the most advanced country in Africa."

42. The Dogbadzi village chief and his council of elders once persuaded me to help resolve a longstanding water shortage. Their plan was ambitious: build a four-meter-high, above-ground cylindrical water storage unit on the mountaintop.

The structure would be made of reinforced concrete, and the water piped in from a small, trickling spring around the other side of the mountain—where we first needed to build a concrete coffer dam. I was skeptical at first. The project seemed too complex. But I couldn't deny the high level of enthusiasm from the villagers.

There were serious challenges, including the absence of sand or gravel at the top of the mountain. But the women rose to the task with incredible energy, collecting sand, gravel, and lumber at the foot of the mountain, then carrying it all up on their heads. Even fifty-kilogram cement bags were split in two so they could be carried more easily. Women stationed along the path acted as sentries, alerting others when materials had arrived below.

Meanwhile, the men expertly constructed the towering reinforced concrete tank and laid galvanized piping around the mountain to a newly built reservoir that caught water from the spring.

Their determination began to convince me that the project was possible.

I delivered the six-meter-long, two-inch-diameter galvanized pipes with couplings needed to complete the system. After months of collective labor, drinking water finally flowed into the village. The inauguration of the water system was joyous. I was deeply moved by what we had accomplished.

I informed the U.S. Embassy in Lomé that their Self-Help funds had been well spent.

Energized by our success, I suggested to the chief and his elders that they consider installing a small generator on the water reservoir to provide electricity, especially for the early mornings and misty nights when visibility was poor.

Their reply was firm: "The night is for other things. The day is long enough. Any light at night would upset the spirits."

43. In 1973, I was taking the old German train from Agu-Gare to Lomé. I sat contentedly on one of the benches that lined the interior walls of the passenger car. As we moved along, the

Togolese passengers chanted a rhythmic song, naming each village where the train stopped.

At my feet, a toddler played with a razor blade.

His mother, seated beside me, watched without concern. I quickly snatched the blade from the child's hands and handed it to her.

To my surprise, she gave it right back to him.

Startled, I said, "I'm afraid he'll cut himself."

She replied calmly, "If he wants to cut himself, let him. That's how he'll learn not to play with a razor blade."

44. One of my Togolese friends from the village once suffered a terrible earache. He went to the mission hospital to get it checked. The doctor examined his ear canal and removed tiny fragments of bird feathers.

He cautioned my friend, saying, "I know villagers often clean their ears using the tips of bird feathers, but be careful. That's what caused this."

45. In 1974, while I was working in the Peace Corps office in Lomé, a madman burst through the front door wielding a machete and tried to attack the Peace Corps Director (PCD).

The office staff managed to restrain him, but when the PCD attempted to call the police, he couldn't get through. After several failed attempts, his frustration boiled over. He slammed the telephone repeatedly against the desk until it shattered.

I looked over at our stunned Togolese office manager, wondering what he would say. He remained calm and simply remarked, "I guess we need to keep the front door locked."

46. One of the gravest offenses in a Togolese village was a child striking their mother. For generations, such a thing had never happened. Then one day, it did, and the entire village was thrown into crisis. They didn't know how to respond. It was treated with the same seriousness as a murder case and referred to the regional court. However, the court found no law on the books addressing this specific situation.

I asked a Togolese colleague what would happen next.

He said solemnly, "Like the rare occurrence of murder, some things are best left to judgment in the afterlife."

47. My African colleagues in French-speaking West Africa often leaned on a saying when under stress: "Life is an eternal combat."

Once, someone tried to comfort the man who said it by responding, "Yes, sea never dry."

Another Togolese neighbor added quietly, "Man proposes, and God disposes."

48. Religion played a central role in the lives of nearly everyone I encountered. I often thought to myself, If you could harness the religious fervor in Africa for development, there would be no limit to what could be achieved.

Most people I met practiced either Christianity or Islam, but nearly all, regardless of formal religion, also participated, in some form, in traditional animist practices.

49. In 1972, a mad scramble unfolded across the country as new laws demanded the adoption of culturally "authentic" names— names many Togolese could never have dreamed of using in their actual lives. The name-change law was a central part of a national campaign promoting Togolese authenticity, but its rollout was chaotic and rife with corruption.

Elderly Christians were especially distressed. I remember one man who told me, "I was baptized Joseph by my Catholic church, and I intend to die with that name."

Not long after, he was beaten by thugs, and his church ransacked.

Another man lamented being forced to give up his name, Moses, while his Muslim neighbor, named Moussa, the Arabic equivalent was allowed to keep his. A rumor spread that the Muslim community had paid off the president to be exempt from the policy. It was widely believed that, despite high illiteracy rates, Muslims held considerable economic power due to their dominant role in the transport sector.

50. The whole situation made ordinary communication more difficult. People were now expected to call others by names they had never used before. I found it nearly impossible. Fortunately, I was always known by my local day-name, Komla—Tuesday's child. But even that posed its own confusion. There were already so many Komlas, it was hard to tell who was who.

51. This name-change chaos wasn't original. It was copied directly from the politics of Mobutu Sese Seko, the president of Zaire (now the DRC). Togo's president admired Mobutu and called him "Big Brother." He openly praised Mobutu's grand palace and the opulent jungle city of Gbadolite—a vanity project that would later be reclaimed by the bush and remembered as a looted monument to excess.

52. In 1971, while serving as a PCV, I was required to travel to the regional capital and line up along the main road to wave at the presidential cortège as it passed. The motorcade included both the President of Togo and his "Big Brother" from the DRC.

Soon afterward, Togo's president launched his national authenticity campaign: renaming mandates, a strict dress code (women were forbidden to wear bras or trousers), and the appearance of state-sponsored 'shock' dancers.

I heard a popular saying from that era, supposedly attributed to the DRC's dictator:

"He keeps three kinds of ministers, one who is a minister, one who is in jail, and one who is in exile. And he rotates them annually."

53. While serving as a PCV in Togo, I tried to domesticate the agouti—a rodent-like species of the genus Dasyprocta, often referred to locally as bush meat. Agouti was the most prized meat in the area. When I left after three years, I handed off the project to a local Togolese farmer, unsure of what would come of it.

Thirty years later, I was attending a meeting in South Africa and happened to sit next to a Nigerian colleague. We began exchanging stories, and I mentioned my agouti experience.

His eyes lit up. "I work in Ghana," he said, "and over there we call agoutis 'grasscutters.' They trace the origins of domesticated grasscutter farming to a region in neighboring Togo—the same area where you worked. It's a major industry now."

I laughed and replied, "After thirty years, I finally learn of my success."

54. In 1973, I was living in Lomé but happened to be visiting my PCV village when a runner came sprinting toward me, urgently calling me to the local mission hospital. I ran there immediately and found the Peace Corps physician, who explained that he visited the hospital every Thursday to perform surgeries. Then, almost in the same breath, he asked, "What type of blood do you have?"

"A+," I replied.

"Perfect," he said. "That's exactly what we need to save your fellow PCV. He's been in a terrible vehicle accident. I assume you're willing to give blood."

I agreed without hesitation. Later, I learned that the American Peace Corps doctor, David Bloom, stayed by the injured volunteer's side—Sidney Bliss—all the way to Lomé and then accompanied him on an emergency medevac flight to Spain.

55. Months later, I was thrilled to hear that Sidney had survived and was recovering at home in the U.S. About a year after his evacuation, I was working at the Peace Corps office in Lomé when

I heard a piercing scream. I rushed out of my office to find our Togolese receptionist fleeing in panic.

"It's a ghost!" she cried.

Confused, I looked down the hallway and saw something incredible: Sidney Bliss, alive and well, walking into the building.

I greeted him, still stunned. "Why are you here?" I asked.

He grinned. "I figured it would be easier to find a job in Africa if I came back in person."

To make a long story short, years later Sidney and I found ourselves working together again—first as colleagues in Niger and Togo, and later in Maputo, Mozambique, from 2001 to 2006. I was honored to serve as best man at his wedding in 2003. In 2005, I visited his mother at a retirement home in Fort Myers, Florida, and in 2011, I last saw him and his family in Maputo. He always introduced me as the man who had saved his life in Togo.

Sadly, he passed away unexpectedly at his home in Maputo on July 20, 2021.

He is one of four Americans I knew who spent their post-PCV lives in Africa and are now buried in the countries where they lived and served. The others were Auggie Aughenbaugh, Al Miller, and Sue Rosenthal. There are still others who stayed for decades in Africa or eventually returned to the U.S., but their time on the continent defined their adult lives.

I should also mention Dennis Ota, the very first Togo PCV from Hawaii. He died instantly in a horrific vehicle accident while my friend was rushing to help settle him into his new site.

56. After my failed attempt at improving chicken production, a Togolese woman tried to console me. "That's okay," she said, "because we don't feed eggs to children anyway. It will turn them into thieves."

I later learned this belief was common in southern Togo. Despite the high nutritional value of eggs, it was widely believed that giving them to children would cause them to become dishonest. Egg consumption was culturally reserved for adults.

57. One night in late 1972, I was jolted awake by frantic shouting from the woman who lived next door. I ran outside to find that our housing compound was under siege by army ants—dozens of coordinated columns were closing in.

The neighbors quickly showed me how to build small campfires at the front of each column. The fire forced the ants to redirect their path and spared my home from invasion. It was an eerie and unforgettable display of both nature's power and local wisdom.

58. That same year, I took a Togolese friend to Lomé. It was her first time visiting the capital—and her first time watching a movie.

We were halfway through a violent American action film when she began to shake uncontrollably. We had to leave the theater, and outside in the grassy area, she vomited.

Once she calmed down, I asked, "What upset you so much?"

She answered, "Did you see what I saw? I've never seen a person kill another person."

I tried to explain that everything on the screen was fiction, actors playing roles—but she wouldn't accept it. "I saw what I saw," she insisted.

59. While living in my PCV village, I observed the detailed, labor-intensive process of making cassava flour, or gari. The women dug up cassava roots, peeled them, cut them into smaller pieces, and soaked them in water to ferment. They dried the fermented chunks—often on the roadside—then grated them into flour.

What fascinated me most was their use of old tin roofing sheets as grating tools. Nails had been hammered through the metal from the underside to create jagged holes, turning discarded roofing into giant grating boards.

60. During my time as a PCV in my Togo village, my breakfast often consisted of a bowl of cassava flour mixed with sugar cubes and water. This simple cereal was typically accompanied by a cup of Nescafé, enhanced with sweetened condensed Peak milk and more sugar cubes.

61. One concern I had while living in the village was my eyesight. Reading late into the night by candlelight seemed to strain my eyes, and I worried they were growing weaker.

62. The rhythmic pounding of fufu near my house caught my attention one day. Three young women took turns wielding large wooden pestles to mash slices of boiled African yam into a gelatinous mound of fufu inside a carved wooden mortar.

Curious, I asked if I could give it a try. They burst into laughter, it was a chore strictly reserved for women and certainly not one they expected a foreign man to request.

They eventually relented, handing me a pestle. On my first try, I pounded too forcefully and sent the fufu flying out of the mortar and onto the dirt. They quickly took the pestle from me, frustrated that I had ruined their meal. The entire process would have to be restarted—peeling, boiling, and pounding fresh yams.

To lighten the mood, they began singing a local ditty that loosely translated to, "Do you want your yam boiled or fried?" (This inspired one of the poems included in Annex C.)

At least the goats were happy, they got to enjoy the yam peelings a second time. But the women's expressions made it clear that my presence was no longer welcome. I learned an important lesson: this was not the place for a man, and certainly not a white foreigner.

63. In the village, children frequently followed me, chanting and asking for five CFA francs—just a few U.S. cents. Some families disapproved of this behavior and would scold the children, perhaps more so because of the term they used: "yovo," the local word for a white person.

I asked many times where this word came from. One explanation stood out: "yovo" referred to the pale inside of a banana beneath its dark skin.

To silence the chants, I'd sometimes respond by calling the children ameyigbo, a word I believed meant "black people" in Ewe, though I seldom heard it used by locals. Interestingly, it was the children—uninhibited and curious—who taught me many of the local words I picked up.

64. In 1973, I had an American friend working in Togo who had previously served as a PCV in Mbandaka, in what is now the DRC. He shared a curious observation: when he lived in Mbandaka, which sits on the equator, he noticed that flushing the toilet produced an unusual motion. Instead of spinning clockwise or counterclockwise, the water just swirled back and forth.

He claimed it was due to the location being precisely on the equator—neither north nor south. Whether myth or science, it was one of those quirky details that added to the folklore of Peace Corps life in Africa.

When I was in the DRC in 2005, I didn't notice any unusual behavior in how water swirled in the toilet bowl south of the equator. However, back in 1975, when I was acting Peace Corps Director for three months in the Central African Republic (CAR), I did encounter something peculiar in its capital, Bangui—my trusty compass failed to work properly.

It turned out that Bangui was affected by a magnetic anomaly that distorted normal magnetic waves. I eventually tucked the compass away and focused instead on other pastimes: attempting to learn the local language, Sango, and joining residents on excursions to see the ocean-going ships along the Congo River or people-watching at the international airport as passengers arrived and departed.

Besides drinking beer in local bars, these quiet diversions made up the main forms of recreation in Bangui, where the open vistas of the African bush began at the very edge of the city.

65. In my early years as a PCV, I immersed myself in the cultivation of local crops, eager to understand both cash and food production. Cocoa trees fascinated me the most. I visited many cocoa plantations but was struck by the fact that I never met a single farmer who had tasted chocolate.

One elderly grower once told me, "When I was young, one man could manage a hectare of cocoa, sell its produce, and buy a car. Now, even if he manages one hectare, it won't fetch enough to buy a single tire."

In nearly every cocoa field I visited, children made up the bulk of the labor force. I couldn't help but wonder how the crop could be harvested if child labor laws were ever truly enforced.

66. I also spent considerable time visiting cocoa and coffee fields, but my own backyard was full of yam mounds, a crop revered and even worshiped in many local traditions. I quickly learned how much care and expertise yam cultivation required.

Planting the seed yams was a job always entrusted to a female specialist. Meanwhile, the construction of yam mounds, a physically demanding task, was often outsourced to laborers from northern ethnic groups. These men worked with large-bladed hoes and were paid based on the number of mounds they created, as well as fed and given drink throughout the day.

To my delight, some of the yams from my own backyard plot were eventually selected for inclusion in the village's annual yam festival, an event that underscored just how much pride and cultural value this root crop carried in local life.

I also learned that in traditional practice, fertile women were the ones entrusted with planting crop seeds—a symbolic and practical choice tied closely to beliefs in generative power. Village blacksmiths, I discovered, used shredded cocoa pod skins as fuel for their forges, while entrepreneurial women found a different use for the discarded husks—turning them into a base for traditional soaps. These details revealed the remarkable resourcefulness of rural communities and how nothing was wasted.

67. Yams were typically boiled in large aluminum pots placed on small, cast-iron charcoal burners known locally as krapot—a cooking device similar to a hibachi. I noticed these pots

everywhere throughout my PCV village and grew curious about their origin. After much inquiry, I finally tracked down the source. On the outskirts of the village, I found men melting down scrap aluminum—usually from old car parts—and pouring the molten metal into wooden molds lined with sand. When I asked, "Where did you get the mold?" they replied, "We inherited it. It's been around for generations. We call it the mother mold."

I often wonder how many of these essential cooking pots were made from that single mold and where they all might be today.

68. From 1970 to 1973, I served as a PCV school construction volunteer in Togo's Agu District, helping to build ten three-room village primary schools. I still recall the wisdom shared by one village chief who said, "We highly appreciate your assistance. We know that one day you'll leave, but you can't take these school buildings with you."

69. That single sentence captured the essence of community development: building something that endures beyond your presence. When I constructed my home in the village in 1972, I installed screened shutters on all my windows to keep mosquitoes at bay while still allowing the cool night air to circulate. The feature drew interest from local villagers. One man who came to

admire the setup remarked with a smile, "That's a good way of keeping the snakes out."

70. Anytime the village chief needed to communicate an important message, he sent the town crier, known in my PCV village as the gong-gong man to roam the village. At each passageway, he would strike his two-pronged iron gong and shout out the message on the chief's behalf. It was a remarkable way of disseminating news—audible, communal, and immediate.

71. Perhaps nowhere did I witness the winds of change more clearly than at an animal traction site nestled deep within the tall savanna grasses of northern Togo. In 1974, I dropped off three new PCVs—Steve Eastep, Marv Wolf, and Tom Callahan—in the middle of seemingly nowhere. Their mission? To pioneer a training center that would teach local farmers how to use cattle for field cultivation.

Animal traction was virtually unknown in the area at the time. The idea had been borrowed from neighboring northern Benin, and these volunteers were tasked with adapting and implementing this unfamiliar practice. I remember wishing them good luck as they stood among the tall grass, far from the comforts of familiarity but full of purpose.

In 1989, I revisited the same spot in northern Togo where, fifteen years earlier, I had deposited three pioneering PCVs in the middle of the bush. I still harbored misgivings about having dropped them there with little more than encouragement and good intentions. But what I saw defied all expectations.

Not only was there a fully functioning training center for teaching animal traction techniques—how to train cattle to plow fields and pull carts, but there was also a thriving community that had grown up around it. These three volunteers had fundamentally transformed the landscape of northern Togo.

I asked an elderly local how such widespread adoption of animal traction had been achieved. He replied, "I don't know all the details, but I do know the first people targeted were the village chiefs and community leaders. And those who first adopted donkey carts earned good money transporting goods for others. Of course, nowadays everyone has a cart, so there's not much money left in transport."

72. My early years in Africa (1970–76) were closely tied to my work with the US Peace Corps. Back then, things were generally going well for most PCVs most of the time. However, there were a few lines we warned volunteers not to cross, particularly when it came

to meddling in the world of black magic or engaging in behaviors that could draw dangerous attention from local authorities.

This was also a time in the US when experimenting with black magic and the early use of marijuana was becoming more common. A few PCVs made poor decisions that ended badly.

In one case, some Togo volunteers stole celebratory signs posted on the main boulevard in front of the presidential palace, meant for the state visit of the French President. In another, a PCV brought marijuana-laced brownies to a party held at the US Ambassador's residence.

The most serious incident involved a male PCV who was caught by the Togolese secret police in a sexual encounter with a minor of the same sex. Such behavior was not only illegal but incredibly dangerous in that political climate.

Our standard response in these kinds of crises was swift: we would obtain custody of the volunteer and escort them quickly across the nearby Ghana border, where Peace Corps Ghana staff would already be alerted and ready to receive them.

Perhaps the most surprising case I heard of was in Mali, where the PCD became so deeply involved in local cult practices that it backfired. She had to be medically evacuated.

73. In the early 1970s, in a village deep in rural Togo, I saw several children with red hair. Curious, I asked a man in the village about it. He laughed and replied, "A red-headed Irishman passed through here a generation ago." I accepted the explanation with a smile, but later, as I drove back to my city home, it struck me, those red heads were a sign of kwashiorkor, a serious protein deficiency.

74. I took pride in how little water I used for my nightly calabash bath. I never felt as clean at any other time in my life as I did after one of those bucket baths. I wanted to stay clean, partly to avoid the common African comment that white foreigners "smelled like wet dogs." I eventually learned this was a frequent observation, based on the belief that white people didn't bathe enough.

Each evening, after the cooking was finished, I would place my galvanized bucket filled with water over the dying embers of the cooking fire to warm. Then, by the light of a kerosene lantern, I'd carry my bucket to the shower stall for a proper, warm rinse.

75. Over time, I noticed something else. After years in Africa, the natural perspiration of Africans began to smell to me like their staple food, cassava, maize, or palm oil. Bad body odor, of course, was easily noticeable when people didn't bathe. Smelling clean and pleasant was a strong cultural value. Wealthy men would

often douse themselves in expensive colognes. Cleanliness extended to their utensils and bodies, even if their homes were made of mud bricks and surrounded by dust.

76. In remote villages, it wasn't uncommon for small children to run away from me in fear. I once asked an African colleague why, and he said, "They're scared because they've never seen a white man. They think you're a ghost. Actually, we all think you look like corpses." It was said without malice, but it stayed with me.

77. Later, while winding our vehicle along narrow tracks through tall savanna grass, we passed a group of young men wearing various U.S. college sweatshirts. It reminded me of the booming secondhand clothing market from the U.S. I asked my colleague what people wore before these used clothes became common. He answered simply, "Nothing."

He went on to say, "I'm lucky. I wear used clothes without anyone knowing they're from the market. When I go shopping, I dress in used clothes so vendors think I'm poor and give me a better price. But no matter what you wear, you'll always get the 'white man's price.'"

I had to admit, I too had bought used U.S. clothing, especially winter gear for trips back to the States. I often wondered how many poor people would be left without clothing if those shipments ever stopped.

Incidentally, in Togo, used clothing was known in the local language as "dead people's clothes." The belief was simple, one would have to be dead to part with such good garments. In the coastal Ewe-Mina language, used clothing was called abruni wawu, which translates roughly to "clothes of the dead." I found the label unsettling and disliked the idea that so many Africans were dressed in cast-offs from the West.

Curious, I did some research and discovered that used clothes were collected from all over the United States, sold to East Coast merchants, and sorted and baled for shipment—often to Igbo traders in West Africa. These wholesale merchants would then distribute the clothing to market vendors in countries like Togo.

Lomé became a major hub for used clothing because the Togolese government had few protective regulations in place to safeguard its own textile industry. The used clothing market in Lomé was dominated by Igbo merchants from Nigeria, who somehow managed to smuggle the goods across borders into neighboring nations. It seemed clear that the mass importation of secondhand clothing stifled any chance for local textile production or the growth of domestic fashion brands.

Still, Peace Corps Volunteers often took advantage of the market, not only to save money but also to compete for the most outrageous T-shirt slogans they could find. The goal was to outdo each other at social gatherings with the most ridiculous or baffling printed messages.

78. I always limited how many rural villages I visited in a single day because of the expected hospitality. The custom dictated that every guest be welcomed with a large calabash of the village's local brew either palm wine, its stronger distilled version, or the effervescent fermented sorghum beer known as tchoukoutou. Refusing to drink was considered impolite, so I did my best to honor the gesture, even when my head started to spin after the first few swallows.

79. More than once, I found myself pulling over on the roadside about a kilometer outside the village, searching for shade so I could lie down until I felt steady again.

I also observed how palm wine was made in my PCV village. Unlike other regions of Africa where the sap was tapped from live palm trees, here the trees were felled. A hole was then carved into the trunk at just the right angle, allowing sap to drip steadily into a clay pot placed below. Every day, the local specialist would light a stick and sear the edges of the hole to disinfect it and keep the flow clean.

When the clay pot was full, the palm wine specialist would deliver it to a local woman seller. Fresh palm wine was best enjoyed straight from the tree, but sellers often diluted it with water, resulting in a more pungent taste. While the process of making palm wine is complex, perhaps it's enough to say that it was the village's most beloved alcoholic beverage.

Palm wine (aha) competed with the cheaper fermented maize liquor known as deha. For the more serious drinkers, there was sodabi, a potent, clear spirit distilled from palm wine. According to local lore, the name sodabi originated from a man from Benin who learned the distillation process while serving in the French military during World War II. He brought the technique home and popularized the liquor, his name, reportedly, was Sodabi.

80. Further north in Togo, the preferred drink was tchoukoutou, a bubbly sorghum beer brewed in the drier savanna regions. I learned that the best time to drink a calabash of tchouk was when

it was freshly brewed and foaming with small bubbles rising to the surface.

81. In late December 1974, I was called to assist with the autopsies of two American men: the pilot and mechanic of President Gnassingbé Eyadéma's jet. Their deaths followed a crash during low-visibility conditions caused by the Harmattan, the dust-laden winds that swept down from the Sahara and collided with Atlantic coastal breezes, blanketing Lomé's airport in haze. The accident was kept out of the press; the president had already been in another crash earlier that year and didn't want the news getting out.

Because the deceased were Americans, Togolese officials insisted an American doctor be present for the autopsies. The Peace Corps physician was tapped for the task, but he didn't speak French. As a result, I was asked to serve as interpreter and had to witness two full autopsies. Later, I also helped prepare and crate the bodies for shipment back to the United States.

82. On a lighter note, I never had my clothes ironed as well as I did in my village. My laundry was washed in galvanized tubs, rinsed, and then dried on rope lines or laid across bushes. Once dry, it was pressed using a heavy cast iron filled with glowing coals.

That iron smoothed out wrinkles better than any modern electric version ever could.

83. I was fascinated by the necklaces of cowrie shells worn by local fetish women during occult ceremonies. When I asked about them, I was told the shells had been passed down through generations. Intrigued, I did some digging and found that the cowries had likely originated from the Maldives, far across the ocean, and had once served as currency in West Africa over a century ago.

These same women also wore colorful glass beads—short, cylindrical, and worn on their wrists, ankles, and around their necks. Though they claimed the beads were also ancestral, I learned many of them were originally Venetian in origin. Some beads were still being produced locally, continuing a tradition rooted in centuries of global exchange.

You can imagine the jolt I get seeing cowrie shells used for necklaces and bracelets in the United States. In West Africa, these shells are powerful symbols—worn only by occult priests and their acolytes. It's startling to see them turned into fashion accessories. Similarly, I often wonder about the tattoos and piercings people wear in the U.S.—do these markings indicate tribal affiliation, or are they purely aesthetic? My instinct is always to ask, "What group do they belong to?"

84. In Togo, I was particularly fascinated by facial scars. Some people bore intricate markings, and I often asked my African colleagues which ethnic group practiced such scarification. They explained the scars were made when the person was still a baby, to clearly mark their ethnic identity. One colleague said, "So their ethnic group can be distinguished from another."

Today, such practices are fading. With fewer facial scars, it's become harder to identify someone's ethnic background at a glance. Traditionally, many in southern Togo wore a small crescent-shaped scar on one cheek. In the distant past, some groups in northern Togo even filed their front teeth into sharp points as a marker of identity.

85. I had grown used to the sound of tools dropping the moment I walked away from a construction site, a sign that work had paused. But one day, it was different. The workers dropped everything while I was still there and bolted. Moments later, I understood why. A loud hum filled the air, and a swarm of aggressive African bees was bearing down on the site. I didn't wait, I ran for my life, hoping to avoid being stung.

86. In my village, I was told the best time to steal something from another village was during a moonless night, especially if it was raining. One such night, several villagers crossed the border into Ghana to raid a state-run tree nursery. They stole saplings of a new variety of cocoa trees resistant to the swollen shoot virus that had been devastating their fields. These men returned as heroes, and the stolen trees flourished.

87. I still remember when a television set first arrived in the village store in 1972. Crowds gathered at night, mesmerized by the images on the screen. Many congratulated me for the United States' achievements in space, beaming with pride as if I were personally responsible. I tried to explain that not everything they saw was real, that Lost in Space was just a TV show. But they would not be swayed. "We saw it with our own eyes," they insisted.

88. The family who lived near me in my PCV Togo village had a gray parrot that could speak a few words in Ewe, their local language. The villagers found this endlessly amusing. The running joke was that the parrot was teaching me their language.

89. Not far from the chief's compound lived a well-respected family. One evening, they invited me to a feast that lasted well into the night. As I got ready to leave, they insisted I stay the night—it

was too late to travel safely, they said. I agreed and settled in. Before bed, they kindly prepared a bucket of warm water for me to bathe. In their shower stall, I used all the water provided, then noticed a clay pot filled with more water sitting on the floor. I assumed it was also for bathing, so I used it to rinse off.

Later that night, I heard a woman scream.

Unbeknownst to me, I had used water reserved for a very specific purpose—cleansing after menstruation. I was mortified when they explained this. Even now, decades later, the memory makes me blush. All I could do was shake my head and mutter to myself, "WAWA"—West Africa Wins Again.

90. Just a few days later, I was summoned by the village chief. A woman had been beating her young son mercilessly, and I had stepped in to stop her. The chief didn't waste words. "Don't intervene when a parent is disciplining their child," he said, and promptly dismissed me.

As I turned to leave, I spotted a woman in the chief's compound tied to a post with a rope around her neck. Alarmed, I stepped back inside and asked, "Why is she tied like that?"

He looked at me calmly and said, "That's how we punish a woman who speaks forbidden words to a man."

I later discovered what those words were. She had said, "I defecate in your mouth."

91. While visiting the chief's house, I couldn't help but notice the numerous bottles of alcoholic spirits scattered around his receiving room. He caught my gaze and explained, "These bottles represent fines paid by people who break village rules. The village court usually imposes a penalty of a bottle or two of Schnapps."

He gestured toward the bottles again and added, "We don't drink them. We use them for libations to honor our ancestors. Any time you drink anything—our local brew, palm wine, or distilled palm wine, you pour a few drops on the ground first. That's for the ancestors."

Just then, one of the women in the compound called out to a child, addressing him as "Bucket." I asked the chief why she would name her child that. He replied, "She has lost several children to bad spirits. By calling her living children unusual names, she hopes to confuse the spirits so they can't find them."

92. After a long, exhausting drive in northern Togo in 1974, I realized with dread that my car's fuel tank was empty. We were miles from the next station, and I knew I couldn't make it. I

stopped in the nearest village, and the local PCV brought me to the village witchdoctor's hut. I explained my situation.

The fetish priest conducted a divination ceremony using sliced kola nuts. After tossing the pieces on the ground, he looked up and said simply, "Go. You will reach the next station."

I followed his advice, and to my amazement, despite the fuel needle being well below empty, I made it.

93. That PCV, Jules Laramee, lived in the village in a house he had built himself. He shared it with three girlfriends—one local woman, his American girlfriend from back home, and another PCV from a nearby village. One evening, the PCV girlfriend was refueling her motorbike using the light of a kerosene lantern. In an instant, the fuel caught fire, and the entire house went up in flames. Everyone escaped just in time, standing outside as the propane gas bottle from their three-burner hotplate exploded, obliterating the home.

94. On a road trip through northern Togo in 1974, we crested a hill and were met with a breathtaking and terrifying sight: a massive bull elephant standing squarely in the middle of the road. My Togolese driver calmly said, "Stay still while I back up."

But instinct took over. I jumped out of the car to take a picture.

The elephant wasn't impressed. It charged.

I bolted back into the car just in time, and the driver reversed us to safety.

95. He shook his head and said, "I told you so."

Along another dusty road in northern Togo in 1975, I spotted a small, hand-painted sign that read: "Coldest Beer in Africa." Curious, we stopped and backed up to find a ramshackle hut. Inside was a man who asked, "You want a cold beer?"

We nodded, and he pulled back the lid of a large clay jar buried underground and filled with cool water. Tied with goat leather cords, bottles of beer bobbed inside. He pulled two out, untied them, and set them before us on a rickety table.

"Here's your cold beer," he said proudly.

I took a sip from my bottle and smiled. "Thanks," I said. "Coldest beer in these parts."

96. At a bank in Lomé in 1974, I found myself standing in a long line. A Togolese friend noticed me, came over, and said, "Come with me. The teller is my cousin—she'll serve us quickly."

Thirty years later, at the same bank, I stood in another long line. This time, a security guard spotted me, walked over, and politely escorted me to the front. Surprised, I asked him why.

"We respect our elders," he replied with a smile.

97. In Lomé in 1975, I began to notice something strange. Around the same time each evening, a thick, dark pall would settle over the city. It carried a distinct smoky smell. After months of observation, it finally clicked: everyone was lighting their charcoal cooking fires at once.

I rushed next door to speak with a woman cooking over her charcoal fire.

"Why don't you use a propane bottle with a gas burner?" I asked.

She laughed and said, "I'd love to, but I can't afford it. Even if it's available, who's going to buy me the propane and the cooker?"

Over the years, I noticed firewood and charcoal trucks in many African cities traveling longer and longer distances to find usable wood. One driver I asked was blunt: "We'll keep going," he said, "until the last tree is chopped down."

98. At a rural health center in Togo in 1974, nearly every woman in town had gathered to listen to an American Peace Corps health

worker. She delivered her talk in Ewe, using flip charts to emphasize her points, washing hands, boiling drinking water, keeping cooking areas clean.

When she finished, an elderly woman stood up and said matter-of-factly, "We don't do any of the things you recommend. And yet, here we are."

99. In every African country I've lived in, the essential sauces served with meals were—at least for me, overly spicy. Most were packed with hot chili peppers. Shortly after arriving in Lomé in 1970, I ate a particularly fiery sauce and had to excuse myself to sprint around and gulp down copious amounts of cool water. My Togolese counterpart watched my antics and said with a grin, "You don't like our hot sauces. Too bad. Chili peppers are full of vitamin A and protect your innards from parasites."

Still, I just couldn't tolerate the heat. Eventually, the women in my housing compound learned this and began preparing a milder, less spicy sauce just for me.

100. In 1974, I explored ways to stay in Togo after my Peace Corps service by attempting several small business ventures. I dabbled in exporting African wood carvings and maize grinding mills, hoping to find a profitable niche.

I thought I'd struck gold with the idea of cultivating papaya fields—not for the fruit, but for the milky latex that oozes from the fruit's skin when scratched. This latex, known as papain, is a key ingredient in meat tenderizers used in the US and Europe. My hopes were high until I discovered that Sri Lanka held a tight monopoly on papain exports. So much for that.

101. There was a stretch of verdant rice fields I used to admire at an upcountry location in Togo. One day, passing by, I noticed most of the fields had been abandoned. Curious, I stopped the car and walked into the area. I found two farmers sitting idly and asked, "What happened? Did your water pump break down and leave you unable to irrigate?"

One replied casually, "No, nothing like that. We need rest. The Taiwan Chinese left, and we can't work like them. We need our leisure time. Besides, the mainland Chinese are supposed to replace them."

That was 1974 or 1975.

102. On another trip that same year, I stopped at a roadside bar in the Togolese countryside. There, I overheard a young African woman saying to an elderly man, "You're too old for me."

The old man smiled and shot back, "But my money is not old."

103. Years later, I attempted to get a passport for my Togolese mother-in-law so she could travel with us to the United States. The passport office insisted she apply with her father, who had long since passed. They then asked for her husband, but she was divorced. Ultimately, after a small bribe, she was issued a passport stating she was born "around 1930."

I came to understand that very few Africans knew their exact age. Birth certificates were rare, and most people were named according to the circumstances surrounding their birth. My mother-in-law recalled a time during World War II when cotton cloth imports were halted, and people had to wear bark cloth. So, her birth year was estimated based on that historical event.

104. There was never any confusion when a letter was sent to me in my Togolese village. One letter was simply addressed to: "Komla Amerika Agu."

As I mentioned earlier, "Komla" is my day-name, meaning I was born on a Tuesday. Day-names were common and culturally significant—one set for boys, another for girls—with further variations for twins or the birth order of siblings. Sometimes, significant events at the time of birth also influenced a child's name.

105. A good Togolese friend of mine had two children—one girl with a dark complexion and one boy who was quite fair. Curious, I asked him about the contrast. With a knowing smile, he said, "Well, she was born at night, and he was born during the day."

106. During my three years (1970–73) as a PCV in Togo, my trusty Honda 50 motorbike (locally called a moto) was my lifeline for getting around. Once, I transported it to Lomé on the old German train, and while cruising the capital's sandy roads, I lost control and fell. Fortunately, I wasn't hurt, and the cars behind me didn't run me over, but the right handlebar snapped clean off.

I took the damaged bike to Marie Gadsden, our PCD at the time. She was a dignified and firm African American woman. I asked if the Peace Corps could cover the repairs. She examined the damage, looked me straight in the eye, and said sternly, "You're responsible for the accident; therefore, you must pay for the repair yourself. Let this be a lesson."

I went to a local welder who charged me a modest fee to fix the handlebars on my moto. He did his best, but the welding job left them crooked. From then on, I had to ride while holding the handlebars at an angle just to go straight. I drove like that for the next two years.

107. But lopsided handlebars or not, I always had my trusty SGGG bag looped around them. The initials stood for the hardware store where I had purchased it, and at the time, owning such a bag was practically a badge of honor among Togo Peace Corps Volunteers. It was ideal for carrying whatever odds and ends you needed on the road.

For me, that included a stack of large yellow envelopes. If I had to relieve myself while out riding, I would veer off the path and duck into the bush, do my business inside one of the envelopes, seal it up, and toss it farther into the brush with the joking farewell: "Air mail."

108. That same moto accident triggered a bold (and, in retrospect, foolish) nighttime escapade. One night, some Togolese friends and I rolled away one of the many abandoned, left-hand-drive green jeeps parked beside the Peace Corps office in Lomé. These jeeps had originally been used by Peace Corps Nigeria but were left to rust when that program shut down during the Biafra Civil War.

The jeeps had sat idle for ages, slowly corroding in the salty sea air. The Atlantic coast was only a block away, and without regular rinsing, the ocean winds made quick work of anything metal.

Rolling the jeep away was the easy part. Starting it was the real challenge. The canvas-covered vehicle had a leaky radiator, which we patched with locally made soap. We couldn't afford a new battery, so I parked on hills and inclines to make it easier to push-start the vehicle. I used it for over a year to deliver 50-kilogram bags of cement to my school construction sites.

Curiously, Peace Corps Togo never seemed to notice that one of its jeeps had gone missing. And when I later borrowed a cinva ram press used for making cement-stabilized earth bricks from a local UN center, it quietly disappeared into the local landscape too.

109. During that same period in 1974, I was working for Peace Corps Togo when a major initiative was launched to recruit more African American volunteers. I was especially pleased to welcome an African American man from inner-city Chicago and settle him into my former village.

I took him to the village on a Friday, but by Monday morning, he was back in my Lomé office, requesting an early return to the United States. Surprised by the sudden reversal, I asked him what had prompted such a quick and decisive move.

"There's no electricity or running water in the village," he explained. "I'm used to a fast life. And once night falls, there's nowhere to go."

Although I regretted his departure, I helped him complete the formalities for his early termination from the Peace Corps. The experience left me with the impression that African Americans from rural backgrounds often adapted more easily to life as PCVs and were less likely to suffer from culture shock.

110. I frequently attended the old German church in my PCV village. Built in 1898, it stood as a testament to Germany's colonial influence. German scholars had been the ones to first put the local Ewe language into writing, and this church, perched partway down a mountainside, was part of a larger effort to persuade mountaintop villagers to relocate to lower altitudes.

111. Those who came down first, however, had no desire to share the fertile land they had found. So, they spread false rumors about an infestation of snakes at the lower levels to dissuade others from joining them. That deception sparked a long-standing feud between the early settlers and those who moved down later. Even after years, I was never entirely sure who the locals meant when they used the term "dalaves"—the snakes.

As a former German colony, Togo had a unique colonial past. After Germany's defeat in World War I, the country was divided: the eastern part became a French mandate and remained so until independence in 1960, while the western region fell under British control.

That western sliver of Togoland later voted through a questionable 1957 referendum—to join the neighboring British colony, the Gold Coast. When the Gold Coast gained independence and became Ghana, those western Togolese became Ghanaian citizens. The arbitrary nature of this division was laid bare each time I visited a border village in my Agu District. Half the village was in Togo, the other half in Ghana. The border literally split families and friends.

Each time I visited, I was reminded of something the President of Togo once said: "You don't cut a people in two like you cut a loaf of bread."

112. On Sundays, I was always moved by the choir singing in that small German evangelical church. The harmony, power, and emotion of their hymns filled the space like a concert hall. One Sunday, I complimented a village woman on her exceptional voice and said, "You should make vinyl records."

She smiled and replied, "We already do."

The quality of their music was so captivating that I quickly learned never to hum a church tune at the worksite. The moment a few notes left your lips, the workers would drop their tools, join in singing, and begin dancing in perfect rhythm.

113. In my PCV village in Togo, I never ceased to be mesmerized by the traditional akpessé dancers. Their flawless coordination, the deep rhythm in their feet, and the way their voices lifted in unison, it was artistry rooted in culture, not choreography. Their innate ability to move together with grace and harmony left a lasting impression on me.

114. Across Africa, dental hygiene was handled with an impressive variety of natural tools. Many used sticks from shrubs or tree branches to clean their teeth among the most respected were branches from the neem tree, believed to be particularly effective. I recall an American friend, Dean Christ, who lived in Togo and had long been a heavy smoker. His teeth had yellowed significantly over the years, but after he decided to quit smoking, he started using these traditional sticks daily. His teeth became visibly cleaner, and his gum health improved dramatically.

I was so struck by this transformation that I brought samples of the sticks back to Washington, D.C., and handed them to my dentist. He sent them for analysis to a lab at Georgetown University. The lab's conclusion? The sticks had no special chemical properties. Still, I couldn't help but feel there was something powerful about their simplicity and effectiveness.

115. My first serious brush with malaria came in early 1972. I was in my PCV village when I fell seriously ill and later learned I had gone into convulsions. The village chief was informed, and he quickly dispatched a few men to carry me to the nearby German mission hospital. The German physician gave me an immediate injection of quinine into my thigh, and within minutes the fever broke and my crisis passed.

I stayed at the hospital for a few days under the doctor's care. We spoke often during my recovery, and he shared many insights about life in the surrounding villages. One topic he discussed with a sense of sorrow was the high number of young women admitted with complications from failed abortions. He explained, "There's a pattern. Nine months after a particularly heavy rainy season, the hospital fills with these cases. People are confined indoors. The rest follows."

I commented, "Even a light drizzle is enough to cancel an important meeting."

He nodded and added that many of the young women resorted to desperate measures—crushing handfuls of aspirin and mixing the powder into small bottles of Coca-Cola to create a dangerously acidic drink. I asked if their mothers were aware of what was happening.

"Some are," he said. "A few women told me their mothers warned them: once the bleeding starts, you can become pregnant."

The German doctor ended our earlier conversation with a revealing comment. "It's commonly believed in the village," he said, "that if you don't have sex by the age of eighteen, you will become deathly ill." The combination of cultural beliefs, isolation, and misinformation often left young women vulnerable to dangerous choices.

116. In 1974, I was invited to Peace Corps headquarters in Washington, D.C., for an orientation program for new Associate Peace Corps Country Directors (APCDs). Wanting to make a good impression, I wore my best safari suit, which I had custom-made in Lome, Togo. At the end of my first day, I stepped into the elevator to head home when a senior colleague looked me up and down and quipped, "Please come tomorrow in other attire than your pajamas." So much for first impressions.

117. Back in my PCV village, I learned an effective way to deal with the seemingly endless plague of cockroaches. I discovered that if I left a small amount of beer in a bottle in the corner of my room overnight, the cockroaches would crawl in to feed on the residue but wouldn't be able to climb back out. In the morning, I'd take the bottle outside and tip it slowly, making sure not a single cockroach made it back inside. It was primitive pest control, but it worked.

118. Like many autocrats, the President of Togo had large landholdings, especially in cocoa-producing regions. In one of the villages I worked in during 1973, the local school director stood out as an exceptional individual—his gardens thrived, and he had impressive success raising chickens and small livestock. During a visit from friends from Lome, he casually mentioned that the president had a large cocoa plantation nearby.

His visitors returned to the capital and, unfortunately, repeated his remarks. Not long after, national police stormed into his house in the dead of night, beat him, tied him up, and threw him into the back of a pickup truck. He was taken nearly 100 kilometers away to a jail in Lome, where he was held for six months and beaten so badly that I didn't recognize him when we crossed paths months later in a distant village.

"I'm free at last," he told me, his face still marked from the trauma. "I've learned a hard lesson: never talk about the president to anyone. Not even to friends. Especially not to friends."

119. In 1973, while staying in the capital city of Lome, Togo, I rented a row unit in a cluster of rustic two-room lodgings. Each room offered a different window into the lives of residents from various Togolese ethnic groups. My first night there was restless, hot, humid, and airless. When I complained to the manager the next morning, she replied, "You chose the room without a window facing the sea breeze. Sleep on a straw mat and fan yourself. All the sea breeze rooms are already taken by my fellow Togolese, of course."

She gestured toward the row of units along the shared veranda. "You can always tell where someone is from by looking at their bucket," she continued. "Northerners' buckets are usually encrusted with filth, while southerners scrub theirs with lime juice. And don't get me started on how the northern women try to imitate the southern ones, never getting the hems right on their wraparound skirts."

I thanked her for the local color and asked where the shower and toilet stalls were in the sandy compound. Following her directions,

I walked barefoot through the sand with a galvanized bucket of water in hand and a towel wrapped around my waist. I was fully undressed and standing under the cold stream in the topless shower stall when I heard laughter overhead. I looked up to see students crowding at the windows of a three-story secondary school next door, thoroughly entertained by the sight of a naked white man bathing.

Fleeing the scene, I made my way to the elevated latrines but was instantly overwhelmed by the rancid stench rising from the large tin bucket used to collect human waste. My need to relieve myself disappeared completely. Back at the lodge, I told the manager about my experience. She handed me a cheap bottle of perfume and advised, "Soak some tissue with this and stuff it in your nostrils. That's how we survive behind the honey truck that comes to collect those big galvanized buckets. Too bad our water table is too high for proper septic tanks."

120. In another episode in 1975, while walking toward the Peace Corps lab to submit a stool sample for examination, I carried the small specimen cup discreetly in a black plastic bag. Suddenly, a teenage boy sprinted past me and snatched the bag out of my hand. I didn't even try to chase him. I just chuckled to myself,

imagining his reaction when he opened the bag and discovered what he'd stolen.

121. Around this same time in Lome, I had a particularly unpleasant encounter with the city's open sewer system. I stepped out of a taxicab and, without warning, found myself knee-deep in the putrid sludge of a roadside drain. Thankfully, I wasn't injured, but the experience was as humiliating as it was disgusting. The taxi driver leaned over and helped pull me out of the muck, casually remarking, "You shouldn't have got out here."

I muttered, "You can say that again."

122. Later in 1975, still in Lome, I experienced another kind of loss—this one more personal. I returned to my house in Tokoin, a northern suburb of the capital, to discover someone had broken in. A thief had forced open the wooden shutters and stolen my collection of long-playing 78 RPM vinyl records, a cherished treasure I used to play on my battery-operated Philips portable record player. Not long after, I heard my records being broadcast on the local radio station, adding insult to injury.

After this incident, I made a firm resolution to follow my own advice: "Don't possess anything that might attract a thief and always park your motorbike inside the house."

123. I'm also reminded of something I said during a multi-country Peace Corps wells conference held in Atakpamé, Togo, in 1974. Heated debates filled the room over small-bore versus large-bore wells, whether to dig-a-meter or pour-a-meter, the use of school roofs as rainwater catchments, or constructing dikes to form reservoirs during the rainy season. The one thing we all agreed on:

"Water is life, and the more potable it is, the better for a healthy life."

124. Living in Togo also deepened my appreciation of the local language and culture. I learned that a rare fistfight was nicknamed a "Katanga"—a nod to the infamous violence in Katanga province of the DRC. If someone really wanted to insult another, they'd call them sapaté, the local word for smallpox. Another popular jab was to call someone an elanto, a meathead.

Interestingly, I had to tread carefully with the Ewe word for "bat," aguto, as it also referred to the people of my Peace Corps village. To avoid the association with bats, the villagers preferred to call themselves aguwo. I always suspected the bat held a deeper symbolic meaning for them, perhaps a hidden village totem best left unspoken.

125. I was always curious about how intimate relationships were expressed in the local language. After some time, I realized that the word used for the male penis was the same as the word for "war." So instead of "making love," the literal translation in Ewe was "making war." That insight told me a lot about cultural framing and how language reflects deeper societal attitudes.

126. While much about local life fascinated me, some elements were darker. Traditional African leaders in Togo, though revered, harbored private grievances against the country's president. However, fear kept them silent. One particularly disturbing practice involved the president's emissaries traveling from village to village with video cameras to record footage of the most beautiful young women. Word would spread in advance, and while no one dared speak against the visitors, many families quietly hid their daughters. The president would later review the footage and summon girls he found appealing.

127. His goal, as it turned out, was to impregnate women from every region of the country. It was said that this biological strategy ensured his influence would be spread through every corner of Togo, his children placed like seeds across the national landscape to safeguard his legacy.

I'm short-statured by American standards, but in Togo, I was of average height. Later, when I worked in Niger, I felt short again. I mentioned this to a Togolese friend who explained, "Yes, we have our coastal physical form and they have what we call a Sahelian form. When they come down here, it's easy to know they are not from this area."

128. In 1972, when I was a Peace Corps Volunteer in rural Togo, the village chief sent word that all adults were required to vote in the upcoming presidential election. I told my compound neighbors that this mandate didn't apply to me, I was an American citizen and not allowed to vote in a foreign election.

This message quickly got back to the chief. He sent a messenger with a curt reply: "The chief's instruction includes you! Even the handful of Germans who've lived here for years plan to vote."

On election day, I made myself scarce, wandering "lost" in the woods. I invented a tale for anyone who asked that I had encountered a beautiful woman I couldn't resist. I later learned that there had only been one candidate: the sitting president.

Voters could choose "yes" or "no." The "yes" votes were cast in the boys' school, and the "no" votes in the girls' school. Everyone knew what that meant.

Anyone who dared to vote "no" faced immediate consequences, ruffians were stationed outside the girls' school, the designated "no" polling place, and they beat anyone who exited from that direction. Unsurprisingly, the president was declared the winner with well over 95 percent of the vote. Rumors spread through the village that the chief had been rewarded handsomely for his efforts, allegedly receiving a large sum of money from the president for delivering such a favorable election result.

129. I was checking out a remote rural village in southern Togo in 1973, and I noticed that one of the earthen abodes had been marked all over with charcoal drawings and words. Upon a closer examination, I saw that these charcoal markings were actually erudite quotes from Greek and Latin classics.

I asked myself, "How was it that such Greek and Latin writings could be displayed on the outside walls of poor, thatched-covered mud huts in a village located well off the beaten track in Togo?"

My puzzlement over this bizarre sight obliged me to ask a villager about these surprising writings, and he said, "Our chief's son was so brilliant in the local catholic school that the German priests once took a promising young man from our village to study in their homeland. He excelled in school, scoring high marks, and was eventually placed in a seminary to train as a priest. But after about two years, something went terribly wrong. He lost his mind completely and inexplicably and was sent back to our village.

"Do you want to see him?" someone asked me. "He's nearby."

I agreed, curious to witness what had become of this once-brilliant student. Just a few huts away, I found him stark naked, completely unaware of his surroundings, jabbering in Greek, Latin, and German as he scribbled frantically on hut walls with a piece of charcoal. His mutterings echoed phrases he had learned in Europe, but now they spilled out incoherently, detached from context or meaning.

No one knew exactly what had caused his mental breakdown, but many villagers believed the cultural shock he experienced in Europe had simply been too great. Whatever the cause, he had been relegated to the status of a village idiot, a role that, in rural Togolese communities, was oddly accepted.

Every village had one or two individuals like him. As long as they weren't violent, they were allowed to roam freely. People generally avoided disturbing them, believing they were inhabited or preoccupied by spirits. In cases where they became aggressive, a heavy log or weight would be tied to one ankle to prevent them from moving quickly or causing harm. Some even committed obscene acts in public, but such behavior was largely ignored, considered part of their tragic affliction.

130. By the way, I was originally slated to be assigned as a PCV in the far north of Togo in 1970, but I had made good friends with the Togolese man who was sent to our Peace Corp training in the Virgin Islands. He changed my assignment so I could be near his father, who spoke English in the southwestern corner of Togo, near the border with Ghana. His father had decided to retire in the last village that his international company, John Holt, had assigned to him. This elderly man was considered in the village to be the chief of all the outsiders.

131. In the village where I lived, anyone born elsewhere or even anyone who spoke with a slightly different accent was considered a stranger. Village identity was tightly bound to birthplace and dialect. Even a person from just five kilometers away was viewed with suspicion or curiosity.

In Togo, it was customary for someone approaching your home to clap their hands outside your door and say "Ago," signaling they wished to be received. (Coincidentally, my intelligent and spirited pet dog was named Ago, which sometimes led to brief confusion.)

Whenever someone clapped outside, I'd often ask my house boy to check who it was. I remember one occasion in particular. He returned and said, "It's a stranger who wants to see you."

I asked, "How do you know he's a stranger?"

He replied matter-of-factly, "He comes from a village five kilometers away, and they speak a little different than we do."

In that moment, I fully grasped just how finely tuned the village ear was to the nuances of language, and how strong the boundaries of local identity could be, even within walking distance.

132. In 1972, while still in Togo, I had not yet given up on the idea of improving local chicken production. Determined to find a better solution, I managed to acquire a kerosene-heated portable incubator with a sixty-egg capacity. It seemed like the perfect innovation until I realized that simply acquiring the device was only the beginning of my challenges.

First, finding enough fertile eggs proved more difficult than expected. I had assumed that if a rooster was present among a flock of hens, fertility was guaranteed. I quickly learned otherwise.

Then came the real work: operating the incubator. The eggs needed to be turned one-quarter of their circumference every two hours to ensure even heat distribution. I carefully measured and marked each egg with pencil lines to help guide their rotation. I placed the incubator right next to my bed, mentally preparing myself for the many interruptions to my sleep during the twenty-one-day incubation cycle.

For the first few days, I kept up the routine, turning eggs day and night. Then, one night, I failed to wake up at all.

I awoke not to the sound of my alarm, but to the sensation of being carried outdoors by alarmed neighbors. It turned out that the kerosene lamp inside the incubator had been steadily releasing carbon monoxide into my small, enclosed bedroom. I had been slowly poisoned while I slept.

That was the last time I experimented with a kerosene incubator.

133. As a former PCV for five years (I served as a PCV for two years in Honduras before going to Africa), I always attended the main swearing-in ceremonies for PCVs in every African country in which I worked. At last count, I had participated in twenty-three of these ceremonies in multiple African countries.

134. There were thousands of American volunteers, but there were no African volunteers. In African communities, it was rare for someone to volunteer to help their communities. This fact made

me think that 'volunteerism' was deeply embedded in American culture. And even if an African was a volunteer, they could not volunteer for a long time as they had to work to gain food for their families.

135. Thanks to the generosity of the U.S. Embassy in Lomé's Self-Help Fund, I was able to assist in constructing numerous primary school buildings and other essential structures throughout my district in Togo. Each time a project reached completion, the entire village would pause its daily activities for a traditional dedication ceremony. I quickly learned that before any new building could be used, the spirits and ancestors had to be properly thanked and honored through rituals conducted by a local fetish priest.

Though unfamiliar at first, I came to respect these deep-seated customs. They did no harm, and in fact, they helped cement a sense of unity and reverence within the community, so I happily went along.

Villagers would gather at the site, forming a wide circle as the fetish priest began the ceremony. He poured libations on the ground, usually palm wine or another locally brewed spirit, as an offering to the ancestors. Then, with solemn precision, he slit the throat of a white rooster and sprinkled its blood around the school building's perimeter. This, I was told, signaled the approval of the spirit world.

Once the priest's work was done, celebration took over. The women danced in perfect unison while drummers played a rhythmic tune believed to please both the living and the ancestral dead. The atmosphere was always joyful, reverent, and deeply communal.

As mentioned earlier, pouring a few drops of one's drink for the ancestors before sipping was a common practice in Togo. Whether inside a home or outdoors, it became second nature to me. Before I drank a drop of anything from palm wine to bottled beer, I would instinctively offer the first drops to the ground. It was both a gesture of respect and a daily reminder of the ever-present ancestral world that shaped village life.

136. While living in my village in Togo, I developed a keen interest in traditional medicine. The wealth of knowledge passed down through generations was fascinating, rooted in plants, rituals, and an intimate understanding of nature. But despite my appreciation for this ancestral wisdom, there were clear limits to what I could accept.

One case, in particular, stood out to me. A woman who lived in my housing compound suffered from a cataract in one eye. Determined to cure herself, she traveled all the way to Lomé to consult with a practitioner at the city's well-known fetish market. She returned energized and confident, believing she had found the answer.

Her treatment involved cleaning out an old wine bottle and pouring a small amount of kerosene into it. Then, placing the opening of the bottle tightly over her left eye, she tilted it, letting the kerosene come into direct contact with the cataract.

The result was horrifying. The burning sensation was so intense that she ran around the compound in circles, fanning her face and crying out in pain. Despite her desperation and endurance, the treatment did not heal her. Instead, it blinded her in that eye permanently.

Witnessing her agony and the tragic outcome was enough for me to draw a firm line. I decided right then and there: if faced with a similar affliction, I would rather go blind naturally than subject myself to such a brutal and misguided cure.

137. In many of my African postings, I became accustomed to sharing my living space with gecko lizards. At night, they would

dart out from behind wall hangings or crevices to feast on mosquitoes and other small insects. I saw them as useful little allies in the fight against pests, quietly contributing to a more tolerable night's rest.

However, not everyone shared my appreciation for them. Many Africans I knew were eager to kill geckos on sight. The common belief was that if left alone, geckos might crawl into a person's body and move around inside, an unsettling notion rooted in local folklore.

The only time I found them bothersome was during their mating season when they emitted a loud, croaking sound that echoed off the walls and often kept me awake. Still, given the choice, I preferred their company over that of the more inoffensive, outdoor red-headed fence agama lizards. I often amused myself trying to count how many times an agama would bop its head before shifting position like a living metronome in the dust.

Of all the lizards, though, it was the chameleon that fascinated me most. There was something magical about their shifting colors and cautious, calculated movements. I considered it a stroke of good luck whenever one fell out of a tree near me. On one such occasion, I gently scooped the startled creature up into my shirttail and decided to keep it in a small cage as a pet—for a while, at least. Watching it observe the world through swiveling eyes, each moving independently, was endlessly captivating.

138. A local fetish woman heard that I was keeping a chameleon as a pet and rushed to see me. She commanded me to release the chameleon to her. She took it to the place where I found it and rammed a slender wooden stick through its mouth until it came out its anus. She then verified with me the exact place on the ground where I found it and implanted the stick in that spot with the impaled chameleon.

She returned days later when the chameleon was dried to a crisp and took it down and ground it into fine particles with her small mortar and pestle. She then poured these particles into a small cloth pouch. She thanked me. Evidently, I had helped add to her occult powers.

139. In my Peace Corps village in Togo, I once noticed a woman nursing a child who must have been two or three years old. Curious and somewhat concerned, I commented that the child seemed too old to still be breastfeeding. Without missing a beat, she responded, "I agree. Give me the money to buy food for him and I will stop breastfeeding him."

Her reply struck a chord. It wasn't a lack of understanding, it was a lack of resources.

Let me be clear: I am a strong believer in the exclusive breastfeeding of every infant for at least the first six months of life. This includes the all-important colostrum, that initial "liquid gold" which is vital for boosting a newborn's immunity and setting the foundation for healthy development. A strong start begins with a healthy birthweight and early nourishment.

Unfortunately, many babies born in Africa would qualify for intensive care if they had been born in the U.S. A significant number enter the world weighing less than 2.5 kilograms. These low birthweights, combined with poor postnatal nutrition, make the early stages of life in many African communities a precarious gamble.

Anemia is also alarmingly common among young mothers, especially those who give birth in their teenage years. This not only contributes to low birthweights but further deepens the cycle of poverty. Poor maternal health leads to poor infant health, and so the cycle continues.

To me, this reality underscores a fundamental truth: the best investment in breaking this cycle is in the formal education of girls. An educated woman is more likely to delay childbirth, access healthcare, and manage her family's well-being with greater effectiveness. In every village in every country, her empowerment holds the key to healthier generations and stronger communities.

140. While I was a PCV in a Togolese village, I learned the art of keeping a small kerosene refrigerator in good working order. This fridge was mostly filled with bottles of beer, but I did keep a small snake bite kit in the fridge. I had received strict instructions always to keep this kit in the fridge. I always wondered how the kit could be used when I was bitten by a poisonous snake in the bush. I would be dead before I could reach my house fridge.

141. I was traveling from Togo next door to Ghana in 1972, and the bush taxi I was riding in stopped at a village market so people could eat. I bought a loaf of locally made bread and was looking for a tin of sardines to spread on the bread. After looking desperately for a flat tin of sardines, I was able to negotiate a price for one tin with a vendor.

I opened the tin, and all the Africans around me yelled at me as if I were a thief. The man standing next to me muttered, "We were using that tin can as a medium of exchange. Ever since the devaluation of our national currency and the introduction of a new currency, we've been using goods as our currency, and you just ate one of the rare exchange items."

142. When I first arrived in my PCV village in 1970, almost no women covered their breasts. During my last visit to the village in 2014, all the women covered their breasts. That is one of many traditional customs that was no longer practiced.

143. One of the biggest problems I had in my Togo PCV village was the noise made by the young African guys loudly playing the Ludo board game outside my shady bedroom window. There was no rest from these nonstop rowdy games of Ludo. The noise they made was incessant. You would think that they were fighting a battle for their lives when they were only playing a kid's game akin to Candyland.

144. There was a day that these same young Togolese men sitting around my house were not playing Ludo, but they were acting oddly. They had grins on their faces and were repeatedly saying, "Meow, Joseph."

I finally figured that they had killed and eaten my pet cat. That was the day that I learned the local people ate cats. At first, I was upset, but as there was nothing I could do, I accepted this fact of local life.

145. While living in my Peace Corps village in Togo, I was eager to participate in the everyday tasks required of villagers, no matter how physically demanding or culturally gendered they might be. One of those tasks was hauling water, a chore traditionally assigned to women and children. Still determined to share in their burdens, I rose before dawn one dry-season morning to join a group of women on their foray to fetch water.

We walked for several kilometers to reach a shallow, muddy puddle in a stream bed—the only remaining water source. The women filled my galvanized bucket and then carefully topped it off with leafy branches to reduce spillage. I helped lift their buckets onto their heads, but when it came time for my turn, I couldn't manage the balancing act. I ended up carrying my bucket by my side.

By the time we returned to the village, their buckets were still full, while mine had sloshed out most of its contents. One woman, trying not to laugh, told me, "Until you are able to carry things on your head, there's no sense in you going with us again to collect water. But if you want, you can help us gather firewood."

I was always amazed by how much weight women could carry on their heads. Using a cloth twisted into a circular cushion, they balanced enormous loads with ease and grace. I often joined others in lifting heavy items, bundles of wood, buckets of water, and even construction supplies onto their heads. Once in place, these women stood tall, almost regal, as if they were international models on a runway. They couldn't lift the load themselves, but once the burden was balanced, they could carry it for kilometers.

It was clear to me: some skills must be learned in childhood, head-carrying among them.

In those same years, I was also determined to learn the local languages of southern Togo, primarily Ewe and Mina. I studied diligently, practicing with villagers and jotting down vocabulary wherever I could. Yet no matter how committed I was, I never quite achieved fluency. Meanwhile, I observed that Africans from northern Togo, speakers of entirely different languages, would arrive in Lomé and, within weeks, be conversing smoothly in the local coastal dialects. Their speed of acquisition fascinated me.

I eventually concluded that Africans, perhaps due to early multilingual exposure, could learn other African languages faster than outsiders like me. I also noted that women seemed to pick up the language more quickly than men likely because they spent more time at the open market, where bargaining and socializing demanded verbal agility.

One of the challenges I faced was the lack of proper instructional materials. At the time, no Ewe language learning books were available in Togo. I had to make a special trip to the University of Ghana at Legon, near Accra, just to find a few texts to guide my learning.

147. I did find that when a Togolese came to the capital city of Lome for the first time from his or her rural upcountry village, they could be lost for several weeks before being able to find their way around in a large city.

148. In early 1974, I had to leave Togo and go to Washington, DC, for an interview at the Peace Corps headquarters for my PCD assignment to Gabon. There were three people who interviewed me. I was shocked when one of them asked me if I had voted for Richard Nixon in the 1968 US presidential election. My reply was, "No. I voted for Hubert Humphrey because he was a big supporter of the Peace Corps."

149. I tried to eat like the people in my PCV village by sitting on stools at low tables, but I preferred to eat my meals at a regular

table. There was a cultural difference at play. They worked from the waist down, while in the Western world, most of the work was done from the waist up.

For example, they cultivated their fields by hand with a short-handled hoe (daba) and a machete. I wondered how Togo could ever advance as long as they farmed with hand tools.

150. It was a proud and highly publicized moment for the President of Togo in 1975 when he stood triumphantly beside a massive elephant he had "heroically" slain near his hometown in northern Togo. The public spectacle painted him as a great warrior and protector of the nation. But, as with many carefully curated political displays, the truth was something else entirely.

What the public didn't know was that the president had shot the elephant from the safety of his helicopter, hardly a feat of bravery. He used that same helicopter to fish, not with rods or nets, but by tossing sticks of dynamite into the rivers below. Still, the narrative was tightly controlled, and the regime ensured only the glorified version reached the people.

The elephant was hoisted onto a flatbed truck and driven across the country, with the president accompanying it on its journey to the coast. At every major town along the route, crowds gathered as he gave short speeches in French, many for the first time, further boosting his image as the benevolent and heroic leader of the Togolese people.

This calculated performance was part of a larger effort to elevate his persona to near-mythical status. In 1976, the government published a state-sponsored propaganda comic book depicting him as a miracle worker, a man of divine power and unparalleled wisdom. Every evening, when I turned on the local television, I was met with the same image: the president descending from the heavens, bathed in celestial light, to land with fanfare on a glowing map of Togo.

He was being cast not just as a leader but as God's chosen gift to the nation.

151. No doubt that the populace feared this long-term president. This fear was supported by reports about his keeping all of Togo's strong fetish priests in the military camp where he resided in northern Lome. It was said he rendered public service by using these priests to detect thieves. He would line up in his camp those accused of thievery and have designated priests to walk in front of

them. The power of these priests would cause the guilty party to fall to the ground.

152. I was honored when, out of over a hundred Peace Corps Volunteers serving in Togo, I was elected by my peers to be one of three volunteer leaders. At the time, I didn't dwell much on the responsibility until a moment of real tension brought its weight into focus.

One day, a village boy rushed to alert me that the Peace Corps Country Director (PCD), a political appointee, had arrived in the center of the village with a rifle in his vehicle. The message was clear: Stay away. The situation was volatile. But I decided to see him anyway.

Only the day before, I had traveled with the two other elected PCV leaders to speak directly with the U.S. Ambassador in Lomé. We had voiced our concerns and formally asked for his intervention to have the PCD removed from his post. The man's erratic behavior, poor leadership, and lack of French language skills had caused widespread frustration among volunteers throughout Togo. His appointment in 1973 came during a controversial shift in Peace Corps administration, when the agency was placed under the domestic ACTION agency, a move that many felt compromised its international focus.

Now, the PCD was in my village, clearly aware of our actions. I approached him. He stayed seated in his car, speaking sharply through the window. I don't remember every word, but I do remember this: "You've stirred up shit, and now you need to clean up your mess."

I said nothing in return. I turned around and calmly walked back to my house, trusting that the villagers, who had come to respect and protect me, would watch out for my safety.

Within a couple of weeks, the ambassador took decisive action. The unfit PCD was removed from his post and sent out of the country. Justice, in this case, had quietly prevailed.

153. In 1972, I was taking the old German train from Agu-Gare to Lomé. I sat contentedly on a wooden bench that lined the side of one of the passenger cars, enjoying the rhythmic clatter of the train and the vibrant atmosphere. As we rolled along the tracks, the Togolese passengers began chanting a sing-song list of the villages we passed, their voices rising in a kind of communal harmony that made the journey feel almost festive.

At my feet, a toddler played quietly. His mother sat beside me, calm and composed. But then I noticed something that jolted me, I realized the child was playing with a razor blade.

Alarmed, I quickly bent down, snatched the blade from his tiny hands, and handed it to his mother, expecting concern or at least surprise.

To my astonishment, she took the blade and immediately handed it back to the child.

Worried, I said, "I'm scared he'll cut himself."

She looked at me and replied, completely unbothered, "If he wants to cut himself, let him do it. That way, he'll learn the harm playing with a razor blade can cause."

Her response left me stunned. It was a stark reminder of the cultural differences in how pain, risk, and learning are understood and of the often harsh lessons that come with growing up in a world where experience is the first teacher.

154. One of my Togolese friends in my PCV village had a terrible earache. He went to the doctor at the mission hospital to have his ear examined. The doctor looked in his ear canal and removed fragments of bird feathers. He cautioned my friend by saying, "Be careful with cleaning your ears with the tips of a bird's feather. I

know this is the usual way villagers clean their ears, but you must be careful."

155. The American Ambassador summoned me to Lome in 1973. He wanted me to use US Embassy self-help funds to build a health center on the foreign minister's farm. I started to object because this was not in my work area, but he insisted on me taking the lead to construct this center. Later, I learned from villagers at the site that the minister was doing this to mollify them because he had confiscated their land.

The completion of the building of the center taught me a number of things. First, I learned that building a health center was easy compared to having it staffed with health agents and stocking it with drugs. The center I helped build stood empty for months in spite of the foreign minister's influence. Anyway, my work helped the ambassador receive a national medal and certificate he wanted before his departure from Togo.

156. My nearest activity to this center was on the edge of my district, and it concerned an earthen dam to provide the community with water in the dry season. Ground water was too deep to make a well and using the school roof to fill a large cistern was insufficient. I was able to persuade the managers of the heavy

equipment school in Lome to come and practice their work by building this dam.

The villagers cleared the land so it could be surveyed, and the heavy equipment arrived. I obtained from the US Embassy's Self-Help Fund the money needed to cover the cost of filters and fuel. Work on the earthen dike was almost completed when the first rains of the season started. In a short while, the dike was holding back the natural flow of rainwater.

I was happy to see villagers collecting water, but I was dismayed when I saw some people from the main village chase away people from a nearby smaller village. I asked a man from the main village why they were doing this, and he replied, "When we wanted the help of that village when we were clearing this area of all brush so the surveyors could work, people from that village refused to work, so they don't have a right to the water in this new reservoir."

157. I always enjoyed visiting the Fon (an ethnic group from the neighboring Benin) wood carvers who lived near the regional capital (about 12 kilometers from my PCV village). They always had interesting carvings to show and sell me. I learned that their profession was a family affair, and you had to be part of the family to know this trade.

I tried to start a business with them, exporting their wood carvings to an American friend in the US who would market them. Among the favorite carvings were made by them was a lion chair sculpted out of a single hardwood iroko tree (Milicia excelsa) trunk.

158. In 1973, I was working as a PCV staff person in the Peace Corps Office in Lome. One of my assignments was to deal with an auditor from the Peace Corps' headquarters in Washington, DC. This auditor found that we had many items in our warehouse that were not in our inventory. So, one evening, he piled these items up in the vacant lot next to our office and set fire to them

The next day, all the Togolese employees in the office were in tears because they thought it would have been better to give them the items instead of burning them.

159. This auditor was also puzzled by the fact that four Toyota pickups were in our inventory, even though there was no authorization to buy vehicles. I told him that the construction PCVs shared those pickups to do their work. One pickup was assigned to each region, and the PCVs shared them on a rotating basis.

We could not buy vehicles, but we could rent them, so I made an arrangement with the dealer to pay a monthly rent fee, and when the fees reached the selling price of the vehicle, Peace Corps Togo owned them. While Peace Corps/Washington appreciated the ingenuity behind this transaction, it was adamant about selling the vehicles and removing them from our inventory.

160. I must convey that I am transported by nostalgia to the early 1970s in Africa. My heart hungers for the old days in the village. In this pre-electronic age, I was happily immersed in a dreamy foreign world. It was like living on a different planet

This was a time of wonder when the great art of letter writing with paper and a pen was the only way of communicating with anyone in the US. I recall writing a letter and carefully addressing its envelope and taking it to the regional post office for the fixation of the number of stamps for its delivery to a place in the far away USA. If I were lucky, and the person I was writing to replied quickly, I could get a reply letter in about six weeks.

I experienced many things in my PCV village that I observed but cannot explain. They happened, but I would not allow myself to believe in these magical events ... they were beyond my understanding. I select below to share with the reader three of my most unbelievable occult experiences in Togo. I saved these mysteries for last place in this section because the words to describe these incredible episodes are a challenge to formulate.

On second thought, maybe I should delete the following because I do not want to try to describe these three impossible episodes which I experienced, and perhaps they are better kept secret and go with me to the grave. Whatever the case may be, the following is my attempt to explain the unexplainable.

161. I helped a man in my PCV village evaluate a parcel of land that he wanted to buy to establish a cocoa plantation. Several days later he asked me if I had left any footprints when I walked through the sand at the edge of a sandy stream that ran through this parcel. I replied that I had walked barefooted on the sandy banks of the small stream.

He immediately asked me to come with him to see if my footprints were still there. We arrived at the stream, and it was clear that my footprints had indeed been removed. When the man saw this, he told me to be very careful. He also said that my footprints were probably taken to a powerful fetisher in a distant village who would conjure up against me a wicked black magic spell.

A few weeks later I heard some noise in front of my house and went to my bedroom window to see what this noise was all about.

It was 2 a.m. (the hour of evil spirits). I clearly saw the glowing wrinkled reddish face of an ugly ogre over the top of my front wall. I was deeply afraid as I peered at the face of this hideous creature.

It was a moonless night and not a sound could be heard. Suddenly a sparkling ball of light came out of one of the ogre's large eyes and flew through the air directly at me. It came at a high speed through my window screen and tried to pierce my body. I instinctively knew if it entered my body, I was good as dead.

I fought it off with all my might and it flew back into the eye of the ogre. After that I sat up the entire night until there was some daylight. I exited my house and tried to explain in my broken Ewe to an old woman who lived in an adjoining building what had occurred. She listened to me and said just one word, "Azé," and then ran off to inform the chief and others in the central part of the village.

Some of the chief's guards arrived at my house in short order to see how I was and asked for many details about what had happened. They all said that I must be very strong to have survived this clash with Azé which had not been heard of in decades.

162. Another magical experience was when I secretly accompanied a group from my PCV village which would climb the steep trail to

a clearing on top of Mt. Agu mountain at every full moon to drum, dance, sing and drink palm wine.

Once atop the mountain, the drum beating and dancing started. For me, it all began slowly but after a few calabashes of palm wine they say I became delirious and danced up a storm.

The next thing I knew I was in my bed and there were a lot of voices outside of my bedroom window. I thought I had passed out and other members of the group had managed to carry me down the mountainside.

The woman who was attending me said, "The others who were with you on the mountain said you rode a moonbeam down to this spot. The people gathered outside want to see you to make sure you're all right. Nobody has ridden a moonbeam for more than a century. This makes you incredibly special."

163. There was another time in 1972 when women farmers ran toward the village, sounding the presence of danger by ululating loudly. The chief's guards came immediately. Some of the women explained to them that there was a 'headhunter' hiding in the high grass. I recalled vaguely somebody saying something about a headhunter season when men would seek and cut off human heads for occult ceremonies.

I turned to an African friend and said, "I'm glad they don't want a white head."

His reply was, "Head is head ... white or black."

The guards (askari) sent a runner to communicate to the head fetisher that he was urgently needed. The head fetisher quickly joined the guards at a spot in the road and did some ceremonies. Upon the completion of the ceremonies, a man dressed in a blue boubou came out of his hiding place and floated in the air over the tall grass until he fell on the dirt road. The guards promptly beat him and tied his hands up, marching him roughly to the chief's house.

(It takes my breath away to describe the above. I am frightened by the recounting of these scary episodes of my time in my PCV village in Togo. This fear tempts me to delete this last part of my initial years in Togo.)

GABON

1. I was working in Gabon in 1975–76 as the Peace Corps country representative. I was obliged to visit PCVs who were stationed about the country. Given the almost roadless condition of this forest-covered country, I had to do my upcountry visits by hiring a small plane.

During one flight upcountry, I peered down into the dense tropical forest below and asked the French pilot what would happen if we crashed, and he said, "We would not even be looked for because there's no way they could get to us."

2. Gabon was a country where it rained almost every day for eleven months out of the year. I had a toddler in 1975, and this was an era when cloth diapers were used. Therefore, these diapers never dried.

I requested that Peace Corps Washington grant me a special authorization to buy a clothes dryer since this item was not an allowed expense. The response I got back was, "While your request is unusual in a number of ways, it is granted."

3. I learned during this time in Gabon to keep a lightbulb on at all times in your closets to diminish the buildup of mildew caused by the high humidity.

4. Starting a new Peace Corps program in Gabon was challenging in many ways. The biggest cultural shock I had in my life occurred in Gabon. I looked at the map of West Africa and saw that Gabon was just down the coast, so I thought it would be just like Togo ... I could not have been more wrong ... it was different in every way.

It seemed the Africa I knew changed when I crossed into the dense forest region where little was the same. I hungered to return to the drier savanna of Africa that I came from. For me, there was something scary about the dark density of this humid forest-covered country. I was accustomed to seeing clear paths cutting through the savanna grassland, but even when paths were present in the dense forest, I could not see them.

5. My cultural shock started in the early morning after my first night in Libreville, the capital city of Gabon, early in 1975, when I heard an unfamiliar clanking noise coming from the street outside of my temporary second-floor apartment. I rushed to the window to see what was going on, and I was surprised by what I observed.

There was a real garbage truck with men emptying real galvanized garbage cans. I could not believe my eyes, especially as the two refuse collectors were white men.

6. There were also adjustments to make in managing a newly re-invited Peace Corps program in a country dominated by the French. Our agreement with the host government was that it would lodge the PCVs, so it lodged one PCV in the capital city of Libreville in a five-star hotel. He liked staying there, but he could not afford to eat there, and the eating places he could afford were a distance from his hotel.

7. There was another case of one PCV who taught English at a school in Libreville and was asked to give private lessons to Gabon's president. I wanted to extricate her from this presidential assignment, but I was overruled by my ambassador. She excelled at this unusual presidential assignment. I had unanticipated problems when the president gave her a car, as PCVs were not supposed to own or drive cars.

8. Perhaps my most frustrating experience in Gabon was when several PCVs based in the southern part of the country spontaneously decided to visit neighboring Congo-Brazzaville. My ambassador was fit to be tied when he learned about this because the U.S. did not have diplomatic relations at the time with that

country. So, there was no way they could be helped if they were detained. Finding these wayward PCVs and returning them to Gabon was something I hope to never repeat.

9. Besides managing a program to teach English as a Foreign Language (TEFL), I had to oversee the primary school construction program, which had earned a high reputation in Gabon when Peace Corps had previously operated there. The Peace Corps was especially remembered for its use of Dodge Power Wagons. In fact, the word "dodge" had entered the local language as a term meaning 'strong vehicle.'

10. The construction PCVs had completed their training and were ready to build schools. I went to see the Minister of Education (the president's brother) to inform him that we were prepared to start and to ask where we should work and how the school construction would be funded. He asked, "How much do you need to build a three-classroom school?"

I replied, "That I don't quite know."

"I estimate that it cannot cost more than the check I'm writing you." He handed me the check and said, "Let me know when you finish the school building. Have a good day."

11. I told the construction PCVs this news and they asked what I would do with the check. I replied that I would have to ask my superiors in Peace Corps/Washington. In any event, we were able to negotiate the check with a local bank and build the first Peace Corps primary school near Libreville. In those days, a check for a million Central African Francs (then equivalent to around 25,000 US dollars) was a large sum to manage.

12. Another challenge for me in Gabon was that the construction volunteers were speaking more Spanish than the French they had learned in training. They could not find local laborers, so they hired "Equatos" from Equatorial Guinea, who spoke Spanish, the language of their home country. (This reminded me that without an imported language, most Africans could not use their local languages to communicate with others from different regions.)

13. I was thankful for the white French woman who assisted me. She insisted that I not only speak French correctly but also produce letter-perfect reports in French. I submitted graciously to her demands to refine my use of the French language, but I never understood why she was paid more than me. She was a local employee, and the warped salary schedule for local employees was higher than that for American employees.

14. I complained to PC/Washington when I found out that the PC/Gabon program was the most expensive in Africa. I simply could not get used to the high costs of living and working in Gabon. I had just paid the rent on my house, and my blood was boiling. Not only was my house super expensive, but I also had to pay a year's rent in advance.

I was so vociferous about this to my Africa Regional Director in Washington that he told me to tone it down because he could not fight over this issue with the Secretary of State. I learned that it was a real feather in the cap of my U.S. ambassador to get the Peace Corps re-invited to Gabon.

I immediately understood what he meant and kept quiet about the high cost issue, though I lamented that the general budget crunch was forcing Peace Corps to reduce the size of its programs in other African countries. Evidently, getting Peace Corps re-invited to Gabon was a significant diplomatic achievement.

15. My youthful Gabonese janitor would always show up for work in the morning drunk. Evidently, his breakfast consisted of a bottle of cheap red wine.

Later, I was invited to the Presidential Palace for an official reception. We were given large tumbler glasses filled with champagne. The ample flow of champagne convinced me that alcoholics ruled this country.

16. The prevalence of this high level of alcoholism in Gabon was confirmed to me several years later when I saw a notice in the duty-free liquor section of a store in the international airport of Abidjan, Côte d'Ivoire, stating that it did not sell any alcoholic beverages to people from Gabon.

Seeing this notice prompted me to ask the Ivoirian store clerk, "Why do you prohibit the sale of alcoholic beverages to people from Gabon?"

The rapid reply I got was, "Because Gabonese will consume the alcohol in the airport lounge right away, becoming inebriated and thus difficult to control."

I learned that if I ever had Gabonese over to my house, I needed to make sure my liquor cabinet was locked; otherwise, they would not leave until every last drop of alcohol was gone.

17. Perhaps the strangest African television broadcast I ever saw was in Gabon in late 1975 when the president of the country pleaded with his fellow citizens to marry non-Gabonese in order to increase the national birthrate and bring under control the high

level of female sterility. He was sincere about raising Gabon's low national population growth rate.

I have always wondered why so many Gabonese women were sterile. Was it because of excessive alcohol consumption, high promiscuity, heredity, or the food they ate? Or was it due to the natural radioactivity that had been proven to exist in Gabon?

18. The president's speech on national TV reminded me that his Ivoirian mistress lived next door with her three children in her three-story villa. I visited their house once and was impressed that they had every electronic gadget imaginable and tons of snow ski equipment. The kids would brag about how their dad had bought the hotel where they stayed at a ski resort in Switzerland.

Their house had everything except food. It was difficult to obtain food in Libreville. They would come to my house to snack.

19. They opened a new modern supermarket in Libreville. There was a meat counter with all the meat wrapped in clear plastic. The meat had been flown in secretly on a plane from boycotted Zimbabwe (Southern Rhodesia).

There was a small sign at the meat counter instructing buyers to cook the meat, and that being wrapped in plastic did not mean it was ready to eat. Evidently, some Gabonese had never seen meat wrapped in clear plastic and thought it could be consumed raw.

20. Incidentally, I had heard that the president imported specially made high-heeled shoes from Italy to compensate for his short stature. He wanted to avoid being called a 'pygmy' by some Gabonese, as this was a serious insult. (In general, pygmies were considered inferior beings in Gabon.)

21. In Gabon in the mid-1970s, any company was obligated to hire any Gabonese who applied for a job. I met Gabonese who had worked for twenty or more companies. Many would take their first paycheck and return to their forest village to splurge. When the money ran out, they would eventually return to the capital, Libreville, or the industrial town of Port Gentil to find another job.

22. Interestingly, most of the work in Gabon was done by foreigners. The marketplaces were particularly dominated for generations by people from Benin and Togo. I was told by the dean of the Daho-Togo (Benin was formerly known as Dahomey) group that he was the first African to build a concrete (en dur) house in Libreville. He had worked for the French administration before Gabon gained independence in 1960.

23. There was a lot of suffering in Gabon when the government decided in 1975 to expel people from Benin and Togo, even though most of them had never actually lived in those countries. There were fears that the school system would be next, as most of the school heads were from Haiti and many instructors came from other Francophone African countries.

24. One of the oddest sights I ever saw in Africa was at a forest clearing where work was underway on the TransGabonais Railway. I was amazed to see hundreds of Pakistanis dressed in their pajama-like work clothes. I was told that other work sites had men from Burkina Faso. Not a single Gabonese worked on the construction through the dense forest and across its many rivers. The 670-kilometer railway took 14 years to build and nearly bankrupted Gabon.

25. I took a break from Gabon in 1975 to serve as acting PCD in Bangui, the capital of the Central African Republic, for a couple of months. A PCV in Bangui had his house vandalized multiple times despite having iron bars on his windows. His investigation revealed that a loose vertical bar allowed the thief to access his house.

The PCV hooked up some electrical wires so the next intruder would get a shock. Sure enough, the thief returned when the PCV was away and was electrocuted.

Local police came to investigate and remove the body. To the surprise of many, the PCV was arrested for murder and jailed. My only option was to bargain for his release and have him sent out of the country.

26. In 1974, I visited the famous Schweitzer Hospital in Lambaréné, Gabon. The national government was in the process of taking it over and integrating it into the national health network. I mentioned to my Gabonese guide, "One of the hallmarks of the hospital when Dr. Schweitzer was alive was that he allowed family members to stay with the patients."

My guide immediately replied, "With all due respect to the foreign missionary doctor, that's a backward idea that goes against modern medical science."

27. I was pleased in 1975 to procure a new wonder — a Toyota four-wheel drive Land Cruiser with air conditioning. This was the first of its kind. The only place I could travel with it was to northern Gabon. So, I set out alone to visit a PCV based in Oyem in the far north. But I got stuck in the mud. I could not get my new car out

of the tracks created by other vehicles before me. This was my first and only overland trip out of Libreville.

28. In Cameroon, I was visiting a Peace Corps training camp for Gabon PCVs in 1975 in Mbalmayo. The Nyong River passed by the camp and there were many fishermen in their pirogues. I asked one of the fishermen if he could take me on a short boat ride. One of them replied, "Of course, if you're willing to make us a small payment."

I got into his leaky pirogue, and we started heading downstream on the fast-flowing river. The pirogue was manned by two men and I noticed a boy bailing water from the bottom with a tin can, as water seeped in. Late afternoon quickly turned into evening. I told the head man, "Let's turn around and go back."

As the pirogue turned to head upstream, the seeping water began to gush. The head man said, "I think it best that you jump into the river and swim to the bank."

I did as he said, swimming frantically, fully clothed to the nearest riverbank. I pulled my soggy body out of the water and started walking back to camp in my slippery shoes. Before I could reach the camp, darkness fell, and I had to feel my way through the bushes. When I finally arrived, one of the trainees who spotted me asked, "How was the boat ride?"

I didn't answer him. I just wanted to change into dry clothes and go to bed.

29. On one of my trips in the mid-1970s to Yaoundé, the capital city of neighboring Cameroon, I spotted a young African man sobbing. I approached him and asked, "What's the matter?"

He surprisingly replied, "What can we do? I've known my whole life but one president, and he is absent from our country most of the time."

I said, "Give it time and you will have a new president."

I felt guilty for saying this, as Cameroon still has had the same second president for 42 years. No succession plan has been made for this elderly man (now 91 years of age), and there are still no firm plans to limit presidential terms. In too many African countries, the president becomes like a traditional village chief who holds power for life, and little thought is given to succession. Aging presidents are referred to as "dinosaurs," and when they die, one of their family members often replaces them.

NIGER

1. I recall hearing of a US Embassy meeting with President Kountché in his office in Niamey in 1976 when one of his military assistants hustled into the room to whisper in his ear. It was thought the courtesy call was over, but he said, "Let's continue our meeting. What I just learned is that a certain major is attempting a coup against me. I know him. He will fail and be arrested. No worries."

I was impressed that just by knowing the name of the individual trying to oust him from power, he was able to so coolly dismiss the attempted coup.

2. During the long dry season, dust storms were common in Niger. These storms would often start at the onset of the rainy season. I was driving to my home in Niamey in May 1976 when a towering blanket of thick dust arrived. I was just a block from my house, so I thought I could make it even though I had zero visibility.

To make a long story short, I ran over a small tree and slammed into the concrete-block front wall of a neighbor. After that incident, I always sheltered in place until after a dust storm passed.

3. It is often said that instead of giving a man a fish you should teach him to fish. Well, I found that not to be so true in Niger in 1977. We had a thriving activity to construct ponds where the water table was high and then stock them with tilapia fish. Then we would teach the Tuareg herders who had lost their livestock in the previous drought how to fish and market their catch.

We thought we were changing the livelihoods of these pastoralists, but after several years the rains returned and the Tuaregs quickly abandoned their camps around the water reservoirs to start again working on rebuilding their herds and living their previous way of life. One departing Tuareg man told me, "We're not cut out for this kind of life ... all the trees make me nervous. And we don't like eating fish."

I find this is an example of how tough it is to change human nature permanently. It takes a true prolonged crisis to get people to consider changing their habitual way of living. We all know of ways to improve our lives but, in general, we do not adopt those ways if we are not obliged to do so for a long stretch of time.

Anyway, an American colleague and I enjoyed fishing with a rod and reel the remaining fish out of the water reservoirs we had stocked with tilapia fingerlings for our dearly departed Tuaregs.

4. My Nigerien work counterpart, Commandant Moussa Saley, frequently used a common phrase when making a critical decision that negatively impacted some people: "You can't make an omelet without breaking the egg."

5. This same counterpart had a fondness for women and would often say the most outlandish things about them, many of which I did not fully understand. For example, during the 1977–1981 period, when we failed to achieve the objectives of our jointly managed activity, he would say, "The most beautiful woman in the world can't give more than she has." I assume he meant that even though we did our best, we could not accomplish everything we had hoped.

He would also say, "My favorite kind of woman is twice my size and half my age."

And when we were camping out in the bush, he once excused himself by saying, "When your car tire has a flat, you have to find a spare."

Many years later (in 1999), I visited him at his home and noticed that one of his two wives was absent. I also heard his grown children calling him "Hadj," an honorific reserved for those who had completed the pilgrimage to Mecca, Saudi Arabia. I asked this Muslim man—who had freely drunk whiskey when I worked with him—what was going on. He replied, "When one gets near the end of his life, he should arrange things."

While I pondered his reply, he excused himself to go pray— something I had never seen him do before.

This man was dear to me. I dedicated my Cornell University master's thesis to him in 1983. He passed away in 2001. I wrote his eulogy.

6. All this talk about Islam reminded me of the time I visited an elderly Imam in Niger in 1978. He told me about the years he had spent walking (da Allah) to Mecca and back. He proudly referred to himself as a "four-star Hadj," and believed that those who made the holy pilgrimage to Mecca by plane were of much lower rank.

7. I'm reminded of a time in 1978 when an American colleague and I took a course on Islamic religion at the Libyan People's Cultural Center in Niamey, Niger. At the end of the course, we were given a thick copy of the holy book, the Quran, printed in both Arabic and English.

Years later, I learned that this course had sparked my white American colleague's interest in Islam. He eventually adopted the name Abdulahi (slave of Allah), completed the Mecca pilgrimage, learned to read the Quran in Arabic, and became an Islamic scholar. I remain in touch with this outstanding man.

8. In Niamey, Niger, I once attended a religious gathering in 2008 where the head preacher said something I've never forgotten: "There are two ways to be happy, either get more or desire less."

9. In 1979, I repeated my instructions several times to a Nigerien employee in Niamey. He finally understood, and a female colleague listening in said, "He understands fast when you repeat many times."

10. One of my prized possessions hanging on the wall of my Texas home is a decorative red goat-leather frame displaying, under glass, twenty-one silver Agadez pendant crosses handcrafted by Tuareg artisans. Each cross represents a different Tuareg town.

11. There was a clause in Niger's revised constitution that prohibited legal action against anyone who had seized power by toppling the national government. When I asked why such a clause was necessary, the reply I received was: "Without that clause, there would be no constitution."

12. When I left a major town in far eastern Niger, some residents wished me a safe trip "back to Niger" as though the rest of the country were foreign to them. In general, people in eastern Niger knew little about the western part of the country. If they traveled at all, it was to nearby towns across the border in Nigeria. Their

goods, currency, and connections came from the other side. Though their homes were technically in Niger, their villages straddled the Nigeria border.

13. In 1976, I drove east of Zinder along the new blacktop highway—"Route de l'Unité"—funded by Canada. My route took me through Gouré and on to Nguigmi, on the edge of Lake Chad. The road ran through a vast, desolate landscape devastated by a prolonged drought, evidenced by the carcasses of big-horned Kuri cattle strewn across the land. My objective was to visit Geoffrey Bergen, a lone PCV teaching English at a secondary school in Nguigmi.

I found him, and he welcomed me into his small house, half-buried by a shifting sand dune. He lived with one of his Nigerien students, the tallest Nigerien I had ever met. (Years later, I saw Bergen again in Niamey, where he was working as the World Bank representative. His former student, Ali Bety, had become a senior official at the French development agency.)

Nearly thirty years later, I returned to Nguigmi and was dismayed to find that the Route de l'Unité had almost disappeared under the desert. It was easier to drive on the sandy tracks beside what remained of the highway. Evidently, there had never been a plan to maintain it.

14. Initially, I drove alone across Niger, but the flat, vast, treeless terrain made it hard to stay awake. The monotony was numbing, and heat waves dancing off the road surface made it worse. I soon learned to always travel with a local driver accustomed to navigating these open, arid spaces.

15. We tried to establish rudimentary radio stations in rural Niger. They were well received but hard to maintain. The tall antennae gave them a 25-kilometer broadcast radius, and villagers would gather around radios to hear pre-recorded discussions from neighboring communities. Sadly, the harsh climate rendered some of these stations inoperable within just a few months.

16. My American office mate in Niamey once said of me, "He writes too much. We need to send him somewhere where there's nothing to write about."

Our African colleague responded, "That resonates with me. I'll send him deep into the desert. There's nothing there but sand."

I did as instructed and traveled into the vast emptiness. I returned with a 20-page paper describing the shapes, sizes, and colors of the sand I had observed.

17. I visited the Sultan of Agadez, Niger, in 1976. His house was located near the centuries-old, famous mud mosque. When I

visited him again in Agadez in 2008 (protocol required me to see the Sultan), I was surprised to find that it was the same man I had met in 1976.

On his wall were portraits of all the presidents of Niger. I remarked, "You've lasted longer than any of the presidents on your wall."

One does not speak directly to the Sultan but only through his assistant, who remained on his knees before the Sultan's elevated throne. The assistant spoke to the Sultan in a language I did not understand. Through the assistant, the Sultan replied, "Those were politicians. My role is entirely religious, and I'm careful not to say anything that impacts politics. I'm acutely aware that if I say anything political, the people will follow it."

18. I learned in 1979 that Niger was the first country in the world to implement an upcountry educational TV system. In the most remote areas, you could see hangars with a TV set encased in a wooden cabinet powered by solar panels mounted next to the building. I gloated, "Niger is ahead of the times!"

Thirty years later, while working in Niger again, I attended a meeting at the Ministry of Education to discuss the challenges of delivering basic education to rural areas. I brought up the educational TV installations I had once seen, but none of the

Ministry officials knew what I was talking about. Evidently, Niger's innovative TV program only existed now in unread reports buried in the Ministry's dusty documentation library.

19. The same can be said about solar energy in general. Back in the 1970s, there was a national center in Niamey for manufacturing, repairing, and installing solar appliances—mostly solar water heaters. But when I passed by the center in 2014, it was shut down and resembled a graveyard of abandoned solar equipment.

20. While on the topic of solar energy in the blazing sun of Niger, I once enjoyed the peacefulness of my Nigerien counterpart's riverside garden when he lamented, "I planned to retire here and live by the river with its seasonal ups and downs. But now, my retirement has been ruined by a nearby solar irrigation installation that allows year-round farming. Don't they understand we're supposed to rest during the dry season?

"I guess we'll have to get more Gourmas," he added, referring to the Gourmantché ethnic group from neighboring Burkina Faso, "but I don't like doing that, even though they're the only ones who can handle gardening work."

21. Years later, I returned to the same spot on the bank of the Niger River and saw a heap of water hyacinth snagged along the shoreline. I asked the Nigerien with me when these weeds had

invaded the river. He replied, "Several years ago. They just keep spreading. It's feared they'll soon make the river unnavigable."

Later, I realized that this invasive species—Pontederia crassipes, a South American aquatic plant, was beginning to clog lakes, rivers, and waterways across Africa.

22. In 1979, President Kountché participated in the inauguration of a new water reservoir and used the occasion to sharply criticize his own ethnic group, the Zarma. He declared, "This is a very nice expanse of water, but I do not see one single lettuce plant growing around it—because you consider gardening to be beneath you."

23. In the mid-1970s, I attended meetings in Niamey at the Niger River Commission (NRC) where the construction of the Kandaji Dam—planned for the northern section of the Niger River near the Mali border—was discussed. More than three decades later, in 2008, I returned to the NRC and found that they were still discussing the same dam project. I understand the dam was officially completed in 2013. However, after hearing about it for over forty years, I remain skeptical that it was ever fully completed and utilized as originally planned. Still, Nigeriens assure me it is done.

24. In 1980, while traveling in a four-wheel-drive vehicle with my Nigerien driver, we nearly ran over a Tuareg man and his young daughter. We had just come around a steep curve on a dusty laterite road when they suddenly appeared, standing silently in the middle of the road. The driver slammed the brakes and slid to a halt. He immediately got out of the vehicle to scold the man in Hausa, the lingua franca.

But the man didn't respond. Noticing something was wrong, my driver fell silent. They stood there for a moment, two ragged figures against the dry landscape. Then the man spoke haltingly. He explained that his entire family had died of starvation and that he did not want his daughter to share their fate. He begged the driver to ask me to take the child and raise her as my own.

Though moved, I had serious misgivings. I told the driver to explain that what the man was asking was not permitted by my employer. Still, I handed over a small sum of money, hoping it might help. The driver relayed the message and gave him the cash. The man looked at it and said, "You have condemned us to death. There's no use for this money, and there is nothing to buy in this God-forsaken place."

That moment still haunts me like a Biblical plague. It remains one of my deepest regrets. I live by the principle of doing no harm, but on that day, I failed.

25. On that same trip, we had just left a camp of women and children farther north, clustered around a single water well. I tried to persuade them to move farther south, where food was more accessible. But they refused any assistance, saying, "We must remain here. This is our home, and when our men return, they need to find us."

I responded, "But there's nothing to eat here."

One woman replied, "There are plenty of cram-crams."

I recognized cram-crams as similar to the goat-head stickers I had known growing up in Kansas, but I had never considered them edible. There were indeed many cram-cram grasses in the area. The woman demonstrated how, by opening the sticker pod, one could find a tiny seed inside.

"These are the seeds we are eating," she said.

Never in my wildest imagination had I envisioned this as a survival strategy.

26. In 1978, we thought we had found a solution to Niger's ongoing fertilizer challenges. The country had large deposits of rock phosphate, and we believed this material could improve the mineral deficiencies in local farm soils. We identified test plots and trucked the phosphate long distances to those fields. However, the farmers were reluctant to apply it due to labor shortages.

Moreover, the cost of transporting phosphate was beyond their means, and in the end, phosphate alone wasn't sufficient. The soil required more than just phosphorus—it also lacked nitrogen and potassium.

Ideally, a proper laboratory analysis of the soil from each field, along with crop-specific recommendations, would have been the best approach. Unfortunately, that analytical capacity didn't exist at the time.

Some farmers found satisfaction using urea fertilizer manufactured in nearby Kano, Nigeria. It was heavily subsidized, and due to a favorable exchange rate, Nigerien farmers could reportedly purchase five 50-kilogram bags for the cost of one.

27. I relied heavily on my academic training in soil science, especially from a textbook that guided much of my thinking: *The*

Nature and Properties of Soils by Nyle Brady and his co-authors. Years later, I met Professor Brady in Washington, DC. He mentioned that a new edition of his book had just been released.

Impressed, I asked, "When do you find time to work on it?"

He replied, "I get up every morning at 4 a.m. and work at my desk under the basement stairs until 7 a.m. before heading to work."

28. In 1983, I wrote a paper arguing that the incredibly low crop yields in Africa could not be significantly improved unless affordable and appropriate chemical fertilizers were delivered in a timely manner. Environmentally friendly fertilizers should certainly be explored, but without the extra push provided by chemical inputs, yields would not rise to the levels needed. As it stands, Africa has some of the lowest average crop yields and smallest farm sizes in the world, along with a deeply entrenched problem of fertilizer subsidization.

29. In Niger, herders were not overlooked, given that the pastoral zone represented a major portion of the country's wealth. This promise led to the deployment of a team of arid land specialists from universities in the southwestern United States. After months of study, the results were eagerly anticipated.

The team's core conclusion was stark: "The pastoral zone is overgrazed, and all people and animals must be removed for ten years to allow recovery." Of course, such a solution was impossible to implement.

Years later, I attended a meeting at Niger's livestock ministry, and they were still discussing the chronic overgrazing problem and the need to change herders' mentalities—to move away from treating cattle as family members and toward a more commercial mindset. There was even talk of introducing modern ranching.

30. Shortly after the American study, we received one of the first satellite photographs of the pastoral zone and were intrigued by a small patch of green visible in the middle of the desert. A team was dispatched to investigate.

They discovered it was the site of an old French colonial ranch. Its barbed wire fencing was still largely intact, which had kept grazing animals out for decades—explaining the vegetation.

Regardless of such findings, one reality remained: Nigeria, with its 1,500-kilometer northern border, still considers Niger its ranch.

31. A striking fact about Niger is that even in its far northern desert, there is an immense amount of groundwater deep beneath

the surface. So far, the cost of bringing this water up has been too high to justify investment.

There was much discussion about the idea of using this water to irrigate vegetable crops, which could then be airlifted to Europe via the international airport in nearby Agadez. Another proposal was to develop a sanitary production facility for bottled drinking water sourced from this subterranean reserve.

32. Most people would not think of onions as being one of Niger's main exports, but they are. Anywhere there is a water source, irrigated onion fields are abundant. Most of these tasty onions are exported for a tidy profit to coastal West African countries. The onions seem to like Niger's dry climate and a ready supply of manure.

33. In Niger in the 1977-1981 period, Women in Development (WID) was an important component of the project I helped manage. We did a study of the many ways women contributed to the functioning of their rural households. This study found that women were busy from early morning until late at night doing essential work for their respective households. This study also speculated that women were expending more calories than they consumed.

34. One of the main activities of this WID component was the installation of motorized grinding mills. We thought the grinding mills would relieve women of the onerous and time-consuming task of grinding by hand millet grain into the flour, which was used to make their major food staple. We were obliged to re-examine this activity when a group of poor women complained to us that the newly installed grinding mills were ruining their livelihoods.

Evidently these women had previously ground by hand the grain for wealthier women in a village. We learned that when a household became wealthy, the women were assigned to their homes, thus removing a laborer from the workforce. This application of 'purdah' was according to Islamic law, which required women to be confined to their homes.

It was clear that the installation of grain grinding mills robbed these poorer women of one of their major sources of income. These wealthier women would now send their grain to the mill for grinding with one of their children or house servants.

35. When we were initiating our project in Niger in 1977, we had made all the arrangements to take delivery on thirteen sturdy UK-made four-wheeled drive vehicles that were commonly used in Niger. I was about to go to the car dealership to take ownership of these vehicles when my supervisors informed me that I had to

cancel this order and purchase American-made vehicles. No matter that there was no place in Niger to repair these vehicles or to buy spare parts for them, it would take a year to get delivery of these US-made vehicles.

This was an example of tied aid at its worst. Tied aid in the US context was when the USG provided funding for an activity but with the obligation that products purchased to implement the activity come from the US. My Nigerien counterpart understood this concept but claimed, "This is Niger. A totally different context."

36. In Niamey, Niger in 1978, we were excited to be invited by the national president to jointly review our project's annual report. In those pre-electronic days, we carefully typed each page on stencils, and a staff member ran them through a black ink hand printer to produce a master copy. We then took those pages to a local commercial printer who bound the report for distribution.

The big day finally arrived, and I accompanied the key project managers to present the report to the stoic military president. We went over the content with him. He made few comments and wished us well with the project's implementation. I did pose one question: "Your Excellency, this report is long, and I fear few people will actually read it."

He replied quickly, "Start a rumor that there is a secret hidden in your report then people will read every page to find it."

37. This was the same military president, Seyni Kountché, who forcefully opened private grain warehouses to stop the hoarding of millet and sorghum during a prolonged drought. Though he came from a village located within our project zone, he refused to allow us to work there, stating he wanted to avoid any perception of personal gain.

Although he served as a military dictator for thirteen years, he remains, in my experience, the most honest of the ten African presidents I've met.

38. I must write that President Kountché honored me during the week of my departure from Niger in July 1981. He awarded me a certificate of Témoignage de Satisfaction (Witness of Satisfaction) in recognition of my five years of service to the country.

I never imagined that his military chief of staff, Ali Saibou, would reluctantly succeed him. I often accompanied my Nigerien counterpart to visit Ali—his cousin—at a military camp in Niamey. The jovial Ali would strip down to the waist despite the heat and guzzle mugs of Johnny Walker whiskey mixed with soda water, ice, and lime juice. We would feast on roasted pintade (Guinea fowl). (Since I couldn't drink as much whiskey as they could, I brought my own beverages.)

Ali was immensely popular throughout Niger. He proudly claimed that during the great drought of 1974, he delivered food to all 5,000 villages in the country. Years later, I reflected on that claim when I learned that by 2008, Niger had nearly 10,000 villages. (A village was typically defined as any settlement with 500 or more people.)

39. In Niger in 1978, we got the brilliant idea of importing white leghorn purebred roosters to mix with the local hens to improve the breed of local chickens, making them bigger. We called this activity 'Operation Cock.'

Within several weeks, the hundreds of imported white leghorn roosters had all died from local diseases. My Nigerien colleague laughed and said, "Our scrawny African chickens are tastier. They may be skinny, but nothing beats the flavor of our local chickens, which survive by scratching the ground for food."

40. Our next idea in Niger in 1978 was to improve the short-legged goats that nearly every rural household owned. These goats were remarkable: they could eat almost anything, never seemed to get sick, and were, of course, edible.

We decided to import a group of red goats from a distant part of Niger. This breed produced more offspring and its hides were valued for leather production. The effort saw moderate success, but progress was limited by the small number of goats and debates around whether they should be sold at cost or given away for free. As usual, things given freely were often less valued by the community.

41. When I arrived in Niger in 1976, I was very eager to learn Hausa, the most widely spoken language in the country. I was heavily criticized for this because I was based in Niamey, the capital city, where Zarma was the dominant language. At that time, I had to travel 180 kilometers outside of Niamey to find a town where Hausa was regularly spoken.

Despite this, I persisted with my Hausa studies. When I transferred to USAID/Niger in 1977, I discovered that learning an esoteric language qualified me for a two-step salary increase.

The local Peace Corps language coordinator tested me, recording the session. This recording was sent to Washington and reviewed by a native Hausa speaker at the Nigerien embassy. Their evaluation was forwarded to the Foreign Service Institute (FSI), which then awarded me a rating indicating basic proficiency in

Hausa. Based on that rating, I received the two-step salary increase.

Interestingly, when I was first studying Hausa, almost no one in Niamey spoke it; Zarma was the norm in the capital's traditional territory. But when I returned to Niamey in 2008, nearly everyone spoke Hausa.

42. While I'm on the subject, I should mention that my transfer from the Peace Corps to USAID in 1977 was not a decision I made lightly. I had a few conditions. One was that I would not have my office located within the U.S. Embassy and would be allowed to establish an independent office outside of it. Another condition was that I could select my own Nigerien counterpart. (My previous Peace Corps experience had certainly influenced this decision.)

To my surprise, all my conditions were met, and I moved across Niamey into a new house furnished with brand-new furniture and appliances. I had a much higher salary, and at first, it seemed I had less work. I had turned down a transfer to Peace Corps/Mali as PCD, but I happily threw myself into my new role managing a major rural development project in the Niamey administrative department.

I was pleased to discover that my new house was surrounded by imported eucalyptus trees and a flourishing garden of lemon grass. The eucalyptus trees were reputed to repel mosquitoes, and the lemon grass offered a convenient source for brewing tea said to help prevent or cure malaria.

There was, however, a last-minute hitch due to a federal hiring freeze at the time. I used to keep two framed letters on my office wall: one stating I could not be hired because of the hiring freeze and another, dated just a day later, confirming that I had been hired. Welcome to the topsy-turvy bureaucracy of the USG.

I note that today, I likely wouldn't be permitted to work outside the new fortress-like U.S. embassies. However, I'm glad to know that Peace Corps country offices are still allowed to operate independently of embassy compounds.

43. During my time in Niger from 1977 to 1981, I was an avid fisherman. I worked hard to catch a big capitain (Nile perch) using a heavy-duty rod and reel in the Niger River. I tried every possible tactic but never succeeded in landing one.

I even had a dedicated "fishing car", a 1967 Peugeot 204 station wagon that I bought from a former PCV mechanic, Auggie Aughenbaugh. I scrounged around for parts to repair it in the outskirts of Paris, France. An American colleague, John Mullenax, and I would camp along the banks of the Niger River in pursuit of the elusive big fish.

The car was painted green, the only non-white vehicle I owned in all my years in Africa. I always preferred white cars for their ability to reflect the tropical heat.

Incidentally, the former PCV mechanic who sold me the car remained in Niger his entire adult life and was buried in 2015 in Agadez, near the home of his Tuareg wife. I'm still in touch with his daughter, Marie, who became a U.S. citizen long ago and now works as a PCD in Eastern Europe.

44. I wondered where all the big fish I saw for sale along the side of the road came from. I asked a Nigerien friend about this, and he said, "The local fisherman go far upriver and set up strong nets to catch these fish."

After a couple of years of trying to catch a big fish, I gave up and bought a fish from vendors on the side of the road. When I arrived at home in Niamey, I lied and told my family that I had caught the fish. They believed my fib and placed the fish in the freezer along with the other fish we regularly bought in the open city market.

45. On July 4, 1976, I was dressed in a locally made suit—my first—and stood behind the American Ambassador's residence in Niamey to celebrate the 200th birthday of the United States. This was a special occasion, and for the first time, fireworks would be displayed near the Niger River behind the ambassador's home.

There was a delay in the fireworks as everyone waited to see if the President of the Republic of Niger would honor his invitation. He had never before accepted any of the many invitations he received to attend national day ceremonies. To the amazement of all gathered for this special Fourth, he suddenly appeared in the circle of honor. The rumor was that he had never seen the sky lit up by fireworks and wanted to witness it.

The fireworks began just minutes after his arrival, and he was spellbound by the dazzling display in the night sky. As he watched, he did something no one had ever seen him do before. This stone-faced military man actually smiled.

46. While helping implement a complex rural development project in western Niger in the late 1970s, I observed that each village visit involved six or more vehicles arriving, with just one person stepping out to give advice. I thought each visitor contributed so little that their roles could be combined into a

single polyvalent agent, which would be more efficient and economical.

I suggested this idea to my Nigerien counterpart. He replied, "Good idea, but exercising it would mean eliminating a lot of jobs and more jobs is what we need."

47. A few days earlier, this same Nigerien counterpart had told me that he had finally figured out what the development process was really about: eliminating excuses for not doing assigned work.

He gave an example to illustrate his point: "They said they couldn't do their jobs because they didn't have vehicles, so we gave them vehicles. Then they asked for fuel, and we gave them that too. Then they needed new office buildings, so we built those. Now they have everything they need to do their jobs, but they still don't do them."

He later admitted that achieving anything was difficult because it wasn't possible to coordinate people who were, by nature, immune to coordination. He often said in French, "Comment coordonner les incoordonnables?"—"How do you coordinate the uncoordinables?"

I replied, "It's difficult to re-engineer society."

And fleetingly, I thought about what Africa might look like if it were populated with Chinese.

48. My Nigerien colleague took me again to his Niger riverside garden in 1978. He plunged an old calabash dipper into the river and drank his fill of water. He saw me observing him and said, "Never drink water from the river as it will make any white foreigner like yourself sick. Even your iodine pills can't purify it."

49. His words reminded me of the slogan often heard in Africa that was started by the World Health Organization (WHO) in the 1970s – "Health for All before the Year 2000." (In French, "Santé pour tous avant l'année 2000"). Of course, that slogan eventually morphed with time into something of a joke.

50. In 1978, we held project meetings almost every week in the mayor's office in Niamey. The boiling hot temperature of the meeting room was unbearable, made worse by the long-winded speeches of many participants. When it was my turn to speak, I kept my comments as brief as possible in the hope of ending the meeting and escaping the hermetically sealed, stifling room.

My refusal to engage in the customary long palaver and my concise interventions earned me the nickname in French, "rigide et sec"— rigid and dry.

51. I also shocked my Nigerien colleagues when I remarked, "Niger can't get ahead as long as its women can't get ahead." (I still stand by this statement today, as it remains widely applicable.)

These long weekly meetings, held in such oppressive heat, were only interrupted by the passing of a plate of kola nuts around the table. This was our substitute for coffee breaks. Like my Nigerien colleagues, I crunched down on the bitter nuts, trying to extract all the caffeine they could offer.

52. I remain deeply concerned about the status of women in Africa. At one point, I invited several senior Nigerien women to a meeting to discuss how they, as highly educated professionals, coped with being relegated to a lower social status in their own homes. All of them admitted they were treated as inferior beings at home.

One woman said she always had to be ready with a bottle of drinking water to offer her husband when he came home. Another added that she not only needed to anticipate his thirst but also had to bring a cool bottle of water with a drinking glass, precisely how he preferred it.

53. In 1980, I led a nutrition survey in Niger. Our findings showed that most children under five (U-5s) were severely malnourished and stunted, meaning they were too short for their age. Since stunting is a permanent condition that causes reduced cognitive ability, I asked myself, "How can a country develop if the majority of its population is stunted?"

In 2005, I found myself asking the same question. Due to fast population growth, the number of children requiring nutritional assistance has tripled. Today, the child nutrition crisis is even more acute than it was decades ago.

54. In 1979, I went on a tour of the US with a group of Nigerien colleagues and other West Africans. We visited the Grand Canyon. As we were viewing its wondrous grandeur, one of these Africans expressed in awe, "God must have been very angry to strike the Earth so hard as to leave such a wide and deep cut."

At the end of our US tour, I asked my West African colleagues, "What are your biggest impressions of the States besides the Grand Canyon?"

One said, "For me, it was the gas burning day and night at refineries. If we had that gas for cooking, that would be revolutionary. It was a reminder that we need refineries."

Another female member of the group said, "My biggest impression is the number of old people who are out and about and doing things. You would never see anything like that in Africa. I also learned that carrying things on your head is considered weird by all those who see you."

Another group member said he was impressed by the number of sidewalks, but he could not figure out why there were rarely people using these sidewalks, whereas in Africa sidewalks were rare, but the sides of the roads are filled with pedestrians.

I see plenty of cars, as would be expected in a wealthy country. You see two or more cars parked outside each house. Yet the houses have car garages. Why don't they park their cars inside their garages?

And where are all the policemen and soldiers? In our country, we have gaggles of them on every street corner."

This observation prompted one colleague to interject, "I can't believe all the large yards are planted in grass. All this land should be planted in food crops. And there are no protective walls around these yards."

This comment caused another member of the group to say, "It's a miracle to me that the mail is delivered to your houses six days a week, and nobody steals it. Also, natural gas is piped into every house. Now, that is development!"

A female African member of our group added to the comments by saying, "I don't want to say anything, but it appears to me as most people here are overweight."

While we were having this discussion, we were waiting to observe the demolition of a multi-story building. After the building was pulverized by explosives, one African in this group said, "Too bad they can't ship those buildings to Africa because they could be used by us for many more years. And many are better than what we currently have."

55. My Nigerien counterpart claimed in 1980 that our project was sustainable because we were laying the "right" foundation. I countered, "Yes, we're making good progress, but sustainability is an elusive concept. We need experienced, independent specialists to conduct a comprehensive post-project evaluation five years after implementation. If nothing else, there will be vital lessons learned that should be widely disseminated."

One lesson I had already come to appreciate was that a project must be designed so that an average Nigerien could implement it. Still, I agreed—we were laying a positive foundation. Alongside similar projects funded by other donors across Niger's southern tier, the country seemed off to a promising new beginning.

That said, our project was too complicated. We needed more focus on essential elements and had to remain mindful of unintended consequences. That's when I reminded my counterpart of the KISS principle—Keep It Simple, Stupid.

Many years after the completion of our well-funded, eight-year, comprehensive rural development project, the positive difference it made was not palpable. The main takeaway was that such efforts must be implemented over 15 years or more and not reliant on annual appropriations from the U.S. Congress.

56. While I was in Niger (1976–81, 1999–2000, and 2007–2010), there was constant talk about building a Green Wall (GW) by planting trees across northern Africa to prevent the Sahara Desert from advancing farther south and degrading farmland. This effort entailed establishing massive tree nurseries and planting neem (Azadirachta indica) seedlings in protective rows.

The neem tree, though not native to Niger, was introduced by colonialists from arid regions of India. It flourished there, providing much-needed shade. The trees were drought-resistant, and both their leaves and seeds had medicinal properties. Their dense foliage prevented anything from growing beneath them, and their insecticidal leaves were often layered in granaries by farmers to preserve their harvests.

57. The importance of the Green Wall was not lost on us, but when we searched for an American forestry specialist who spoke French, only one name came to mind—Fred Weber. Fred had initiated a Green Wall north of Niamey in the late 1960s. It made perfect sense to bring him back as an advisor to us and the host government.

Fred joined us from his home in Idaho. When I asked how long he could stay, he said, "Two weeks." I asked why he had such a short stay, and he replied, "I have to go home to change my socks."

For the reader's information, work on the Green Wall continues to this day, though evaluations of its progress remain mixed.

Part II: The Second Decade (1980 – 1990)

Niger-Guinea-Togo/Benin

1. I had a disagreement with my Nigerien counterpart in 1980 in his Niamey office over whether or not his country was receiving enough external aid funding. His position was that Niger needed more money to develop. My position was that Niger could not absorb more funding than it was already receiving. I also explained that Niger had received more funding since its independence in 1960 than any country in Europe after World War II under the Marshall Plan, but Niger's case was not the same.

I described that what was done in Europe was basically a rebuilding job, and what was needed in Niger was to lay a development foundation. We both agreed that Niger remained mired in the bottom ranks of the UN Human Development Index (HDI) in spite of all the costly efforts made over the years to lift it out of the category of Least Developed Countries (LDCs).

2. During the 1977-81 period I worked in Niger, I enjoyed taking a break from my job and going with some of my colleagues for refreshments at the Rivoli Bar located in the same downtown Niamey building. The bar was a crossroads for those traveling

across the desert. I learned much about Niger and Africa in our conversations.

One time, I was told how you could tell how long a person had been in Africa by the way they treated the pesky swarms of flies and what they would do when one fly would inevitably fall into their beer mugs. If a fly fell into their drink and they pushed it away, not drinking anymore, they were newcomers. If a fly fell into their drink, and they flicked it out with their fingers and continued drinking, you knew they had been in Africa for a while. If a fly fell into their drink and they continued drinking without removing the fly, you knew they had been in Africa a long time.

3. While we were sitting in the Rivoli Bar, a man came in, covered in dust, and proclaimed that he had just crossed the Sahara in the back of a truck. A short time later, another man entered, also shaking off dust, and announced that he had crossed the Sahara on his motorbike. Not long after that, a third white man walked in and sat down. We asked him, "Where did you come from?"

He replied, "I just spent many weeks crossing the Sahara on foot."

Honestly, I didn't care how they crossed the Sahara or where they were from—just as long as they could tell the difference between a goat and a sheep.

4. While on the subject of ever-present flies and their potential to spread germs, I feel compelled to write about my visits to child rehabilitation centers in Niger. One of the things that bothered me to no end was seeing flies constantly swarming on the eyelids of infants, and no effort seemed to be made to shoo them away.

5. In the early part of the new millennium, I visited Olelewa, a village in eastern Niger. I was told that it had once been a reliable source of millet grain, but the rain line had since shifted southward, leaving the village with only meager harvests for several consecutive years.

There was nothing I could do to bring the rains back, but I sensed that this change in rainfall patterns was evidence of climate change. I believe funding should be sought to help villagers adapt. I discussed these thoughts with the village chief, although he remained firm in his belief that the rains would return, and until then, his village would survive.

I left with the impression that Nigeriens were experts at buying time. In March 2001, I wrote an article about this experience titled "Coping with Climate Change on the Edge of the Sahara: A Day in Olelewa, Niger".

6. It was the long dry season in arid Niger, a time Nigeriens referred to as the season of the "skinny cows." Many eagerly

awaited the fall of the first rains, known as the mango rains. During this period, mango trees would bear fruit, and children would rush to knock green mangoes from the branches to eat. This broke the long, hungry season, but many of them ended up sick from consuming unripe mangoes.

My curiosity compelled me to note that mango trees, like many other fruit-bearing trees and plants, did not originate in Niger. This fact made me wonder what people ate before the arrival of Europeans. Of course, the population back then was much smaller. Today, hundreds of tons of food must be imported daily to feed the country's fast-growing population. The dream of food self-sufficiency seems more distant than ever.

7. My favorite Peace Corps group in Niger was fondly referred to as the "rat patrol." The PCVs in this group even called themselves "RATS." They traveled from village to village, teaching communities how to trap rodents that were depleting their household grain stores. This was part of a larger effort to reduce the substantial post-harvest losses in granaries.

8. We visited many livestock watering wells in Niger's pastoral zone. I remarked that these well sites were ideal breeding grounds for mosquitoes. The pools of stagnant water that collected in the

hundreds of surrounding hoof prints were perfect for mosquito larvae to thrive.

9. While we were visiting one of these livestock watering wells, I noticed there were far more women than men. I asked, "Where are your men?"

The reply shocked me: "Some of our men sold a few heads of cattle and headed south to the bordello camp."

Later, I learned more about this camp. Evidently, the enforcement of sharia law on the Nigerien side of the border had led some entrepreneurs to establish vice camps just across the border. These camps included gambling, horse races, prostitution, and other illicit activities—things some men eagerly wasted their health and wealth on.

10. This visit to a livestock water well made me think of what my Nigerien counterpart once said about the project we were implementing years before this visit. He proposed that we set up places where farmers could spend their money. He suggested that such amusement parks would give them the added incentive to work extra hard so they could enjoy the delights of these parks.

11. I was on one of my trips upcountry in Niger when our vehicle broke down near the far northern town of Ingall. There was no way to repair our vehicle so we hitched a ride in the back of a cattle

truck for our long trip to Niamey. The cows were not a problem but the unruly group of Tuaregs caused us to be constantly on alert.

The flat-board sidings on the truck bed were too high for us to look out. The sun's blistering rays bore down on us unmercifully. The floor of the truck bed became slippery as our Tuareg companions spit on the floor as they could not spit out of the high railing boards of the truck bed. The Tuareg saliva situation was made worse because the group of Tuaregs were practicing the fast of the annual Muslim holy month of Ramadan, and therefore they did not swallow their saliva because they believed this would be a violation of the fasting requirements of Ramadan.

After hours on this truck, it stopped and a ladder was sent down into the truck bed to us so we could climb out. Evidently, we had arrived at the city limits of Niamey. But it was past the 7 p.m. curfew hour, and a roadblock had been set up to prevent entry into the city. I could see the lights of my house, but the soldiers manning the roadblock refused to allow me to walk to my house. Therefore, I and my traveling companions were obliged to spend the night sleeping on the side of the road.

12. I spent the night on the side of the road thinking of my bad luck to be stranded like this. I felt like the Ténéré tree, which was growing miraculously all alone in the middle of the desert, but a rogue truck that was off the beaten path managed to kill it by running over it accidentally. After all, the desert should be open and void of any trees.

13. I found it interesting how they defined youth organizations in Niger. There were such organizations in almost every village that were called 'Samarias.' Youth was defined as anyone below the age of 50. I found this unusual in a country where the average life expectancy age was about 60 years.

14. A US journalist came in 1981 to visit the project on which I was working. He wrote an article that was published in a major US newspaper on what he observed about my project and it was much different than I expected. After his visit, I was instructed not to talk again to journalists.

This journalist, Keith B. Richburg, was at the start of a career which allowed him to experience many corners of Africa. He wrote an engrossing book in 1997, entitled, *Out of America: A Blackman Confronts Africa.*

15. In July 1981, my assignment to Niger ended when I was honored to get a long-term training assignment to Cornell

University in Ithaca, New York. This assignment was canceled by the incoming Reagan Administration and I was assigned temporarily to an Africa Projects Office within USAID/Washington which was lodged in the US Department of State building.

Among other things, I was tasked with researching and writing a lengthy paper (126 pages) entitled, "The Development of the African Private Sector" in 1982. This paper was sent to all USAID missions in Africa with the instruction to prepare a project identification document (PID) based on the information provided in this paper.

This paper gave the background necessary to prepare a PID. This approach was in line with the focus under the Reagan Administration on the private sector rather than on basic human needs as was the case under the previous Carter Administration. The writing of this paper and its processing made me more aware of the fickleness of USG aid as it changed its emphasis with each administration.

After a year of working in this office my long-term assignment at Cornell was re-instated. I spent a year at Cornell basically studying the project I had co-managed in Niger. Cornell allowed me to attempt getting a master's degree in international agriculture. I satisfied all the degree requirements in July 1983 with the writing of a lengthy master's thesis entitled "Niamey Department Development Project: Managing Rural Development with Minimal Facts."

16. I proposed in this thesis the use of a process called QUAD – Quick Use of Available Data. I recommended the use of QUAD in the design and implementation of assistance projects where all the facts are not available. The usual practice at the time was to engage US university teams which took a year to undertake a multi-household level study and farming systems survey, and another year to report on its findings. Often times the project would be over before you got the full results of these university studies, and even if you did, these results would make little difference in the outcomes of your project.

17. I dedicated my thesis to my Nigerien project manager counterpart, Commandant Moussa Saley. He had previously been deputy director in the forestry office in the Ministry of Rural Development. He was the highest-ranking official in the forestry office, but he did not have a diploma from France; therefore he was the deputy, as the director had a degree from France.

At that time, a high value was placed on a diploma from France. A master's degree from the US was difficult for the French system to rank. I do recall French citizens going to a university in the States to study. This was referred to as 'récyclage.'

18. After the Commandant retired, I was working in Niger in 2000 for an NGO, and I hired him to investigate the village forestry assistance activities that had taken place in Niger since the 1960s. He and a colleague did an intensive study and found that village woodlots that had been started by PCVs decades earlier were the most durable of all the activities promoted.

19. Before I finish writing about Niger, I want to mention two American scholars who were fluent in Hausa and authored insightful books about the country: Professors Robert B. Charlick and William F.S. Miles. The book by Charlick that I most cherish is Niger: *Personal Rule and Survival*, published in 1991. The illuminating work by Miles is *Hausaland Divided: Colonialism and Independence in Nigeria and Niger*, published in 1994.

Incidentally, Professor Miles served as a Peace Corps Volunteer (PCV) from 1977 to 1979 in Yekuwa, a small community in eastern Niger on the border with Nigeria. He later published another book based in Niger with his son in 1999, titled *My African Horse Problem*. He once shared an amusing anecdote about finding for sale on Amazon in 2013 the same Hausa dictionary he had used as a PCV in Niger.

20. I must admit that my favorite book on Niger — and on other West African countries that benefit from the Niger River — is *Strong Brown God: The Story of the Niger River* by Sanche de Gramont, published in 1991. (I'm sure there are other excellent books I've overlooked.)

21. I should note that the books mentioned above don't include all the Americans who have written about Niger. Nearly all of these works were written by former Niger PCVs. Since the Peace Corps established its presence in Niger in 1962, around 3,000 PCVs have served there. Unfortunately, the violence perpetrated by extremists forced the Peace Corps to close its long-standing program in Niger in 2011. That leads me to wonder: Who will write future books about Niger — or about other African countries from which the Peace Corps has been obliged to withdraw?

22. I encourage readers to visit the Peace Corps Worldwide website, which provides daily updates on hundreds of articles and books written by former PCVs. Congratulations and sincere thanks to John Coyne and Meredith Hailey Beil, both PCVs in Ethiopia from 1962 to 1964, for founding this site in 1989 and maintaining it to this day.

GUINEA

1. I arrived at dusk in early November 1983 with my family at Conakry Airport, the capital city of Guinea, not knowing what to expect. The airport was dimly lit, and tufts of grass grew through the many cracks in the runway. Overall, the scene reminded me of being plucked straight out of Graham Greene's 1936 novel Journey *Without Maps*, which was about Liberia, Guinea's neighbor.

2. It began to rain as we approached the dark building near the runway. Members of my family were allowed to enter one by one, disappearing behind a filthy curtain. I protested, "It's against Geneva protocols to separate family members," but my words only made the armed soldiers guarding the airport entrance smile. I was relieved to find my four family members on the other side of the curtain, waiting near a pile of luggage that workers had dumped in the center of the dim warehouse floor. The building was poorly lit by a single bulb, and it was a chore to identify our suitcases. Fortunately, an embassy vehicle was waiting for us and transported both us and our luggage to our assigned house. The streets were flooded by torrential rains. The Guinean driver laughed and said, "You may need a boat to get to work during the

rainy season." I note, for those unfamiliar, that Conakry can receive up to four meters of rain during Guinea's annual rainy season, which lasts from May to November.

3. I traveled to the U.S. in 1984 with a group of Guineans, visiting a number of cities, including New York City. In that city, we entered a famous large department store. My group was in awe of the store, and one of them remarked, "Your government made a good decision to operate such a grandiose place." I explained the role of the private sector in the U.S. economy. They could hardly believe their ears, as Guinea had no private sector—everything was controlled by the government. They had assumed that was the norm everywhere.

4. In 1985, the waiting room at Nigeria's international airport near Ikeja was packed, yet officials kept letting more passengers in. The room became so crowded that the plate-glass wall shattered, injuring many. Ignoring the injured, I joined dozens of others running across the tarmac toward the plane preparing for its return to Guinea. The disorder escalated, and soldiers were called in—they used whips to try to control the mob swarming the stairwell to the plane's open door. When I finally fought my way on board, all the seats were taken. Fortunately, there was a folding wall seat in the pilot's cockpit, and I was invited to sit there. The

co-pilot turned to me and said, "It's always like this. You'll find the next airport a contrast."

He was right, and I asked a Nigerian passenger, "Nigeria is richer, bigger and more advanced than Côte d'Ivoire, why can't its airport be as calm and organized as that one?"

He quickly replied, "Here they're doing things like their former colonizer ... in our airport, we are doing things in our own way."

His comment made me think that the colonialism practiced by the French was different from that practiced by the British.

5. Upcountry in Guinea in 1985, I and about thirty other plane passengers were nearing the end of our patience with a single overbooked passenger who refused to disembark. It was a remote area of Guinea, and the heat and humidity were stifling. I thought the man might be forcibly removed by the other passengers, but the flight attendant pleaded with everyone to wait until the local police arrived.

It took the police several hours to reach the airstrip because they had no transportation, and the airstrip was located several kilometers from town. When they finally arrived, they escorted the man off the plane, and once the door was shut, there was a collective sigh of relief and a resounding, "Thank God."

6. That incident reminds me of when Guinea's long-term president, its first, who ruled for 26 years, passed away in March 1984. He had been preparing to host a summit of the Organization of African Unity (OAU) and had commissioned special red cloth banners bearing his image for the event.

After his death, I managed to obtain samples from the textile mill where parts of the banner had already been printed. Today, one of these keepsakes remains hidden in my Texas home. I cannot bring myself to display it—it bears the image of Guinea's bloody dictator.

7. In 1983, Guinea's market women displayed their power in an unforgettable protest. They lined up in front of the presidential palace (formerly the French colonial governor's office) and lowered their skirts to expose their bare rear ends to the authoritarian president in response to his unpopular policies.

This act was considered the ultimate insult, and the women shouted in unison, "Down with the regime."

Remarkably, the regime was shaken by this mass act of defiance and ultimately relented on enforcing some of its policies.

8. My assignment to Guinea in 1983 was prompted by a headline in a Washington newspaper that read, "Black Hole in the US Assistance Program in Guinea." At the time, the US Government

was trying to take advantage of a policy shift in the Guinean government, which had long resisted the private sector, especially in agriculture. Additionally, the US had important bauxite mining interests in Guinea.

USAID had contracted two American companies to construct a new agricultural school. However, due to the overwhelming dominance of Eastern Bloc countries in the local economy, all construction supplies had to be imported from the US. This led to a range of logistical challenges. For example, an excess of form lumber was ordered, and much of it was stolen and used as firewood for local cooking fires.

For context, Guinea had been largely isolated after gaining independence from France in 1958. Snubbed by Western countries, it turned to the Eastern Bloc for assistance. Many of the goods it received were ill-suited to local conditions, most famously, snowplows from the Soviet Union, which became the subject of countless local jokes in this tropical country.

A USG audit was scheduled to assess the construction activity, and the bad press had already begun. To make a long story short, I became heavily involved in responding to the audit and ensuring the successful completion of the project.

There was one final hiccup: the electrical generators wouldn't start. Upon inspection, it was discovered that mice had chewed the internal wiring to pieces. Once repaired, the generators functioned, and the school buildings were finally inaugurated.

Incidentally, the two US contractors later filed legal suits against my employer. The cases were quietly settled out of court, and I was instructed never to speak of them again.

9. Rice imports were at record levels in Guinea, which had exported rice prior to its independence in 1958. Various West African rice-belt countries have varying taste preferences with regard to the type of rice. Some countries prefer broken rice, while others like long-grain rice. Whatever the country, plates are piled high with rice. I could never finish the rice on my plate, so one African colleague said to me, "You don't like our food?"

I replied simply, "I like your food, but it is too much for me to eat. I don't know how you manage always to clean your plates that are piled high with rice."

For these rice-belt coastal West African countries, if a person had not eaten rice, they had not eaten. Of course, the argument continues as to which country offers the best jollof rice dish.

10. I was driving in central Conakry, Guinea, in 1986 to pick up a birthday cake for my daughter. I placed the cake carefully on the passenger seat next to me and walked around my car to get into the driver's seat. I sat down behind the wheel and looked over to check out the decorations on my cake, but all I saw was an empty seat.

Evidently, someone had stolen my cake. I got out of the car and looked far and wide but I did not see my cake. We held the birthday party without a cake.

11. After the death in 1984 of Guinea's long-serving authoritarian president, many Guineans living abroad began returning for visits. Two Guinean professors came to see me in my Conakry office, one was teaching at the University of Senegal in Dakar, and the other at the University of Chicago in the US. They were pleased to find me working at the US Embassy, as prior to the president's death, no Guinean would have dared enter the embassy.

I emphasized how much Guinea needed people like them and encouraged them to stay. A few returnees had already accepted positions as ministers; these were often referred to as "imported Guineans." One of the professors responded, "I suppose it's fine if you return as a minister, but for me and my family, I can't see how we could live in Guinea. There's no housing, no proper schools for my children, and when I want a cup of coffee, there are no coffee shops."

12. One thing I found interesting about Guinea in the mid-1980s was that even the unschooled people could speak some French. My previous experience in Francophone Africa was that you could not speak French unless you went to school.

13. I saw a few weeks later the Minister of Plan, Edouard Benjamin, who had previously worked at the World Bank in its Washington headquarters, but he was born and raised in Guinea. We had a lively conversation. In closing, I asked him, "What kind of development assistance is best now for Guinea?"

He responded, "Just roads. Help us build good roads, and we'll do the rest."

14. The port of Conakry was like an open market. We had arranged for two shiploads to deliver 20,000 tons of U.S. long-grain rice—the type preferred by Guineans. What unfolded at the port was chaos. Thieves ran rampant, employing every imaginable tactic to steal rice. Some slashed the sacks with razor blades as the trucks passed by. The truck drivers themselves were among the most active thieves, hiding bags of rice under their seats.

People even boarded the ship to loot rice, smashing the mock video camera my American colleague, Robert Hellyer, had set up as a deterrent. The situation became so unmanageable that the ship's captain had no choice but to undock and head back to open sea. Things had clearly spiraled out of control.

I managed to persuade the Prime Minister to dispatch a contingent of elite special forces to disperse the crowd and recover as much rice as possible. When the troops arrived, the crowd quickly scattered and the looting came to a halt. The forces gathered all the rice they could and stacked it high in an empty port warehouse.

Pleased with the outcome, I returned early the next morning to check on the rice—but the pile was gone. Alarmed, I rushed to the Prime Minister's office. He looked at me calmly and said, "I'm sorry, but that rice was the payment for the intervention of our elite forces."

15. As noted previously, Guinea's longtime, strong-arm dictator, Ahmed Sékou Touré, died suddenly in 1984 after 26 years in power. He was evacuated on an Aramco plane with an American Foreign Service Officer aboard from Saudi Arabia to Cleveland, Ohio in the US, where he drew his last breath. His family quickly moved to Morocco. His funeral at the Grand Mosque (the largest

in Sub-Saharan Africa) in Conakry was attended by many heads of state and dignitaries, including the vice president (VP) of the US. So many outsiders came to the funeral that there was no room at the airport for any more planes.

We had been told the day before that non-Muslims would be allowed to enter the Moroccan-built mosque, but at the last minute, all the non-Muslims were instructed to go outside. Initially, in preparation to enter the main Mosque, we were all squeezed into a small side room. I tried to stay near our VP, George H. W. Bush, who towered above the other dignitaries and was the only one who did not perspire even though we were all dressed in suits and ties and the temperature and humidity were high. I held tightly in my arms the VP's shoes as well as my own. My ambassador, James Rosenthal, was pushed to the other side of the packed room and thus was unable to join us.

There was a sense of panic as we all bent over to put on our shoes. I bumped heads with the President of Benin, Mathieu Kérékou. The outside doors to this side room were opened, and we were led around the mosque to the other side, where folding chairs were spread under some big shady trees. After a short while, we were told that the funeral service was over. Many people quickly rose from their seats and got into their cars to race to the airport. But the elderly president of Côte d'Ivoire refused to budge until he signed a book of condolences. Such a book was found, and he signed it. To this day, people wonder what words he wrote in this book.

16. There was some speculation that the President of Côte d'Ivoire, Félix Houphouët-Boigny, made a subtle reference in his book to a statement he had made years earlier to Guinea's now-defunct president. It is reported that he said, "You take the socialism route, and I'll take the capitalism route, and we'll see in 20 years which of our countries is the most advanced."

A rumor circulated in Conakry that during a recent visit to the Ivorian capital, the Guinean president was so shocked by the country's impressive level of development that it triggered his heart attack. Other rumors linked his death to the full moon and a rare earthquake centered in Gaoual, a village in the far northwestern corner of Guinea.

To this day, some still wonder whether the Guinean president was truly buried near the Conakry Mosque or if his body was secretly flown to Morocco for burial.

(For further reading, see my article on this subject published in the February 2011 edition of Foreign Service Journal, titled "The Grand Syli's Funeral.")

17. After Guinea's stern dictator of 26 years died in 1984, the Guinean managers of the massive American-owned bauxite mine in Kamsar approached me with a pressing question: how should their country be managed moving forward? Given the U.S. interests in the mine, most of these managers had received advanced training up to the master's level at the University of Pittsburgh.

I responded, "Run your country the same way you run this mine. It operates around the clock, 24 hours a day, without missing a beat. Also, manage your nation like the cargo ship that arrives monthly from Wilmington, North Carolina, bringing in the goods this enclave community needs to survive—and like the ships that transport your bauxite ore to Jamaica for smelting into aluminum."

I should note that many people outside the mining enclave also benefited from the goods imported each month. There was a steady leakage of these products into the local economy. In fact, I often found the same items being sold by roadside vendors in

Guinea that I used to purchase at supermarkets in the United States.

18. Mentioning the University of Pittsburgh Francophone Management School makes me think of its dynamic creator … David Gould. I saw him several times in Francophone West Africa. I last saw him in Togo in 1988. He was in a rush to return to his work in Pittsburgh and changed to earlier flights. Sadly, he was among those in the tragic downing of PanAm flight 103, which was blown out of the sky by a bomb over Lockerbie, Scotland.

19. In Conakry, Guinea, in the mid-1980s, it was after dark. I grabbed my flight bag full of almost worthless local currency, Syli, and went out on the streets to hail a clando-taxi to take me to a clando-restaurant. They were both referred to as clandestine businesses at that time because operating a private business in Guinea was illegal.

No signs or markings indicated their locations so as to avoid being found out by local authorities. However, many of them had to pay bribes to local officials to stay in business. I paid for the taxi and the restaurant with a stack of ragged local currency which needed no individual counting as long the stack appeared high enough.

20. In Guinea, during this same period there was a coup shortly after the strong-arm first president died. At the time, this former president of Guinea was the only leader in Francophone Africa to say 'no' in 1958 to the President of France's offer to have independence but in close association with France. His 'no' outraged the French, and they left in a huff with all they could carry and damaged all they could before they departed.

21. The coup in Guinea was orchestrated to overthrow the government that had assumed power following the death of the country's long-term dictator. I had just returned from our large July 4th celebration in 1984, held at the most expensive and only modern hotel in Conakry, affectionately nicknamed "Gonna-Cry." As was my habit, I turned on the local radio, but all I heard was martial music. I immediately used my two-way radio to contact the ambassador and said, "I think something serious is happening, local radio is playing nothing but martial music."

The ambassador quickly got dressed, fixed the flags on his official diplomatic car, and drove to my house to pick me up. As we headed toward the embassy, we were stopped at an intersection by soldiers who were either drunk or drugged. They jammed their rifle barrels into our faces. I feared they might kill us and take the ambassador's car for a joyride.

Fortunately, the ambassador managed to persuade them that we meant no harm and only wanted to reach the embassy. Once safely inside, another colleague informed us that the ambassador's deputy had been jailed on the other side of the city. We later discovered that the very top officials who had attended our July 4th celebration just hours earlier were the same ones who had staged the coup after leaving our reception.

22. The coup-makers rounded up the former top officials of the national government and executed them. A few days later, we went to see the new prime minister, who was laden with fetish protection amulets. We cordially greeted him and waited for him to reply.

All we heard was loud snoring. After a few minutes of this, we assumed he was asleep and withdrew from the darkened hall. My ambassador said after we were outside, "That's the strangest introduction to a new government that I could imagine."

23. After the coup occurred, the city was in an uproar. I stayed overnight in the US Embassy in Conakry with my colleagues. When morning arrived, I volunteered to take an unmarked vehicle in the embassy parking lot to see if calm had returned to the city. I drove around the central market as people ran to and fro to loot all they could carry.

It was an atmosphere of pure pandemonium. I was unmolested, so I decided to drive around this area, but I was stopped by a security guard in a uniform who had a gun. As he pointed his gun at me, he said aloud, "Turn around and get out of here."

In my rearview mirror, I observed him firing the gun at other people who dropped their looted goods, which he picked up and stuffed into his car.

24. We did see the same Prime Minister a couple of weeks later. This time, he was wide awake and talkative. We thought the worst was over for him. His parting words to us were, "There are spies everywhere. I don't know whether or not I'll be sleeping in my bed at home or spending the night in prison."

25. In 1984, I was designated by my embassy in Conakry, Guinea, to deliver the U.S. government's formal expression of displeasure to the new Minister of Justice, Jean Traoré, regarding the execution of all the ministers from the previous regime. The minister listened politely as I recited the official U.S. human rights position on the matter. When I finished, he calmly replied, "Where was the United States when all my family members were killed by our initial long-term president?"

He then showed me to the door. Once I was a safe distance away from his office, I softly muttered to myself, "Where was the U.S.?"

26. It was an exciting time for me. I was feeling lucky when I was informed that the ship transporting from France my new Peugeot 504 station wagon, which I had bought in Paris when the exchange rate was favorable was due to dock soon at the Conakry Port. My sense of good luck increased when I was told that my car was the only one not damaged when the ship was subjected to a violent storm a few days earlier.

I was at the port when they lifted my car off the ship. My car was descending nicely down to the wharf when it swung and hit the side of the ship. Its collision with the ship's side broke its front windshield. It took several months to get a new windshield from France, which was promptly fitted into my car so I could drive it for the first time.

27. One of my duties in Guinea in early 1987 was to go to a hilly spot near the Conakry International Airport runway with a pair of binoculars to count how many Russian Aeroflot planes were ferrying soldiers from Cuba. These planes would refuel before taking off for the final leg of their journey from Havana to Luanda. Counting the planes gave us an estimate of how many thousands

of Cuban soldiers would be fighting in Angola's protracted and massive civil war.

The Cubans were everywhere in Angola, along with their Soviet advisors. Their presence was easily detected via aerial photography, as one of the first things they typically built was a baseball field.

The Cuban presence left a lasting impact on Angola. To this day, there are weekly flights to Havana, and so many Angolans were trained in Cuba's medical system that more Spanish is spoken among medical personnel in Angola than the national language, Portuguese.

It was a long and bloody civil war that lasted a quarter of a century. It was also a confusing one. The U.S. supported the losing side, which ironically was trying to damage the very offshore oil interests the U.S. hoped to protect.

I was assigned to Angola in 1996 for two years, but the renewal of the civil war prevented that assignment. When I finally spent six months in Angola in 2018, what I learned during that time only deepened my confusion about the country.

28. An example of a blatant corruption scandal occurred shortly after the coup in 1984. There was an excellent source of natural

water near the capital city of Conakry that could be used to produce bottled water. Two French entrepreneurs unknown to each other had paid hefty bribes to two different ministers for the rights to this source. They did not learn they had been duped until both of the companies showed up at the source site to begin work (Big private sector investors from the US withdrew from their proposed investments because of the bribes requested by Guinean officials.)

29. I can recall starting many reports about Guinea with the words ... "Gorged with many natural resources but doomed by gross mismanagement and corruption" ... I understand that after over forty years, Guinea is still unable to exploit its impressive natural wealth rationally.

30. In late 1998, I returned to Guinea for six weeks to undertake a 56-page study entitled "Guinea: Potential Sources of Conflict and Instability." This was an early warning paper on the triggers that might lead Guinea to go down the same violent path as neighboring Liberia and Sierra Leone.

This study determined that Guinea's strong Islamic institutions, beliefs, and practices would keep it from being torn apart like these two countries. Of course, there were also other key factors.

One of which was keeping long-grain rice available on the market at a price the average Guinean could afford.

31. In Guinea, after their first president died of a heart attack in 1984, external donor agencies worked with new host government officials to reform the operations of Guinea's key institutions. They considered that without strong functioning institutions, Guinea could not develop, and they determined that the creation of such institutions required competent people staffing those institutions.

On behalf of the donor agencies, the UN organized competency tests for existing Guinean civil servants to see which ones needed training to upgrade their job skills. Almost all those taking these tests failed. This mass failure of Guinean civil servants posed insurmountable hurdles to making key institutions in Guinea basically functional. This mass failure of hundreds of Guinean civil servants caused the host government to call off any more tests of this nature.

32. I will always remember what the World Bank representative told me in Conakry, Guinea, in 1985. I asked him. "What next? You have already reformed the entire financial sector, especially putting the banking sector back on a more stable footing."

He replied, "There is always a new phase in the development of a country. My only regret is that we did not close the Central Bank and start anew. It has been like lifting the carpet and finding underneath it additional levels of gross mismanagement."

33. When I was in Conakry, Guinea in the mid-1980s. I passed under the Castro Bridge twice a day on my way to and from work. I was told that this was the bridge from which the first authoritarian president had hung the bodies of his opponents, serving as a reminder to all of what could happen to them if they went against him.

Near this bridge, there was a large metal green sign with large letters in white that read, "Culture = Productivity." A little farther down the road was another similar sign that read, "Productivity = Culture." To this day, I continue to ponder the meaning of these signs.

34. I took a short-term assignment and was sent from Guinea to Ethiopia in 1985 for six weeks to help with the drought/famine relief effort. Twenty years later, I was watching a BBC documentary on my TV in my hotel room in Nairobi, Kenya, about two guys who had been integrally involved with the 1985 drought relief program in Ethiopia.

They went back to Ethiopia to see the people they helped save from dying of hunger and what those people were doing today. Their last words in this hour-long documentary were, "We saved these people so they could become today's beggars."

35. Visiting nearby Dakar, Senegal, in 1985, I came across a different kind of street beggars who were referred to as Talibés. They were young boys who grouped on the streets with their tin begging cans. These boys were attached to Koranic schools (madrasas) and they were collecting money for the heads of these schools. I heard that punishment was meted out to those boys who did not bring to their master some money. It was reported that there were thousands of these Talibés on Dakar's streets.

36. In Guinea, the harshness of the government forced many people to vote by their feet, i.e., they walked to neighboring countries. Some have been tortured in the infamous inner-city Camp Boiro. One case had been tortured to tell the truth. He told the truth repeatedly, but his torturers said, "We don't want your truth. We want the minister's truth."

The former lines were cited in a book, *La Verité du Ministre* (The Truth of the Minister), written by Alpha-Abdoulaye Diallo and published in 1985. He spent ten years in the infamous Guinean gulag of Camp Boiro in Conakry. After he was released, he walked many days north to Guinea-Bissau, a neighboring country.

37. I would get my US diplomatic pouch mail with other mistaken Guinea addresses. I received mail addressed to the following countries: Guinea-Bissau, Equatorial Guinea, and Papua New Guinea. I was told that Guinea was an ancient name for Africa.

38. In the mid-1980s, I had an American colleague who lamented being assigned to Conakry – Guinea, saying, " The only thing they can do worse to us is to assign us to Guinea-Bissau."

39. Guinea was a challenging country in which to live and work. But the embassy had a cabin cruiser which was used to visit the islands off Conakry's shore and to do some deep-sea fishing in Guinea's rich fishing waters. The intended use of the cabin cruiser was to serve for evacuation purposes.

Some houses also had swimming pools that were referred to as 'emergency water supplies.' The tennis court at the ambassador's residence was dubbed an emergency helicopter landing pad.

40. I have to say that, of all the places I have worked and lived in Africa, Guinea was by far the most challenging. The lack of a reliable supply of electricity and water created constant obstacles. Simply getting to work each day, navigating long distances

through thick traffic packed with ramshackle vehicles, was an effort. Paying a full year's rent in advance for substandard housing was exorbitant, and shopping for anything locally was almost impossible. For fresh food, we had to place weekly orders through SABENA, the Belgian national airline, which flew into Conakry. (SABENA, incidentally, was jokingly said to stand for "Such A Bad Experience Never Again.")

41. All these challenges lent themselves to offering every six months a break in Dakar, Senegal, for one week. These breaks were called 'dentavacs,' although no dental work was intended.

42. When I was in Conakry, Guinea, in 1984, cholera was endemic and the cause of the death and illness of thousands. I learned that cholera had first started in Africa in 1970 at the Conakry Port by an infected person on a Russian ship that had come from Mecca, and from there, it spread to the rest of Africa.

Cholera spread rapidly across the continent, and in 1972, while I was serving as a Peace Corps Volunteer helping to build a health center in a remote village in Togo, all work came to a halt when a skilled laborer working on the site died from the disease. At that time, people in the village were unfamiliar with cholera and called upon their local gods and spirits for protection from this new and frightening illness.

Although there were other skilled workers available, none were willing to return to the site. They believed the location had been hexed by the death and feared the mysterious sickness. Most of these laborers had learned their construction skills in Ghana during the post-independence economic boom that followed Ghana's break from the United Kingdom in 1957. However, they had returned to Togo after Ghana's economic fortunes declined.

I was especially amused by their uncanny use of construction terms in Ghanaian pidgin English, terms like "bigler" for bricklayer. (I had been told that Peace Corps Volunteers in Ghana who picked up pidgin often lost the ability to speak standard English properly.)

42. Once in Conakry in early 1984, the authoritarian president—who had ruled for twenty-six years, announced that he would give a speech at the People's Palace Square in two hours. The palace, built by the North Koreans, was one of only two new buildings constructed in Conakry over the last two decades. The other was the prime minister's office. It was often said that, in terms of infrastructure, Guinea was living off the "fat" left behind by the French.

Curious, I joined the thousands who had quickly gathered for the speech, thanks to the efficient, pyramidal structure of the country's single dominant political party. We were all made to stand in the vast open-air square in front of the palace and pay attention under the punishing sun. The president delivered his long-winded address from the high steps leading to the palace entrance.

Anyone not visibly paying attention was prodded with sticks by the attendants. The extemporaneous political speech, what locals called a discours fleuve, or "river of words"—dragged on for several hours. When it finally ended, I swore I would never attend one of his speeches again.

Everything he said echoed the content of numerous books he had authored outlining his political philosophy. I was told these books were studied in schools and that knowledge of their contents was required for university students.

43. It was no wonder to me that when the population was sure their first president was dead, they happily destroyed all facades and signs glorifying the only political party and burnt his books in huge bonfires. For me, the joyous reaction of the Guinean people reminded me of that scene in the 'Wizard of Oz' when the population was sure the wicked witch had died.

44. I learned in Guinea (1983 – 1987) that the best surname that a Guinean could have was 'Camara.' With that name no one could identify your ethnic group. (The main ethnic groups in Guinea are Malinké, Peuhl-Fulani, and Sousou.)

After the harsh Malinké dictator died suddenly in 1984, everybody thought it was the turn of the Peuhl-Fulani to rule, but to the surprise of many, a Sousou took power and lasted as long (26 years) as the first dictator. And after his death he was followed by another Malinké. To this day, I have been told that the Peuhl-Fulani are the majority ethnic group, but they are still waiting for their turn to have one of them to be president.

45. I also learned that the Peuhl-Fulani group only had six surnames, and you could often tell by their last name from which geographical area in Guinea their families originated. In addition, I learned that in this Islamic country, it was customary for a married man of any ethnic group to take if he could a second Peuhl-Fulani wife. Evidently, these women were coveted, but their men were not good enough to run the country.

46. As noted, when the ruthless Guinean president died in 1984 and the national government was overthrown, Camp Boiro ceased to exist as a detention, torture, and execution camp in the middle of Conakry. It was opened to the public, and everyone flocked to

the camp, particularly to see the cell of Diallo Telli, the first secretary of the OAU, who died from the 'black diet.' (The 'black diet' was the total absence of food and water while your enclosed cell was locked tightly until you died.)

During my reverent visit to this cell, I said, "What a terrible way for such an erudite man to go."

The Guinean man standing next to me said, upon hearing my doleful statement exclaimed, "What a terrible way to run a country."

47. One highlight for me in Guinea in early 1984 was encountering the well-known American black rights activist Stokely Carmichael, who had fled the US with a price on his head. He had come to the US embassy to pay his fines, which had accumulated over the years while he took refuge in Guinea ... a paradise for all leftist radicals. He was allowed to pay his fines with Guinea's national currency, the Sily (elephant), at the official rate which was a fraction of the parallel rate which most people used.

After his fines were paid, the US embassy issued him a passport with his new name, Kwame Ture, which he took from two of his African benefactors, the Presidents of Ghana and Guinea. Incidentally, the President of Ghana was overthrown in 1966 and took refuge in Guinea, where he was made honorary Co-President until he died in 1972.

Although the regime that welcomed Stokely had ended, I was told that he continued the practice employed by the old regime of addressing everyone as 'comrade,' and every time he answered the phone, he said that regime's usual expression, 'prêt pour la revolution' (ready for the revolution).

48. An interesting tidbit about the wide gap between the official Guinean exchange rate and the parallel rate you could easily get from black market money changers is that departing official expats would sell everything in their houses that was imported duty-free and exchange their proceeds at the parallel rate. Then, they would buy gold, which was plentiful and cheap, and have it made into jewelry. They would exit Guinea weighted down by their gold jewelry at the end of their tours and when they got to their destinations, sell their jewelry for a small fortune.

49. I recall when I lived in Conakry, Guinea, in the mid-1980s and drove through the city late at night, I always saw the streets filled with people. I asked my Guinean driver, "Why are all these people not home sleeping?"

He replied. "They do not have a place in which to sleep, and if they sleep inside, they wait for their turn to use the sleeping place. There is just not enough housing for all these people."

I awkwardly replied, "I have noticed that Africans sit outside of their houses in the day, but these people are out of their houses day and night. I assume they continue to have their kitchens outside and that they also eat outside.

50. In Guinea in 1985, we had access to a large sum of local funds made available through the revised banking system. These funds had accumulated over many years from the sale of U.S.-supplied food aid. At the request of the new Minister of Plan, we used the funds to finance the construction of roads and bridges.

The Yugoslav private entrepreneur selected for this infrastructure project visited our office and remarked, "My workers in the far southeast of Guinea don't want to be paid in money. They say there's nothing to buy and insist on being paid in goods they can actually use, like cement and tin roofing sheets."

51. Traveling up country at the time in Guinea was an ordeal. You had to put big barrels filled with fuel on top of our American Jeep Wagoneer vehicle and drive slowly to avoid the many potholes. There was an extra Guinean passenger in the vehicle, so I asked, "Who's that?"

Our Guinean driver replied, "He's here to clean the fuel lines periodically. The fuel vendors add some water to their fuel, and we have to purge the fuel lines periodically of any water so our vehicle keeps running.

52. In Guinea, I asked myself how they kept their big boubou gowns so white. Every man wanted to dress in these ample white gowns as they were mandated as the official dress of the single political party. I wondered about the quantity of clothes whitener (Eau de Javel = Clorox) they had to use to keep their white boubous spotless. Certainly, the quantity of cloth needed to fabricate one of these gowns was beyond the budget of the average Guinean, especially if the cost of the tailor were included.

It must be a challenge to iron and care for these gowns. And if they traveled on an airplane, how many of these voluminous outfits could they fit into a single suitcase?

53. I cannot leave this section on Guinea without admitting to my addiction to buying colorful African shirts. I must have more than forty of them crowding my closet. In Africa, I wore them to work, they were everyday wear. There was often a friendly competition among Americans to see who could find the best local tailor to make a shirt (and sometimes matching pants). In the U.S., I avoid wearing them as I get too many stares.

Many of my African shirts are older than my grown children. I am especially proud of one shirt hanging in my closet that I bought in Conakry, Guinea in 1985. It's special because it's made from the distinctive blue, indigo cloth for which Guinea is uniquely known.

TOGO-BENIN

1. An American man in Lomé, Togo, was making millions off a novel idea: producing construction rebars from abandoned railroad rails scattered across West Africa. He collected rails from throughout the region and shipped them to Togo by coastal barge, where he melted them down at his foundry in Lomé's industrial zone and recast them into various sizes of rebar.

His business was thriving, and his exclusive deal with the president to protect him from competition was proving highly profitable. I remember him telling me once in 1988, "The real definition of an entrepreneur is someone who sees a money-making opportunity where the average person doesn't."

2. I don't know if this story is true, but it was circulating in Lomé, Togo, during the time I lived and worked there from 1987 to 1991.

The story goes that the president of Togo was visiting his Asian counterpart, who proudly invited him to his luxurious villa in the mountains. As they enjoyed drinks on the terrace, the host gestured toward the freshly paved asphalt road they had traveled on. Leaning in, the Asian dignitary whispered, "Ten percent."

The Togolese president understood immediately, it meant his host had received ten percent of the cost of the road contract.

Years later, the Togolese president returned the favor and invited his Asian friend to visit him. He also brought him to his own mountain villa, and while they were having drinks on the back terrace, he said, "Look down there and tell me if you see any paved road."

The guest scanned the landscape for a long time and finally said, "I don't see any road."

The Togolese president chuckled and replied with pride, "Of course you don't. One hundred percent."

This story, whether true or not, serves as a stark reminder that corruption exists everywhere, and that efforts to control it must be constant, deliberate, and courageous, no matter the risks.

3. I have often thought that external donor agencies should consider helping local Africans complete the many buildings and houses that were started but never finished. In Lomé, Togo, for example, I noticed countless homes that remained unfinished for years. Across Africa, similar abandoned construction projects can be found, and skeletal structures left to deteriorate. It occurred to me that perhaps private companies could step in to complete these

buildings and then rent them out for a set period to recover their investment and earn a modest profit. In any case, the completion and rehabilitation of these partially built structures deserve serious attention.

4. When I was in Togo in the late 1980s, I held fond memories of my Peace Corps village from the early 1970s. I also remembered with affection the old German train that used to travel between Kpalimé and Lomé. Knowing it once passed through Agu-Gare, and since we were nearby, I told my driver, "I think I'll get off here and take the train the rest of the way ... this should be fun."

I walked to the station house to buy my ticket, only to find it full of goats and sheep. I asked a woman passing by where I could purchase a ticket, and she laughed, saying, "The train hasn't run in years, this station was abandoned long ago."

Fortunately, my confused driver had lingered and was still waiting.

I reflected then on the definition of a poor country. Surely, a country without a functioning railroad or even a bottling plant qualifies.

5. Sometimes, established religious sects in Africa get mixed up with traditional religious practices. In 1989, my urban

housekeeper in Lome, Togo, went to her church every day. She spent more time on her knees praying with her vial of corn kernels than she did standing up.

One day, I became exasperated by her behavior, and when she was not looking, I stole her vial of maize seeds. She immediately panicked, accusing me of stealing her vial. She said sternly, "You are risking death if my vial of seeds is not quickly returned."

After a brief reflection on her uncharacteristic words, I quickly returned her vial and walked off like a dog with its tail between its legs.

6. Street food was always plentiful in Lomé. The roadside eateries, mostly run by women, did a brisk business. My favorite snack foods at the time were aloko (fried plantains), koliko (fried African yam slices), and agbeliblanko (turkey tails). The latter was shipped in large frozen bundles from the U.S. if you've noticed, turkeys sold in the States often have their tails clipped off. In fact, turkey tails and used clothing might be among Togo's largest imports from the U.S. I've read that tapioca made from cassava tubers is one of Togo's major exports. (These topics merit further research.)

There was no shortage of options if you wanted a full meal. The main traditional dish was fufu, made from either cassava or yam flour. Every dish came with a spicy stew-like sauce, and meats like fish, beef, pork, or chicken were typically available.

In general, it was said that in Togo, wealthier people ate rice because it had to be purchased. Fufu was eaten occasionally, while yams were saved for special occasions and stored in cool places. The daily diet of most southern Togolese consisted of agblé, white maize flour boiled into a gelatinous glob, served with a vitamin-rich sauce. One popular version was made from the green leaves of a local plant called adema, with okra pods and sometimes small fish known as adewi. I found that the more I adopted the local diet, the healthier I became. The sauces provided all the vitamins I needed, and the starchy staples delivered sufficient carbohydrates.

7. I was visiting my PCV village in Togo sometime in 1988 when I overheard a group of young people talk. I heard some words that I knew were not part of the local language, so I asked a man sitting at the edge of the road, "What language are they speaking?"

The man laughed and replied, "They're speaking Hindi. They've watched many times the Hindu movie shown daily in a nearby shop."

8. I found myself in Togo's single political party building in 2000, getting things arranged to present to Togo's president a special American presentation on the country's demographic challenges in the future. The local staff had gotten the seating arrangements all wrong, and the US Deputy Ambassador (DCM) was irate, complaining harshly to the Togolese staff.

In response, the Togolese staff laughed, and this made the DCM even more upset. I intervened to cool him down by saying, "Laughter is their attempt to diffuse the situation. It's a local cultural thing."

9. In Lomé, Togo, in 1989, I was taking my children to see the central market. As we neared the bustling area, my 12-year-old daughter exclaimed, "What's going on here? Are they having some kind of carnival?"

I chuckled and replied, "No. This is how the market always is."

On that same trip to Lomé's crowded central market, we got stuck in traffic. A man approached my car, holding a fistful of colorful postcards. I rolled down my window to take a closer look. As I was negotiating the price with him, I noticed a slight dip in the rear of my car and got out to inspect the tires. Sure enough, the right rear tire was flat. The postcard vendor quickly said, "Luckily, there's a tire repair shop just across the road."

That's when I realized I'd been the hapless victim of a scam. It was clear the postcard seller had distracted me while an accomplice punctured my tire. There was nothing I could do at that point except have the tire removed and repaired.

10. In Lome, Togo, every time the host government expected special guests from outside the country, the beggars would be rounded up and taken out of the city. Each household was required to clean the roadsides where the official motorcade would pass. Also, all the trunks of trees aligning the roadsides would be whitewashed.

11. To be fair, I should cite other books and movies on Africa, but that could possibly be excessive. But during my years in Togo, I always kept accessible my French version of Robert Cornevin's foundational book, *Histoire du Togo*, which was published in 1969.

I kept Cornevin's book next to an English version of Jakob Speth's voluminous 953-page tome entitled *The Ewe People – A Study of the Ewe People in German Togo* that I found in a bookshop in

Accra, Ghana, in 2016. Speth's book was originally published in German in 1906,

Perhaps the most popular book on Togo was written by a former Togo PCV. I am referring to George Packer's book, *The Village of Waiting* which was published in 1984. George collected the information for this book when he was a PCV English teacher in Lavié, Togo in 1982-83.

12. Perhaps the most useful book I possessed was the handbook of USAID's Office of Foreign Disaster Assistance (OFDA), which is entitled *Field Operations Guide for Disaster Assessment and Response*. During my first assignment to Niger in 1977, I was given this red-covered handbook by the Washington director of OFDA.

13. In 1988, I finally saw in Benin the old village, Ganvié, which was built on stilts in the middle of a big low-water lake. Evidently, people sought refuge long ago from slave traders and warring African parties by wading into the wide expanse of water and discovered novel ways to remain and thrive in this watery refuge.

14. I cannot cite all the marvelous touristic places I visited in Africa, but I was profoundly touched when I paid my first visit to the old slave fort on Gorée Island in Senegal in 1985 and saw the

'door of no return' where captured Africans would depart as slaves for the New World.

I visited several other old colonial forts built along West Africa's coast, mostly for the slave trade in the 18th and 19th centuries.

The omnipresent Mina people in Lome, Togo, had originally fled violence around the area of Fort Mina in Ghana (called the Gold Coast prior to independence) and adopted and simplified the local language, Ewe. Now, everyone along the Togolese coast speaks Mina.

15. When I was working in Lome, Togo, during the 1987-1991 period, I would obtain newspapers from nearby Ghana. I liked to read the odd way they often used the English language in some of these papers.

There was an article from one paper that I kept. It lamented that after decades of generous external assistance, Ghana was still an underdeveloped country. (See the Financial Times dated November 25, 2004, and read the article, "Stuck in Poverty after 40 Years of Aid: If Ghana is stalling, What Hope for Africa?")

16. In 1990, in Cotonou, Benin we were celebrating the election of its first democratically elected president. One of the first edicts of this new president was the start of an inventory of all multi-storied

houses in Cotonou to see how they were funded. Many applauded this effort, but they were saddened when this inventory was stopped due to the pressure brought by the 'big fish.'

Too often in Africa, it is okay to prosecute the 'small fish,' but I have never seen any African who had wealth and political influence legally prosecuted in any African country successfully for blatant big corruption cases. None of these 'big fish' were imprisoned.

17. As I often said, "A thief stealing a handkerchief from a street vendor would be pounced on immediately by members of the surrounding crowd and either beaten or burned to death with a flaming old tire around his neck. But a minister could steal large sums from the national treasury without suffering any consequences."

An African man once explained to me that I was talking about two very different cases. One, he said, was private thievery, and the other was stealing from the government. Evidently, the latter wasn't judged as harming an individual. In other words, stealing from the government was somehow okay.

I countered by saying, "But it's your tax money that government officials are stealing." He laughed and said, "Nobody pays taxes.

Most of the economy is in the informal sector. The main job of our government is to keep prices of goods low so people can afford to buy them. Our purchasing power is what counts."

After he said that, I kept quiet, realizing I had a lot to learn about how the local economy really functioned. I knew I'd have to wake up very early in the morning to learn all that local entrepreneurs needed to know just to stay in business.

18. Everyone at the funeral of the president of Guinea wanted to see if the President of Benin entered the mosque as a Christian or a Moslem. Obviously, in spite of his conversion to Islam, on that day, he decided to adhere to his Christian roots.

Much later, he changed his politics from a Marxist-Leninist approach to the promotion of democracy. I heard that at the end of his life, his special project was to give every citizen of Benin a Bible. His change of politics and religion earned him the nickname of 'Chameleon.'

19. One story floating around was that the President of Benin did not want to be viewed as the president of his western neighboring country of Togo. He had served as a military officer in the pre-independence period in the French army and the president of

Togo had served in a lowly ranked French military position. (It was reported that he was a kitchen aide.)

These personal relations need to be taken into account in considering the early days of post-colonial Francophone Africa. It was often said in post-colonial West Africa that its first generation of leaders were mostly made at the national military schools of the United Kingdom at Sandhurst or France's military school at St. Cyr, or the London School of Economics.

20. Before we leave the bit on personal relations among presidents, I note that the president, Jerry Rawlins, at the time of Togo's western neighbor, Ghana, did not like the president of Togo because when he was rebelling against his government in Ghana in the 1970s. He took refuge in Lome, and Togo's president put him in jail. He reportedly never forgave the president of Togo for jailing him.

21. During my last visit to my PCV village in 2014, I saw that the coffee berries had not been harvested. Evidently, the market price for coffee was so low that it was not worth the effort to harvest the coffee berries. And still, it was rare to meet a cocoa farmer who had tasted chocolate candy.

(My African Trilogy books are based on my time in this Togolese village, and there is much information on each of Africa's 54 countries in my three-volume *Africa Memoir*).

22. In Togo in 1990, I proposed a project to fund a novel activity with an entrepreneurial Togolese man called TRASH (Togo Recycling and Sanitation for Health). The idea was to use barges to transport excess refuse from New York City (NYC) across the Atlantic Ocean and dump it into the vast excavation pits left behind by years of phosphate mining.

These pits were located near a coastal port. To me, it was a "win-win" initiative—NYC would offload its waste, the massive mining pits would be filled, and the recycling of US trash would bring economic and environmental benefits to Togo.

However, when the President of Togo heard about the project, he vetoed it. He didn't want Togo to gain a reputation as a dumping ground for the world's waste. His rejection of the TRASH project also extended to a companion initiative called LITE—Light in Togo for Everyone—which aimed to replace high-energy bulbs with energy-efficient lighting throughout the country.

At the time, Lomé was noticeably darker at night compared to the neighboring town of Aflao, Ghana. Thanks to the Akosombo hydroelectric dam on the Volta River (the former colonial border with Ghana), electricity in Ghana was cheaper and more plentiful than in Togo.

23. My office in Lome in 1989 tended to be dreary so I purchased some artificial tropical plants to brighten the place up. One day, I was surprised to see the Togolese office janitor watering these plants. I told him that he did not need to water these plants. With a puzzled look on his face, he asked, "How they going to stay so nice without water?"

Evidently, he had never seen such artificial plants before.

24. I knew this man had received a master's degree from the National University, so I asked him. "Why don't you look for a higher-paid job?"

He replied, "You want me to continue my search for months for a job with my belly button stuck to my backbone? The small salary of this janitor's job is better than no salary."

25. In 1990, my ambassador asked me to accompany him to meet with Togo's long-serving president following the president's decision to reverse his earlier promise of transitioning to a democratic regime. During our conversation, the president

declared emphatically, "I'll burn Lomé (the capital city) to the ground before I leave the presidency."

His words triggered widespread unrest across the city. Clashes between civilians and the armed forces became a daily reality, with tear gas thick in the air. One morning, the ambassador called an emergency meeting in his office. From the second-story window, we watched as a procession of people from a nearby neighborhood approached, only to be met by government troops.

In the crowd was a dump truck carrying bodies, mostly women, many with lifeless babies strapped to their backs, victims of a violent raid the night before. As the armed forces opened fire again, panic spread, and the truck abruptly dumped its tragic cargo in front of the embassy's main gate.

The ambassador, Rush Walker Taylor, Jr., ordered everyone to go home for safety, but we couldn't leave, the exit was blocked by the heap of bodies. We remained inside the embassy all day, waiting for the host government to remove the dead.

A Togolese colleague turned to me and said, "I never thought I'd be kept from going home because of dead bodies at the gate. But we need more people killed."

Shocked, I asked, "What do you mean?"

He replied, "I just heard that in Bamako, Mali, a pro-democracy rally succeeded in overturning the government after their soldiers killed a couple hundred protestors. Here in Togo, they're only killing ten to fifteen a day. We need a massacre. We need to show we're not tame sheep."

26. I enjoyed frequenting a bar named "Café Love' in Lome, Togo, when I was living there in the late 1980s. I would always drink one big bottle of Bière Benin (BB).

Years later, that bottle was reduced in size and was called a 'conjuncture.' Evidently, this smaller but same-priced bottle was due to a devaluation of the local currency, the CFA franc, which was tied to the value of the French Franc. The latter fact prompted one African man to say, "We were granted political independence but not monetary independence."

27. Koffi (Friday's male child) was the name of my favorite bartender at Café Love. Years later, I was in Bar Bukom in the Adams Morgan area of Mount Pleasant in Washington, DC and the barman was the spitting image of the Koffi I knew in Lome. I approached him and asked, "Koffi, is that you?"

He replied, "I don't use that name anymore. Here, I'm called Davis."

It was clear to me that he recognized me, but he was either too busy, or he did not want to answer my many questions on how he got from Lome to here. I gave up trying to talk to him but enjoyed a night of live Reggae music and the delicious African food. I also enjoyed my expensive smaller bottle of BB (labeled Ngoma – Kiswahili for drum) for export to the US.

I went to Bar Bukom every time I was in Washington, DC. I never went there without seeing someone I knew in Africa. The owner of the bar was from Ghana, and it was named after his hometown in that country.

28. I would go to Bar Bukom in the 1980s by taking a city bus to Dupont Circle and walking several blocks to get there. During these walks, I noticed that almost all the people I passed were from Ethiopia. They reminded me that many of these people had been granted asylum as they escaped war in Ethiopia. Today, I understand there are over 200,000 people in the DC area of Ethiopian origin.

I also noticed in Bar Bukom many people from Liberia and Sierra Leone (Salome). It was as if people from African countries which had suffered violent conflict had taken refuge in the US. You could tell where violent upheavals in Africa had spawned successive waves of US asylum immigrants. They were all present in this bar.

29. I look back on the 1980s as the best time in Africa. Three reports supported the forward movement for the continent. These reports were: "Lagos Plan of Action for the Economic Development of Africa, 1980 – 2020;" Elliot Berg's 1981 World Bank report, "Accelerated Development in Sub-Saharan Africa: A Plan for Action;" and President Jimmy Carter's 1980 "The Global 2000 Report."

These three reports embodied what we were all about. Sadly, these reports stayed on bookshelves, collecting dust, and were forgotten about. I still joke that I am still waiting for the implementation of the Lagos Plan of Action of 1980. Nobody laughs anymore because they do not know what I am talking about.

30. I was happy about the progress being made by our water well-drilling project in central-southern Benin to eliminate the Guinea worm (dracunculiasis) by providing potable water to the local people so they would not have to fetch water in stagnant dirty pools during the dry season. These worms thrive in such pools.

I often saw villagers who drank from such pools wind up on wooden twigs and Guinea worms that were exiting their bodies through their lower legs. An excruciating slow procedure.

31. In the meantime, efforts were afoot to eliminate the black fly which inhabited the banks of the Niger River, causing River Blindness (onchocerciasis) to the extent that many people living nearby were blind, and thousands of hectares of fertile land were unsettled and thus uncultivated.

32. I also learned that African tropical soils are loaded with germs that could cause serious infections. I always wore rubber thongs while my fellow Africans were barefoot. The soles of their feet are so thick that I thought that hookworms could not penetrate through them.

I was concerned about touching the soil and contracting a staph infection. (I learned that washing your hands frequently prevented many infections.) There are also diseases transmitted by the bites of sand flies (Cordylobia anthrophaga) on Africa's many attractive beaches.

33. In Lome, Togo, in the late 1980s, I kept a US treasury check in the office safe for four years, renewing it each year. This check was for the purchase of our office building, which had undergone substantial, expensive upgrades. Since foreigners could not own property in Togo, we had to get permission from Togo's president to buy our building.

We never heard from the president, so I decided to go with my ambassador to see him about this. We raised the issue in a face-to-face meeting with the president, and he said, "Oh yes. I've made my decision on that. I disapprove of your request for security reasons. Your office building is too close to the border with Ghana."

I could not believe my ears ... the entire capital city of Lome was a security risk because of its close proximity to Ghana.

34. Oddly, I thought about this meeting much later when I was hiding under my desk in my Lome office as the tear gas wafted through the building. I stayed there all night. Togolese government armed forces were clashing with street protestors who had constructed roadblocks and were moving the barbed wire fence that separated Togo from Ghana farther into Lome. As they moved the barbed wire border fence into Togo, they were hurling insults directed at the Togolese president. One of the most frequent insults inferred that the president had no academic diploma (sans diplome).

35. Days later, local groups were rioting in the city streets. My car windshield was busted by a large rock thrown by one of the protestors. I stopped my car and cried out to him in the local language, "Why did you do that."

He replied, "Because we thought you were French."

From that time on, I sported a decal image of the American flag on my windshield.

36. In 1990, we were worried in Togo that our successful cooperative savings program was going awry. Most of the loans were going for unproductive, grandiose traditional ceremonial purposes, principally for funerals, which could be held years after the person had died.

Even when the loans were productive, they were often given for equipping local bars that bought and sold alcoholic beverages. We questioned loans for the dead and those that contributed to intoxication, and, of course, we were told that we were culturally insensitive.

37. I overlooked communicating another African proverb.

There was once a white man who wanted to cross the river, and he hired a rowboat managed by a young African man to do so. When they were about halfway across the river, the white man started to voice his superiority by telling the Africans how he was educated, had a well-paid job, etc. The African boy interrupted him by asking, "Do you know how to swim?"

The white man became infuriated because this boy, whom he considered an inferior being, was asking him a question that had no relevance to anything he had said, so he asked the African man, "What the hell has that to do with what I said?"

The African man said, "Well, the boat has sprung a leak, and we'll have to swim to the bank."

The moral of the story: always respect the dignity of every person and value practical knowledge.

38. I once visited from my location in Lome, Togo, in 1987, an international agricultural research center located near Ibadan, Nigeria (one of 15 such centers spread around the world). I was pleased to see a man who had been a Nigerian professor, Bede Okigbo, at the Cornell University I attended in the US. He was the director of this center.

He told me in one of our many conversations, "We know we're producing improved plant varieties when thieves climb over our fences at night to steal our crops."

I reminded my Nigerien professor friend of what he had said to me years ago at our US university. He had said, "The secret of farming in Africa is in the women's household gardens."

39. In 1990, I traveled to a village in northern Togo to observe the annual traditional ceremony for virgin girls. This was an important step in their passage to womanhood. The undressed young girls had to walk in single file up a hill to sit on a boulder like generations of young girls had done before them on this date.

I observed that few girls were participating in this initiation ceremony. I asked one of the local men. "Why are there so few girls?"

He chuckled and said, "Yes, there are many more young girls in our village, but they are not virgins. You have to be a virgin to sit on the rock. Years ago, all the young girls in our village sat on the rock."

40. Indirectly, this reminded me of the time that I returned to my PCV village in Togo in 1990 to observe the annual cleaning ceremony of the village. This ceremony required that every nook and cranny of the village be swept clean and all the debris collected be thrown east of the village.

I knew that all the filth was cast in an easterly direction because it was believed that all the bad spirits came from the East. That made sense to me since Togo's eastern neighbor was Benin, the birthplace of voodoo.

I went early to observe the village's annual cleansing ceremony. I wanted to see the chief fetisher lead the procession up the hill with his traditional palm branch with a chick tied on one side and a toad on the other to the place where they dumped all the debris they had collected in the village.

The procession passed, and I did not see a man with the ceremonial palm branch. I asked a villager standing next to me why this was so, and he said, "The old men die, and with them die the knowledge of the old ways because our young people are no longer interested in the old ways."

41. Sometime later in Lomé, Togo, I was playing tennis with a Togolese man who had briefly held a ministerial post. After our match, I asked him, "You were only a minister for eight months?"

He quickly responded with a big grin, "Eight months was long enough."

I didn't say anything, but I understood exactly what he meant. His brief tenure was long enough to steal the money he needed to support himself and his family for the rest of their lives.

Once again, I was reminded of how deeply entrenched corruption was across Africa. Even salaried professionals had little hope for the future. Their wages were unlivable, pensions were meager, and the legal minimum wage was a joke. There were no real safety nets. All the conditions were in place to make corruption not just a temptation but a perceived necessity, a system that normalized and rewarded greed whenever an opportunity for personal enrichment arose.

42. In 1990, I was chatting with a good Togolese friend in Lomé who could have easily emigrated to the United States but chose to remain in Togo. Curious, I asked him why he hadn't moved to the U.S. with his family. He laughed and said, "Well, if I went to the States, I couldn't sit around every day chewing the fat with you and others. And there's never cold weather here."

I replied, "Sure, but if they were handing out free visas to the U.S., there'd be an endless line of people ready to go. Everyone wants to go to America to find work and go to school. It's still seen as the land of plenty, where everything is available, and you enjoy a kind of freedom you can't have here."

My friend nodded and said, "Yes, I know all that. But it's still a society dominated by whites, and many people carry guns. Here, everyone is black like me. I admire your country's diversity, but I feel more comfortable staying at home in my 'all-black' society."

43. His words reminded me of the words I heard from an elderly man in my PCV village. He said, "I don't understand why young men want to go to Paris to sweep the streets when they could opt for a much easier life in the village where it's always warm, there is plenty of food, and they fit in."

44. In today's Africa, I am lost. The fast-growing demographics are more than I can deal with, and the growing expansion of urban centers hides

neighborhoods I once called home. The large, youthful segment of the population scares me. I lament that Africa is the only continent that had not achieved a demographic transition (the shift from high birth and death rates to lower rates) and how that squared with economic development.

I also asked myself where all the people live, especially as the poor always had a problem finding housing, even in the best of times. I was told that some urban areas were growing by ten percent annually.

45. Initially, following independence in 1960, I was told in Togo that in the early 1970s, the neighboring country, Benin (then named Dahomey), had a rotating national presidential system. For a couple of years, Benin would have a president from the south followed by a president from the north, and then a president from

its central region. Although this system has been discarded for several decades, I have always thought that something like it was appropriate for Africa's multi-ethnic nations, especially since presidential succession was always a difficult hurdle for many African countries.

46. While we are on the subject of Benin, I would like to draw the reader's attention to Ouidah, a coastal city of Benin that was for years a Portuguese enclave and formerly served in the 1800s as a port for the shipping of slaves. There's an interesting book on this subject entitled *The Viceroy of Ouidah* by Bruce Chatwin that was published in 1988.

47. I used to collect books and movies on Africa, but with my many moves around the continent, they have been lost. I have lived in some sixty places over the fifty years covered by this book, counting only those places I have lived in for more than three months or more. I have also taken seventy transatlantic flights to and from Africa.

48. I was impressed by the peaceful way a multitude of ethnic groups lived side-by-side in Lome in an atmosphere of tolerance. However, I was more impressed when there were deep-seated conflicts, and everyone sided with their own ethnic group. What's more, they possessed traditional weapons that were hidden from

sight. This made me think that there were rumblings under the surface. These undercurrents need to be taken into account.

49. It was early in 1990 when local employees in my office in Lomé were joyfully singing a celebratory song. I asked what had made them so happy. One of them replied, "Nelson Mandela has been released after 27 years of imprisonment."

I instantly recognized the significance of the moment, but I was surprised that Mandela's release would spark such elation in faraway Togo. After all, he had been imprisoned in his home country of South Africa.

One Togolese employee remarked, "He was fortunate to have been a prisoner in South Africa—if he had been in one of our jails, he would have died a long time ago."

50. A delegation of village chiefs dressed in royal regalia arrived at my Lome office in 1999 and demanded to see me. I warmly welcomed these distinguished gentlemen into my office. One of them pinned on the wall a large map showing in red the part of Togo that was joined to Ghana after a referendum in 1957.

One of the chiefs stood up and pointed to the red part of the map and said, "That is our main development problem. The richest part of our country was given to Ghana."

51. I had heard that there was a Togolese man who almost died of a snake bite and, therefore, was looking to reside in a country where there were not any snakes. His research on this subject indicated that Greenland was such a country.

I thought it was fanciful for any Togolese to consider residing far away in remote Greenland until I came across a book entitled *An African in Greenland*. This book was published in 1981 by a Togolese named Teté-Michel Kpomassie.

52. I have already cited the dust storms that blew from the Sahel Region to the West African coast, causing low visibility. But I have not written that this dust crosses the Atlantic Ocean to reach Brazil and the Amazon forest, where it settles on the trees, providing them with needed topsoil. In any event, West Africa's loss of topsoil is to be bemoaned because it has so little that it can afford to lose.

53. The loss of topsoil is not the only problem facing Africa's generally poor-performing agricultural sector, which is still waiting for a productivity transition to occur. Most Africans still depend on cultivating the soil as their main livelihood, but often, that soil has been depleted of nutrients and suffers from a low level of organic matter.

There is also the growing problem of aging farmhands and the shrinking size of farms as rural population density increases. This shift obliges a move toward intensification rather than the traditional swidden (slash-and-burn) cultivation methods. Compounding this is the fact that few farm families have secure rights to the land they cultivate. These combined factors contribute to low crop yields, even when improved seeds or drought-resistant plant varieties are used. As a result, while the productivity of the average African farm declines, food imports continue to rise.

In the arid regions of Africa, farmers have historically planted small fields in multiple locations in hopes of catching rainfall from sporadic cloudbursts. But, with the onset of climate change, rainfall patterns have grown increasingly erratic. These days, it's either too much rain causing floods or none at all. Rainfed farming systems across Africa are slowly disappearing.

In areas where rainfall is adequate and timely, farmers still require the right type of chemical fertilizer delivered at the precise stage in the crop's growing season. But this fertilizer must also be affordable. Meeting these conditions often demands that national governments step in with significant subsidies. Unfortunately, whether subsidized or not, fertilizer rarely arrives when it is needed, especially in areas with short growing seasons, and labor to apply it by hand is increasingly scarce.

Mechanization is often proposed as the next step in improving productivity, yet very few farmers can afford tractors and their necessary attachments. Moreover, every farmer needs access to such machinery at the same time due to the brief, rain-dependent cultivation season. Only a small minority of farmers benefit from access to year-round irrigation.

Farming in Africa carries enormous risks—sickness, poor seed quality, weed infestations, drought, floods, pests of all types, and the increasing unpredictability of the climate. While African smallholders are typically risk-averse, it's the lucky few who manage to avoid disaster in a given season. This is not the place to write a full treatise on African agriculture, but I wanted to offer the reader a glimpse into the daunting challenges faced by countless African farming families.

I once discussed this very topic with the Prime Minister of Burkina Faso. He said, "As long as the main farming instrument is the daba (a short-handled hoe), Africa can never develop."

(This lengthy digression into the subject of African Agriculture is not only because of its importance but reflects my devotion to the subject and a lifetime of experience in this field. The importance

of this subject prompts me to add in Annexes A and B at the end

of this book summaries of my core views on this vital subject.)

Part III: The Third Decade (1990 – 2000)

Somalia-Tanzania-Kenya-Burundi-Rwanda-Zambia-Malawi-Senegal-Niger

SOMALIA

1. As my Angola assignment was eventually canceled because of the renewal of its Civil War, I spent time in the Somalia crisis operation room at the State Department and touting the award-winning 62-page paper that I wrote in 1992 at NWC entitled, "Redesigning US Assistance to Africa in the Post-Cold War Era." I expected that this insightful paper would have an impact on the US administration of aid to Africa. I was disappointed that it did not have any impact.

2. In early 1993, I was in a meeting where the decision was made to assign me to Somalia. This meeting was mostly consumed by a discussion of what kind of vehicle I should have in Somalia. This discussion involved deciding what kind of armor my vehicle needed without making it so heavy that it would sink into Somalia's sandy soils.

The discussion turned to me, and I was asked, "Since you'll be using this vehicle, what do you think?"

I replied, "If it is so dangerous in Somalia, perhaps nobody should be assigned there."

3. Anyway, I left for Somalia in early March 1993 for a meeting of its warlords in Addis Ababa, Ethiopia, at the AU Africa Hall to end the fighting. We thought we did just that, and the USG's money was well spent on the air transport of the warlords and the payment of their Hotel Ghion lodging expenses.

I thought maybe with peace among the warlords achieved that, I could forgo this unwanted assignment. But, alas, the warlords returned to Mogadishu (Mog) and renewed their fighting as if there had never been the Addis meeting. I buried my wishful thinking and went to Mog after a few days of consultation in Nairobi, Kenya, the staging area for all crises in East Africa.

4. My first trip into Somalia was in March 1993, departing from Wilson Airfield near Nairobi, Kenya. I was flown in on a small aircraft operated by an international non-governmental organization (NGO). Aside from my locally purchased, cheap suitcase, I had been instructed to pick up three items, each housed in a sleek case engraved with the logo "NEC."

I asked the young American pilot if he knew what these cases contained. He casually replied, "Looks like new laptops to me."

I had never heard the word laptop before, but I nodded and acted as if I knew exactly what he meant.

At the time, I even wondered if laptops were meant to be used like disposable suitcases. I had been specifically told to buy a cheap suitcase from the local market because it was likely I'd have to abandon it in the event of an evacuation.

5. I said to my ambassador (Special Envoy to Somalia), Robert B. Oakley, "We got plenty of US soldiers now ... we should disarm these suckers."

He laughed and replied in his deep Texas drawl, "Why, son, it would be easier to disarm the State of Texas."

6. The US Congress authorized exceptionally 100 million US dollars for Somalia but 25 million of the amount was given to Mozambique to disarm its rebel movements. Somalia did not follow any of the classical disarmament, demobilization, and reintegration (DDR) norms.

7. I did find that it was impossible to do any classical development work in Somalia. However, there was much need for rehabilitation and reconstruction work. The World Bank balked at funding anything in Somalia until the country was stable at peace, and

these necessary foundations for development were sufficiently advanced.

8. In Somalia, we would frequently get visits of staffers from Congress (the Hill). We would take them to see a group of the main representatives of NGOs working in Somalia. They were well received by these representatives. They discussed with each member of this group their views on Somalia's future. All the members expressed negative views on the future of Somalia. The staffers turned to the NGO leader and asked, "Is there no one who is optimistic about Somalia's future?"

The leader replied, "Only those people who have been here for less than two weeks."

9. We had a program in Somalia to trade food grain for guns. All the guns that were exchanged were old and unworkable. I asked, "Where are their good guns?"

A Somali man replied, "They put their good stuff in plastic bags filled with camel fat and bury them underneath the dead bodies in the cemetery."

After that, we changed our food aid policy to give food only to women over forty years of age ... no matter how many times they got back in the receiving line.

10. In Nairobi in 1997, I learned that if I wanted to acquire a book banned by the host government, I could go to a certain shopping center and inquire at a Kenyan Indian-operated bookstore. If he had it, he would provide the book wrapped in plain khaki paper. This is how I acquired the book written by our Ambassador to Kenya, Smith Hempstone. His 1997 book was entitled *Rogue Ambassador: An African Memoir*.

This politically appointed ambassador said when the US entered Somalia in late 1992, "It would be like a tar baby."

He was right ... it is still a tar baby from which the USG cannot extract itself.

11. In Mogadishu (Mog), there was so much constant fighting in 1993 that goat and sheep shipments from southern Somalia could not make it to the dhow port. Their shipments represented a major source of revenue for Somalia. In peaceful times, the dhows would have transported in season thousands of these animals across the Gulf of Aden to Saudi Arabia and Yemen. This had been done for decades, if not for centuries.

We encouraged the warring parties to call a truce for twenty-four hours. During this truce day, thousands of animals were herded through the dusty streets of Mog to dhows lined up in the ocean water at the port. This successful event of getting ruminants to the port was called at the time the "Great Goat Rope."

12. In the following year, I was in Kampala, Uganda, having dinner with the American Ambassador, Michael Southwick. He had previously served in Kenya as deputy ambassador. Most of the talk was about his efforts to dissuade the host government from pursuing its one-party democracy policy.

I asked him about the profile of our new ambassador in Kenya, and he replied. "They wanted to get someone completely different than her politically appointed predecessor."

I assumed from his words that they did not want anyone who would "rock the boat."

13. My roommate in Mog was a peculiar American type. His job was to monitor the hundreds of tons of food aid arrivals at the port, although the famine was over. His main peculiarity was that he arrived with a large military duffle bag full of scholarly books. He was a bearded and overweight slob who talked in an ugly sort of language. I could never square his unruly demeanor and looks with his constant use of his spare time to read his many scholarly books.

I found him to be a fount of information about all the happenings in our housing compound, so I asked him, "How do you know so much about what's happening in our compound?"

He replied, "That's easy ... the 125 Fleet Anti-Terrorism Security Team (FAST) Marines guarding us around the clock tell me everything since they learned I'm a Viet Nam vet."

I said, "Wow. You fought in Vietnam, and you came out alive?"

He said in a soft voice, "Yes, it was a success for me because I'm still alive. Never ask me to talk about this subject again. Good night. Not enough hours in the day or night."

14. This abrupt sign-off from my highly intelligent roommate reminded me of the guy who was originally assigned to my post. He had refused to go to Mogadishu because he didn't want to share a bathroom with others. I often wondered how he would have handled such an unconventional roommate, not to mention the calisthenic whistles from the Pakistani troops in the camp next door or the five-times-a-day wailing from a nearby loudspeaker calling the faithful to Islamic prayers.

One thing's for certain, he would have quickly learned the importance of carrying an ice pick when taking a shower. The water in Mogadishu was so heavily calcified that the showerheads constantly clogged. An ice pick was the only tool that could clear the calcium deposits and allow water to flow again.

15. At first, we lived in houses in southern Mogadishu rented from one of the top warlords in Somalia. The top dollar was paid to this warlord who lived down the street. It was like we were supporting the violent conflict with another warlord by paying our warlord cum landlord. Such extortion was the rule in war-torn and perverse Somalia. (For more about this subject, see my book, *Dead Cow Road*, published in 2017.)

16. For several months, the US Army had been trying without success to capture a top warlord, Mohamed Farah Aideed. As Halloween approached, I jokingly suggested we hold a look-alike contest for the warlord, arrest the winner, and call it a day. That bit of humor was quickly laid to rest when a Blackhawk helicopter was shot down.

We later learned that Mujahideen fighters from Afghanistan had taught Somali militants how to plant RPGs in the ground to target helicopters.

17. Anyway, I thought the dropping of thousands of leaflets on Mog from a helicopter, which offered a handsome reward for the capture of the top warlord, would be a success. However, the

warlord came out with its own leaflets offering in derogatory terms a bigger reward for the capture of the American head of the UN's Operation Restore Hope.

18. Later, we moved onto the US Embassy complex, which had been taken over as the UN headquarters. The large grounds of this complex followed a new security plan for US embassies, but this new expensive structure was barely occupied before all its assigned personnel had to be rescued and evacuated. The Somali fighters invaded it and did RPG rocket target practice on the bullet-proof glass entrance windows.

19. I discovered another Viet Nam vet. There was a helicopter pad next to the portable room I slept in. I would often take the helicopter to the airport to catch a flight to someplace elsewhere in Somalia or to Kenya.

One time, when I was coming back to my home compound, the helicopter dropped from the sky in a rapid spiral movement. When we hit the pad, the pilot said, "That's how we did it in Vietnam to avoid incoming fire."

20. My nickname among Americans in Mog was 'chopped liver' because I could go anywhere in Somalia while none of the 25,000 US troops in Somalia could be outside their Mog camps. I could

be killed, and it would not make the news. But if one US soldier were killed, that would be big news and be broadcast by all the major TV networks.

21. Of course, when I left our compound to visit a Mog site, I would have to go dressed in combat gear, with fifteen Marines and three military Humvees, which were driven at top defensive speed. One of the Marines told me, "The biggest threat we face is from the 'Future Looters of Somalia.' These kids throw rocks so hard and accurately that US major league baseball teams should recruit them."

22. The Somalis gave me the nickname of 'Redbeard' (cad cassan). I had put red henna in my beard, which was a custom among adult men in Somalia. I did this as a friendly sign of appreciation for their culture. As soon as I learned the Somalis had given me the nickname, I quickly shaved off my beard because I did not want to make it easier for trigger-happy Somalis to identify me.

23. One time, I was not feeling good, so I went for the first time to the sprawling US Army inflated huge tent hospital on our compound to get a medical checkup. I was astounded to see, as far as the eye could see, soldiers in hospital beds being given IVs, so I asked the nurse attending to me what was going on, and she said,

"All these soldiers are suffering from dehydration caused by Somalia's hot climate."

24. The first and only time I used a firearm in Africa was in Somalia. We were visiting a town in northern Somalia when we started to be the targets of incoming gunfire. We thought this was an unusual way to welcome the American delegation they had invited to come to their town.

We took refuge in a small house. One of the soldiers on our team shoved a 38 pistol my way and said, "If we're going to get out of here alive, we got to fire back."

I found it easier than I thought to fire at those who were firing at us. I was appreciative at that moment of the monthly practices we had at our Mog shooting range.

When the firing settled down, we rushed to our plane in the rain. We were afraid the plane could not take off because the earthen runway had been made soft by the rain. We all sighed with relief when our plane took off. Our long flight successfully returned to Mog.

We did not know whether to laugh or cry when we heard the news that it was all about mistaken identity. A colleague told us, "They thought we were UN personnel and not representatives of the

USG. They don't like the UN and love America. Do you want to go again?"

The head of our mission upcountry said, "Are you kiddin'?"

25. We were constantly puzzled by the Somalis who were pirating ships in coastal waters off northern Somalia's shores. After weeks of this menace, we finally learned the names of the two Somali men leading the pirating. We traced their names to two guys who had worked at a 7-11 in Arlington, Virginia. Evidently, they had returned to Somalia to make their fortune illegally.

26. Before I left Somalia in March 1994, a Somali asked me, "How should we manage our country once all the foreigners have left?"

I replied, "You should manage it the same way you manage the khat trade."

Khat is a perishable crop flown in daily from Kenya, and somehow, it's sold and distributed with remarkable efficiency to eager consumers across the country—no delays, no confusion. It's illegal in the US, but in Somalia, the narcotic effects of chewing its leaves and stems are deeply appreciated.

We didn't dare go out in Mogadishu in the afternoons because the armed fighters, high on khat, were always dangerously trigger-happy. But the point stands: khat is a vital commodity in Somalia, and if you can manage your country as well as you manage the khat trade, your future is bright.

27. Peace was returning when I visited the well-watered Shabelle Valley in southern Somalia in 1993. Water canals were being cleared so that farmers' fields could be irrigated regularly. I noticed that the farmers looked different from the Somalis I had previously known, so I asked one of them about this. He explained, "We're descendants of slaves brought from the Tanga area on the northern coast of Tanzania. A Somali does not work the soil as we do, although they own this land. We have no choice but to work for them."

His words disturbed me, and I couldn't help noticing that he had a pet dog—something unusual in Somalia. I immediately saw that these people were indeed different from the Somalis who lived farther north. A noble Somali would never keep a dog, as Islam forbids contact with them. Likewise, despite Somalia's long coastline and rich fishing waters, Somalis traditionally do not eat fish. I had also heard that Somalia had more camels than people, yet the camels were not ridden. I don't know if it's true, but I was told there isn't even a word for "please" in the Somali language.

The indentured farmer saw my curiosity and added, "These cultural differences put us in a low-class position of servitude. But that's not our biggest problem. Our biggest problem is that the water in the Shabelle River is less than it used to be because of a dam built upstream in Ethiopia that's blocking the flow."

From this farmer, I learned a great deal about the complexities of life for those trying to survive on land they do not own.

28. While visiting this area of Somalia, I was made aware of what people called the "charcoal wars." I asked a local farmer why there were no trees in sight. He replied, "They cut them all down to make charcoal."

I asked, "What do they do with the charcoal?"

"They make a lot of money exporting it to neighboring Kenya, either overland or through one of the coastal ports. Armed militias are constantly fighting over who controls the charcoal and banana trade in southern Somalia. Right now, the militia in charge is led by the Butcher of Hargeisa, the son-in-law of Somalia's former president. He's said to have been responsible for the deaths of up to 100,000 people in 1988 when he bombed the city of Hargeisa in the far north."

29. I was curious and inquired, "How do they make charcoal?"

"They dig a big hole in the ground and fill it with the trees which have been cut into small pieces. They then set the pieces at the bottom of the hole on fire and cover them with straw and dirt in a way that burns slowly. When it has finished its slow smoldering burn, they uncover the charcoal, cool it, and bag it."

I asked, "What do they do after there are no more trees to cut."

"They go somewhere else. They never think of planting new trees."

I looked across the wide treeless expanse and told myself, "War and greed are ravaging the country in more ways than one."

30. When in this part of southern Somalia, I was obliged to sleep a night in the barracks of Belgium troops because my plane did not return to pick me up. The next day I was dropped by the local airstrip early in the morning to wait for my flight. I ended up waiting all day and slept the entire night on the airstrip before a plane from Mog arrived to pick me up. Needless to say, this was a scary experience.

31. I was visiting this town, Kismayo, in southern Somalia because I had heard the local townspeople were shooting internally displaced people (IDPs) when they tried to leave their refugee camp to return to their home villages. Evidently, the townspeople did not want to see the IDPs leave because they would diminish the supply of food aid that they depended upon.

32. I was in another town in Somalia in 1993, near the Ethiopian border, and we drove around the town. When we passed an open field, I saw bits of clothing protruding from the ground. I could not imagine the local people throwing away their clothes, so I asked our Somali driver about this, and he replied, "That's where hundreds of people were massacred by Ethiopian soldiers several years ago. Nobody has dared recover the bodies. It's a stark reminder of the perilous circumstances in which we live, especially next to the Ethiopian border.

33. This ugly scene reminded me that Somalia had waged a war against Ethiopia in 1977 to regain the Ogaden territory, which it claimed belonged to it. Somalia was on the verge of winning this war when the communist regime that controlled Ethiopia called on its Russian friends for help. The Russians brought in thousands of Cuban soldiers who defeated the Somali army and restored the lost territory to the Ethiopian government.

One of the five-pointed white stars in the center of Somalia's blue flag represents the Ogaden in Ethiopia. And two others represent Somali populations in Northern Kenya and the country of Djibouti. The heartland of Somalia dreams of recuperating someday all Somali people under a single national flag.

34. While assigned to Somalia in the 1993-94 period, I had a seasoned Somali driver but no car for him to drive. Eventually, my armored vehicle arrived via helicopter from Dubai. By the time it arrived, we were confined to a secure compound, so the only place I could use my driver was between my office space and the mess hall.

The estimated 100-yard walk between these two places gave me the exercise I needed to help shed the pounds I had put on due to the consumption of the delicious plates of food catered by our Bangladeshi kitchen staff provided by a Dubai company. I was constantly ribbed by my colleagues for using my car and driver, but if I did otherwise, this long-serving driver would be out of work.

35. In Somalia, our compound was frequently shelled at night by incoming mortar rounds. Each time this happened, we had to take refuge in an underground bunker. One time we joked about how the mortar shelling saved us from eating one of the delicious desserts prepared by our super kitchen staff made up of men from Bangladesh.

We all gained weight because there was nothing to do but work and eat within the confines of our well-guarded compound. And most of the Americans assigned to Somalia became smokers of cigarettes.

36. An American man, John Marks, who collaborated with me in Mogadishu had been a Peace Corps Volunteer (PCV) in Mog in the 1960s. At that time, the city was known as "The Pearl of the Indian Ocean" and was the largest recipient of USAID assistance in Africa. He asked to visit the house he had lived in during his Peace Corps service.

Fulfilling this request required me to cross the green line into northern Mogadishu, which was controlled by a rival warlord. We crossed the line with little difficulty, took a quick look at his former PCV residence, and then sped back into southern Mogadishu, which was controlled by an opposing warlord.

My colleague recalled how people used to travel from far and wide to enjoy the beauty of Mogadishu. Many would visit the once-glamorous seaside Nido nightclub to enjoy a good meal and admire the strikingly attractive Somali women, many of whom could have easily been international fashion models.

We both lamented how two rival warlords, Mohamed Farah Aidid and Ali Mahdi Muhammad—each from different sub-clans of the same clan, had reduced this once-vibrant city to ruins. Their bitter fight for control of Mogadishu resulted in an estimated 50,000 deaths, widespread destruction from small arms fire, and the looting and export of anything of value, especially factory equipment and copper wiring.

37. I found Somali women attractive, but after the slaughter in 1993 of UN Pakistani peacekeeping soldiers who were attempting to capture the radio station of one of the warlords, I looked at them differently. I was told that clan pride prompted a group of Somali women to pounce on the dead Pakistani troops, cut off their genitals, and stuff them into their mouths.

38. Somalis claim to be descended from the same common ancestor, and Somalia is a rare African country that uses one language. But Somalis are divided into clans and sub-clans and are willing to fight over the slightest differences. The warlike Somali culture had discouraged early explorers from transiting Somalia.

It took me six months to begin to understand the all-important clan system in Somalia ... the frequent shifting of alliances made this a constant pursuit. I referred to this as the shifting sands of Somalia.

39. Perhaps the closest I came to dying in Somalia was the time I was on a refitted turboprop plane headed to northern Somalia

(Somaliland) to meet with its president. Since the flight distance was too great to cover in a single day, we planned to overnight in Djibouti at the Sheraton Hotel.

Before reaching Djibouti, on the empty, seatless plane, I decided to eat the peanut butter crackers from a Meals-Ready-to-Eat (MRE) package. The crackers became lodged in my throat, and I began to choke, unable to breathe. I crawled toward the pilot's cabin, and the crew immediately recognized the problem. They handed me a bottle of water, which I drank, thankfully dissolving the blockage in my throat.

I tried to make light of the incident afterward, but it was, for me, a genuine near-death experience.

40 . I arrived safely at the Hargeisa Airport but found it controlled by a sub-clan militia that occupied the airport grounds, and they required I pay them for a visa to enter into the nearby city of Hargeisa, the capital city of Somaliland, which claimed independence from southern Somalia.

I was well received by the President of Somaliland, Muhammad Egal, and his top advisors. I have always believed that Somaliland should be recognized as an independent country. But I was told as long as the Africa Union did not recognize it, no country could recognize it. I always thought its different historical background and separating it from the chaos in southern Somalia was a good course to follow.

41. While in Somalia (1993–94), I often thought about the young men fighting for the various factional militias. I asked myself, "What else would I have them do? What better jobs are they qualified for? And where are the jobs, anyway?"

These illiterate young men were handed an AK-47 and an endless supply of bullets. Many were given a new motorbike, a daily ration of fresh khat, some pocket money, and access to the spoils of war.

What more could they ask for? This had been their way of life for a generation. It was all they knew. Despite the danger, their best hope was for the violent conflict among clan and sub-clan militias to continue because, for them, there were no alternative livelihoods.

42. In Mog in late 1993, there was an American contractor who came to my portable cubicle sleeping unit to fix my faulty shower head. I observed him at work, and I noticed he would take frequent swigs from a bottle of gin he carried in his oversized pants pocket, and I said, "You really need to drink water to avoid dehydration."

He grinned and said, "No water for me ... it rusts my pipes."

43. We were confined to our guarded living and work compound, but we closely followed events in downtown Mog on TV almost nonstop, thanks to the advent of CNN. For the first time, this cable news channel broadcasts the hard facts of warfare into the living rooms of the American public. Its broadcasts on Somalia were an indispensable tool for us.

44. One surprise we had was when we were watching a CNN broadcast of a weekend rally of the warlord of southern Mog was of our cook cheering on this top warlord.

45. Perhaps one of the most amazing things that happened in Somalia was the presence in a US military uniform of the son, Hussein Farrah Aideed, of one of the main warlords in Somalia. Even more amazing was that his son, a US citizen, eventually replaced his father as the leader of a major warring faction after his father was killed in battle. Formerly, his son had been in Somalia as an interpreter for the US Marine Corps.

46. My closing words in 1994 on my time in Somalia in my End of Tour report were, "It's only by a few minutes and dumb luck that I'm still here to write this report."

Years later, I related some of my close calls in Somalia to an American missionary friend in Africa, and he said, "It was by the grace of God that you survived."

47. I forgot to mention while I was in Somalia (1993-94) the US Department of State sent a special team of former ambassadors to evaluate the status of the US' heavy involvement in Somalia. This team was referred to as the 'Tiger Team.'

I asked the head of this team what she thought of the American imposed by the USG to lead the entire multi-national UN Operation Restore Hope in Somalia. Her reply was quick and in no uncertain terms, "Miscasting of the century."

48. One of my favorite souvenirs from Somalia is a T-shirt with the emblem of Hard Rock Café in Mogadishu crossed out with the words "Closed for Repairs." Of course, this shirt and what it displayed was all a joke, but it reflected the deep state of disrepair that Mogadishu was in.

TANZANIA

1. Many local Tanzanian people participated in an open workshop with donor agencies in Dar es Salaam, Tanzania, in 1995. One elderly Tanzanian woman listened intently to all the presentations, and when it came time for questions and comments, she stood up and said loudly, "If we could eat all the words contained in all your reports, there would be no more hunger."

2. I asked my Tanzanian driver who he was going to vote for in his country's upcoming presidential election in 1995. He replied with a name I did not recognize, so I asked, "Who's that?"

"He's the only real African among all the crooked politicians who are running. He's a Masai."

3. As part of my job, I had frequent discussions with the Minister of Finance. No matter the subject, he would always have a textbook answer to any of my questions. I got the impression he was playing with me. I thought he treated all donor representatives in the same way. No doubt that his overriding concern was to keep donor aid flowing.

4. In Dar es Salaam (Dar), Tanzania, I was sitting under a shady big kapok tree (ceiba pentandra) in 1994 and asked the waiter, "Why do they call this place the batshit hotel."

He replied, "Just wait, and you'll see."

He had no sooner finished his words than I heard a loud splash on the tabletop. I looked up and saw many fruit bats hanging from the tree branches. I quickly moved from the shade provided by the big tree to a sunny spot beyond the tree's branches.

5. Also, in Dar, at about the same time, I enjoyed a sumptuous meal while a live band played popular music. I looked around and saw that I was the only one in this spiffy place and asked the waiter, "Where's all the people?"

He replied, "Oh, the local people can't afford this place ... only white foreigners can afford our prices."

6. In Tanzania in 1995, I had a colleague who was a lovely Muslim woman from Zanzibar who wore the latest fashions from Paris. I asked her, "Do your people at home accept your dress?"

She replied, "Don't be silly. I wouldn't dare wear these clothes on my home island. I change into traditional black Islamic dress, Bui-Bui, on the hydrofoil boat before arriving home."

7. The American Ambassador, J. Brady, in Tanzania, was upset in 1995 because of the popular jingle that was broadcast on all the local media to promote the sale and use of Salama condoms. This jingle did not sit well with him, as he was against such promotion of condoms.

He insisted on offering his apologies to the Minister of Health, a prominent Muslim woman. The ambassador saw the minister, and before he could bring up the subject the minister said, "I want to extend to you my thanks for the work you are doing to promote Salama condoms. You know my teenage daughter is named Salama, and she enjoys wearing the Salama t-shirt."

8. I was delighted to get one of the cell phones that just came on the market in 1995 so I could make phone calls within Dar. The local phone service seldom worked, so the advent of cell phones was much welcome.

The local US Embassy Tanzanian guard saw me with my new cellphone in my hand and said, "You need to hide your cellphone because the ambassador doesn't have one yet."

9. At a seaside restaurant in Tanzania in 1995, I was dining with a group of colleagues from across Africa when one of them remarked, "I don't know why, but when I first got here, none of

the women looked attractive to me. Now, after a few weeks, they all look beautiful."

Another colleague grinned and chimed in, "If you can't be near the woman you love, you'll love the woman you're near."

The group then turned their attention to me, the only white man in the group. One of them asked, "What kind of woman do you like?"

Caught off guard, I hesitated. But I could see by their expressions that they were genuinely curious and expecting an interesting answer. So, I said, "I suppose I'm drawn to a woman who's well-proportioned and round where she's meant to be round. I admire someone who carries herself with confidence, whose natural scent is pleasant, and who has a unique kind of presence. Ideally, she's someone kind, a bit mysterious, and endearing. Maybe a mix of Marie Curie, an African jungle woman, and the girl next door."

At first, they were silent and wide-eyed then the entire table erupted in applause and laughter. I ended the moment with a final comment: "I don't know why, but for me, a woman from my own cultural background would feel too familiar, like being with my sister."

10. In 1995, my Tanzanian driver could see how much I enjoyed Dar's weather. He asked me, "What's your favorite weather?"

I replied, "My favorite kind of weather is where you can go out night or day in shorts, a tropical shirt and sandals without feeling a chill."

11. This conversation with my driver reminded me it was time for my routine pilgrimage to Bagamoyo Beach in Tanzania, just a short drive from the capital city of Dar es Salaam. I'd go dressed simply in shorts, a T-shirt, and leather sandals, armed with a stack of local newspapers and work papers, ready to sink into a lounge chair and read the day away.

The only interruptions came from waiters refilling my glass and serving up sumptuous plates of food. It was pure heaven. As I once told a colleague, "I should pay for the delight of coming to Bagamoyo Beach, it's shameful that it comes with the job."

An American colleague reminded me that Bagamoyo was also steeped in history. It was the port from which the remains of the famed explorer-missionary, David Livingstone, were transported halfway across the continent by his loyal African attendants, Susi and Chuma, in 1874 beginning the long voyage to London, where he would be buried in Westminster Abbey.

12. In 1995, I was a US election observer on the island of Zanzibar, ostensibly a part of Tanzania. The joke back then was that Zanzibar was big enough to be a country but not big enough to be a region of mainland Tanzania.

It was a hotly contested election that all boiled down to the origins of the people ... were you descended from Africans from the mainland or from Arabs from Oman? I broke up a conflictual discussion by saying, "You all look the same to me."

The leader of one group replied loudly to my comment, "We know where our fathers come from."

13. There were jokes on the mainland of Tanzania about their first and most revered president, Julius Nyerere. One joke was that he gave them TV but not electricity. Another was his only mistake was his Arusha Declaration (which contained his entire political framework).

Even years after he resigned from the presidency many of the people upcountry believed he was still president. I explained to them that he was no longer president, but one of his students was. They said, "That's okay. As long as one of his students is president."

14. In Tanzania, the Chinese constructed a railway in the early 1970s that stretched deep into the southern neighbor of Zambia. In 1995, I was invited by the head of the Tanzam (Tazara) railway company to take the long journey, over a thousand miles to the Zambian border. Riding in his personal, well-appointed luxury train car was an out-of-this-world experience. The two-day trip passed so smoothly that it felt like a single day. At one point, I asked my companion, "When will we get out?"

He chuckled and replied, "Why get out? We have everything we need right here."

As we passed through the Tanzanian countryside, he pointed out the scenery through the large windows. When we stopped at one town, he remarked, "This is the mosquito capital of the world."

His comment reminded me how malaria was—and remains—the most common reason for medical consultations in Tanzania, a constant and deadly presence in the region.

15. In Dar es Salaam, Tanzania, in 1995, I was speaking with my houseman, who lived with his family in a small house behind my larger one. I mentioned that I had spent time in Somalia, and he responded, "My parents escaped slavery in Somalia to return to their home in Tanga, a northern coastal town in Tanzania. Many

people were taken from my hometown years ago to work as farmers in the Shabelle River area of southern Somalia. They were taken because the noble Somalis owned the land but did not work it. Their culture dictated that they should not get their hands dirty."

This was, by far, the most interesting thing my houseman told me during my two years (1994–96) in Tanzania. In one statement, he confirmed everything I had heard during my time in Somalia.

16. I knew a Tanzanian man in Dar es Salaam in 1995 who had recently been reassigned from the United Nations in New York City back to his home country. He was informed that the shipping container with his personal belongings had arrived at the port. Confident that all the contents were properly exonerated, he arranged a meeting with the customs agents overseeing the container, expecting a straightforward release.

Instead, the two customs agents bluntly told him that if he wanted his container, he would have to make under-the-table payments. He refused, insisting on adhering strictly to the laws governing such imports. Over the following days, he stood firm in his determination to follow all legal procedures.

In response, the customs agents began to open his container and sell off its contents piece by piece on the local market. Realizing that honesty was getting him nowhere, he finally gave in and paid the requested bribes. His container was released immediately.

17. In Dar, Tanzania, in 1995, I was told that anyone could see the former long-term first president, Julius Nyerere, in his house. I was reluctant to go see him, but I admired him greatly for what he said in his farewell speech after serving as president for fourteen years. He said, among other things, "African socialism was on the whole a noble cause, but it was not practical."

He said those words after he tried and failed for years to shape Tanzania into a self-reliant utopia, providing for the world with a good example of what was possible in a low-income country.

18. When I was in Tanzania, I was alerted to the killing of albino Tanzanians and using their body parts in occult ceremonies. In general, Tanzanians believed the body parts of albinos possessed magical properties.

The host government and local organizations campaigned actively against this practice, but it was difficult to eradicate. Albino Tanzanians lived in fear, taking extra precautions to prevent their deaths at the hands of those who believed that the absence of their skin pigmentation made their body parts exceptional and valuable in the treatment of certain ailments or transmitted magical powers.

19. In Dar es Salaam in 1995, I was invited to dinner at the home of one of the wealthiest men in the country. The house was a massive, three-story structure with spacious rooms furnished with the latest décor and furniture. It was undeniably impressive.

But upon reflection, the luxury felt like a mockery. The lights were powered by a private generator, and the plumbing only functioned thanks to rooftop water storage tanks. The toilets worked because of septic systems. The road leading to the house was rough and barely passable. Trash disposal was a constant challenge. There were no reliable public utilities or services provided by the city.

I concluded that renting a modest apartment in the U.S. was far better—you get electricity, running water, internet, and functioning appliances, all supported by efficient municipal services. The paved roads, sidewalks, and modern sewage systems in the U.S. are remarkable achievements. After all, the annual budget of a single large U.S. city often exceeds the entire national budget of many African countries.

20. We did not venture out in 1994 in the afternoon into the large Rwandan Benaco refugee camp, circa 500,000 refugees (the second largest urban area in Tanzania), at Ngara in the northwest corner of Tanzania because all the men would be drunk from drinking an excess of banana beer. We wanted to complain, but enterprising women made the beer. I asked an African colleague what we should do, and he said, "Nothing because the making of banana beer is a thriving women's enterprise in the camp."

21. The camp was near the Kagera River, which delimited the boundary between Rwanda and Tanzania. I stood on an old colonial bridge that crossed over the river and stared down into the rushing waters. As I looked at the swirling waters below me, I thought about how the Hutus had thrown the bodies of Tutsis they had killed so they could ride the river currents northward. The agricultural Hutus believed the origins of the pastoral Tutsi were in the distant north.

22. One of the challenges in meeting with refugee camp leadership groups in 1995 was identifying who was formerly with the Rwandan military. I informed my African colleague that the best way to tell if they had been part of the Rwandan military was to look for their wearing of boots. They would trash their military uniforms, but they would never give up their black military boots.

When we came out of a meeting with camp leaders I asked my colleague, "How many former Rwandan military were there in our meeting?"

He replied, "All of them."

23. There was a Belgian citizen working in the camp, but we were careful to refer to him as Canadian because we knew that Rwandans hated people from Belgium, their former colonizers. The refugees loved him as long as he was known as a Canadian.

24. The most heartbreaking sound I heard in Africa was at night when I could hear small children crying because of hunger and disease. Our camp was perched on a cliff above the Benaco refugee camp, and this sound was easily heard, causing sleepless nights.

25. In 1995, I accompanied my Ambassador to a meeting with the President of Tanzania, Hassan Mwinyi, and his Minister of Security. We were there to propose that Rwandan refugees be permitted to remain in Tanzania. Our core argument in support of the refugees was that the Rwandans were skilled farmers who could contribute significantly to the development of this remote, under-populated corner of northwest Tanzania.

The president remained silent, but his Security Minister responded forcefully in Kiswahili, making it clear he was opposed to our suggestion. He said, in no uncertain terms, "We cannot allow those people to stay in our country. They will contaminate our God-fearing Tanzanians with their radical behavior. The way they kill other human beings is something we can never accept."

26. I was surprised that the current Catholic Church in Zanzibar was built over the former slave market. I was also surprised by the existence of a guest house on Unguja Island for official Americans. I learned this house was the former long-term US Consulate, which was one of the first in the world and one of the USG's longest operational consulates.

27. I had many nicknames given to me in Africa. In Togo, I have already noted that as soon as they learned in 1970 via the chief district administrator that I was born on Tuesday, my name was henceforth 'Komla.' In Kenya and Tanzania, I was often referred to as 'mwasali mingi,' which in Kiswahili meant "many questions."

I recognized from this that curious Americans asked more questions than the average African. In general, it was considered impolite for younger Africans to ask many questions of his or her elders. I was allowed to ask questions that African youth could not. In that way, I learned things that they did not know. I also learned that politeness was valued in general over intelligence by Africans.

The reader already knows what I was called among Americans in Somalia — "chopped liver" — and for a time by Somalis as cad cassan ("red beard" in English). In Tanzania, the guards at my front office door called me Kijana mzée, which translates roughly to "young old man." During a 2005 meeting in Kinshasa to help design a new health project for a region of the DRC, an African participant suddenly said, "I'm pleased to see the rainmaker is here."

Later, I learned this man — a stranger to me — had used the nickname "rainmaker" because he'd heard that wherever I went in Africa to help develop assistance activities, those projects were always funded.

Of course, I was always "the white man" wherever I traveled in Africa — referred to in local languages as yovo, muzungu, anasara, toubab, and so on, depending on the country.

I was at the Kinshasa, DRC airport in 2005. I had been warned that I would have to bribe my way through. I was pleased to have avoided at least half a dozen payoffs and had just reached the door to the waiting lounge when a uniformed man stepped in front of me, saluted, and said, "I'm Commandant Chaka, and I've heard you didn't pay anything to get this far. Pay me twenty US dollars before you take another step."

I was so close to leaving the DRC that I reached into my pocket, pulled out a twenty-dollar bill, and handed it over without a word.

28. Yes, I was in Tanzania for two years in the mid-1990s, but I did not climb Mt. Kilimanjaro, Africa's tallest mountain. I wanted to climb it and saw it many times, but I needed six days to climb it, and I simply did not have the time to hike up to cold heights that I did not like. I enjoyed seeing the mountain from a distance and I always sat on the sides of the Nairobi-bound planes that offered the best view of the mountain.

I settled for forays of a few days into Tanzania's many game parks, including the great Serengeti Plains. I saw the Ngorongoro Crater and the Olduvai Gorge, where the remains of one of the earliest humans was discovered.

29. Our Tanzanian employees were too laid back, so we devised a course that would teach them to be more assertive. After the course, we found that our employees were more assertive, but they intervened at the wrong moments. Their interventions were so inappropriate that they came across as artificial. It was clear to me that 'assertiveness' was alien to their culture.

KENYA

1. In 1982, I had an overnight stop in Nairobi, Kenya. I was staying at the Hilton Hotel in central downtown Nairobi when a bullet pierced the window of my fourth-floor room. Evidently, a group of Kenyan military personnel was attempting a coup against the sitting president. The panic of the moment was quickly brought under control, as the host government rapidly suppressed the surprising attempt in what had been a relatively stable African country.

For the reader's information, I stayed at this hotel many times over the years. I eventually learned to request a ground-floor room in case of a power outage, which could disable the elevator in the multi-story hotel.

2. I was in Nairobi, Kenya, in late 1994, and my Indian Kenyan assistant dampened my ebullience over the possible election of an opposition candidate to be president. She told me bluntly, "The candidate you want to win the election can never be elected because he comes from an ethnic group that does not circumcise its boys."

This made me wonder about our US President because his Kenyan father came from this same ethnic group.

3. On a drive through a wealthy white neighborhood in Nairobi, the capital of Kenya, I asked a Kenyan woman riding with me in the minibus (matatu) what she thought of the people living in those luxury houses with expansive, manicured lawns. Her reply was short, frank, and to the point: "We believe you could eat the shit of these people with no ill effects."

This same woman told me that you could tell a woman was serious about a man if she washed his dirty underwear by hand.

She also lamented that she had not yet found 'Mr. Right.' With a wry smile, she added, "You have to kiss a lot of frogs before you meet a prince."

4. In Nairobi, Kenya, in 1997, I wondered why my Kenyan driver was always better dressed than me. Like many of his colleagues and friends, he always wore a suit and tie. And when I went occasionally to the horse racetrack on the weekends, the black and white Kenyans dressed as if they were in London.

I asked my driver about this, and he said, "Yes, we copy the English because our indigenous dress would be inappropriate if we can remember what that was like."

I replied, "In West Africa, they have outstanding cloth out of which they make impressive clothing."

His comment on my statement was, "Yes, West Africans have style … we don't."

5. It was in 1994, in Nairobi, Kenya, that this bizarre incident occurred. "No people in there," my Kenyan colleague said after being sent into a restaurant by a group of our friends to check it out.

I was hungry, so I said, "Let me go in and see if they can find seats for us."

I came back out and said, "What do you mean by 'no people'? There are lots of people in there."

The reply I got was, "Those are not people. Those are Indians."

I asked, "You don't like Indians?"

"No, I don't. They control most commercial activity, own all the shops, and pay us low wages."

At that point, another African guy in our group chimed in, "I think it's time to foment another riot so we can vandalize the Indian shops. I need a new fridge."

I said, "Wait a minute. The Asian population has been here for a couple hundred years."

"Yes, but they never integrated. How many mixed marriages do you see?"

I tried to change the topic by suggesting we take a cab to a popular restaurant, The Carnivore. My suggestion elicited big laughs from the group.

I asked, "Why do you laugh?"

"It's Thursday night. That's what we call Bombay Night—so the dance floor will be crowded with Indian men."

I found that peculiar and said, "They've got a right to dance with their women."

Again, my words triggered laughter, and one of them said, "No, men dance with men. Their women stay at home."

The Carnivore was thus scratched as an option, and I would once again have to forego enjoying its tasty selection of wild game meat.

6. I had the honor of hosting a group of Kenyan university students in Nairobi in 1997 to present the first ten clauses—the "Bill of Rights"—of the U.S. Constitution. When I finished my talk, a Kenyan woman came up to congratulate me on what she called a wonderful and informative presentation. She also said, "How

great it is that your country included the right to food in its Constitution."

I replied, "What do you mean?"

She answered, "Well, you told us all about the 'Bill of Rice.'"

I was taken aback by the idea that all the students had thought I was talking about rice and not rights the entire time.

7. I was walking down a crowded street in Nairobi, Kenya, in 1993 when I spotted a white American man I had once helped get out of jail in Lome, Togo. He had been a big-time money changer in Lome, saving many people from paying the high bank fees by exchanging currency for them.

I remembered dropping him at the border near Benin after he'd been expelled from Togo. I had once asked him why he changed money at a rate lower than the banks, and he replied, "That was the only way I could make any money." He added, "It was the Lebanese business community that got me expelled—they didn't want any competition. The president relied on them for cash gifts."

His son was with him then, and although still a young man, he looked twice his age from the constant trips he had to make to Europe to exchange money.

Anyway, I asked what he was doing in Nairobi now, and he said, "I'm a boxing promoter."

My thought at that moment was simply: It takes all kinds.

8. In Nairobi, Kenya, in 2003, I attended the burial of a young Kenyan colleague who had died of AIDS. I was shocked to see all the fresh graves in the cemetery. An elderly Kenyan saw that I was looking at the new graves and said solemnly, "We're losing our upcoming generation."

I replied with an inappropriate comment, "I'm sure glad that HIV/AIDS did not exist when I first came to Africa."

9. I was in Nairobi in 1999 and enjoying a cup of tea in a sidewalk café when I noticed that most of the cars parked in front of the café were BMWs. I asked the Kenyan waiter about this, and he said, "There is the belief among the upper class that if you want to pursue marriage, you must offer first the chosen woman a BMW, which in our country stands for 'Be My Wife.'"

10. In this same country, I picked up an American friend from the Nairobi airport. It was his first time visiting Africa. While driving him in the night the few kilometers to the city, he commented, "It is very dark here."

His comment forced me to reflect on Africa's lack of electricity. Truly, in terms of electrical lights at night, it is a dark continent. But Nairobi was one of the best-lighted cities in Africa.

11. I was again in Nairobi, Kenya, when I overheard two white guys talk about the recent thievery of their vehicle. I joined their conversation and interjected, "Did you get your vehicle back?"

One of them replied, "Yes, the same day."

"Great. How did you do that?"

The other guy explained, "We left a bottle of scotch whiskey laced with strychnine between the two front seats. We knew they would drink it and die, and then the police could easily find their location."

12. Their story reminds me of one I heard in Nairobi. There was a hit-and-run accident, and the guilty party had driven off. Crowds had gathered at the scene of the accident, and the police came and interrogated them. They asked, "Was the driver drunk?"

A person standing close to the police replied, "Definitely."

A policeman said, "How do you know?"

"He drove straight. A normal person would not drive straight so they could try to avoid the potholes."

13. In Nairobi, Kenya, I was talking to a group of university students about their post-graduation job prospects. One said, "The top graduate from ten years ago is still looking for work, but the last graduate in his class was the nephew of a minister, and he was offered a job as soon as he graduated."

Another said, "The university is a factory for producing the unemployed."

These words made me understand better how Africa was losing its best and brightest talent to other countries that offered them jobs with decent salaries. This 'brain drain' of its professional class was slowing development progress in their home countries.

14. Promoting democracy was a hallmark of many of my efforts in Africa. In 1998, I had an opportunity again to talk with a group of university students in Nairobi. Kenya. I was delighted to present the US democracy as a model. One of the students asked me, "If the one person, one vote model of the US is to be followed, what role does the Electoral College play in the US? And why does each US State get two senators regardless of its population or geographic size?"

To this present day, I wrestle with good answers to these two questions. It was apparent to me that the model of democracy we promoted in Africa was different from what we practiced in the US.

15. There are some restaurants in central Nairobi, Kenya, that I frequented. The Trattoria has been serving good food for fifty years. Another favorite spot of mine was a café where I often enjoyed a cup of coffee, Thorn Tree.

As the name suggests, the café featured a tall acacia thorn tree growing in the center of its outdoor seating area. This tree doubled as a message board for travelers passing through, covered with scraps of paper bearing handwritten notes and messages for fellow adventurers about where they'd gone or where to meet. It was a well-known crossroads for backpackers traveling through Nairobi.

16. The best haircut I ever had was at a barber shop behind the Hilton Hotel in central Nairobi. The Indian barber spoke a language unintelligible to me, but he cut my hair expertly and topped the haircut off with a deep scalp massage.

17. In 1997, a Kenyan man told me as we were enjoying a cup of green Kenyan tea that his country could never become as destabilized and violent as other countries in Africa. I asked him, "Why do you say that?"

He replied, "Our middle class has become so large that it won't do anything to jeopardize what they got."

18. I attended a Christian conference in Nairobi, Kenya, in 2005, and one of the African participants asked me about my home church, and I responded, "I'm Catholic."

His reply was, "Too bad you're not a Christian."

19. A big problem for many African cities is the high number of street kids. For example, it is estimated about 50,000 children are living in the streets of Nairobi, Kenya, a capital city with an estimated population of about two million.

This number is growing and is considered part of rapid urbanization growth in Africa. The main question on my mind is: "What is the future of these children, and how can a country progress with such a burden?"

20. A few of these kids would fill discarded syringes with liquid excrement and threaten to inject motorists backed up in their vehicles at one of Nairobi's congested intersections if they did not give them any money. This is where armed bandits hijacked some cars.

I overheard that the Kenya PCD had two of her official cars hijacked within a short period as she drove to a weekly country team meeting at the US Embassy.

Uncannily, this reminded me of when I covered Togo and Benin. In Togo, I was obliged to attend country team meetings at the embassy twice a week. When in Cotonou, Benin, I complained to the US Ambassador about the obligation to attend country team meetings twice a week, and he informed me that he had country team meetings every workday.

21. One Kenyan colleague was driving home at night with his wife from a church service when two men stopped his vehicle and told him and his wife to get out. He tried to pacify them calmly and soothingly, but they shot him dead, and his wife fled in terror down the street. This vicious hijacking attack and killing of such an upstanding man weighed heavily on me.

22. This sad event occurred at the time of another tragic death of an expatriate in Nairobi in 1993. The city's transport network depended on the ubiquitous 'matatus' ... small locally made minibusses. One of these matatus had a terrible accident, and among the dead was Emma McCune, a British aid worker in Sudan and wife of Riek Machar, one of the leaders of the Sudan People's

Liberation Army. Her life was immortalized in a 1998 book, *Emma's War*, by Deborah Scroggins.

23. I learned of these events related to South Sudan, Africa's newest country, which came into being following the end of over 30 years of bloody war with northern Sudan, thanks to the signing of the Comprehensive Peace Agreement (CPA). At the time, in 2004, I was working on a development assistance strategy for South Sudan to be implemented once it gained independence and hostilities ceased.

I took a UN flight that passed through Lokichogio, a small border town in Kenya, en route to Juba, the capital city of South Sudan. However, most of my work on the strategy was done in Nairobi, Kenya. The expectation then was that once independent and at peace, South Sudan would become one of the wealthiest countries in Africa.

Unfortunately, while hostilities with the North ceased, protracted fighting broke out between the main ethnic groups in the south. Senseless bloodshed and rampant corruption derailed all plans for developing this new African nation.

24. I went into one of the most popular bars in central Nairobi, Kenya, in 1999. I was thirsty for a cold beer. The waiter asked me what I wanted to drink, and I said, "Of course, a beer."

He replied, "Cold or warm."

I had never been offered a warm beer, so I was puzzled by what he said but replied, "Of course, cold."

An African man sitting at the bar interjected, "I never drink anything colder than my blood temperature."

25. In 1997, I heard a language I had not heard before in Nairobi, Kenya. I expected to hear Kiswahili or one of Kenya's local languages. But instead, I was hearing words that I did not know existed. I asked a Kenyan friend what the guys next to us were saying. He replied, "That's 'sheng.' It's a slang language that mostly young Kenyans use."

26. In 1997, on a lark, I took the long nine-hour nighttime train ride from Nairobi to the coastal city of Mombasa. This train ride occurred during a night that was pitch black and made frequent stops. I wanted to see the towns and land we were passing, but the obscurity made that impossible. I complained of this to one of the train agents and he replied, "You're better off not seeing the lay of the land."

BURUNDI – RWANDA

These two countries were former colonies of Belgium and have a similar ethnic composition. They are at the heart of Africa's Great Lakes Region, so I recount some of my experiences in them in 1997-98 together.

1. While working in Bujumbura, Burundi, I drafted an email for widespread dissemination. In that message, I referred to Rwanda as a tiny regional hegemon in Central Africa. I was put in the doghouse for this message, and I was instructed not to write any more reporting messages.

I learned from this discouraging incident that official US policy was of a realpolitik nature, linking the presidents of Rwanda, Uganda, Ethiopia, and Eritrea, and no dissent to this policy would be tolerated. Now, almost thirty years later, I still stand by my original message, which ignored the US' fictive political alignment of presidents in the region.

This occurred in 1997. All the presidents of these countries remain in power except in Ethiopia. The president of this country died unexpectedly of a brain tumor.

2. Later, I tried to redeem myself by writing an extensive paper entitled "Central African Briar Patch: Shifting the Balance of Power Amid a Tangle of Ambitions, Interests, Fear and Hatreds."

This paper fell on deaf ears except for a highly regarded specialist, René Lemarchand. This professor emeritus of the University of Florida/Gainesville praised my paper. He published his seminal book on Rwanda in 1970. He has published many works on this troubled region of Africa over the past five decades.

3. Perhaps the underlying sentiment of the bloody ethnic conflict between the Hutu and Tutsi in Central Africa was best summed up for me in Bujumbura, Burundi, by an African colleague who said, "We have to kill them before they kill us."

I responded. "I can't tell the difference between Hutu and Tutsi. How do you tell the difference?"

He replied, "At times, we can't tell, but after we talk a while, we know."

4. I was asked in 1998 by the commander of a visiting US military group in Bujumbura what the Tutsis understood. I responded, "A hard punch on the nose."

5. I went to Burundi in 1997 to close the USAID Mission, a process that required hiring a dozen local men to empty the warehouse

and liquidate the furniture from various rental properties. At the time, I didn't know to which ethnic group these workers belonged. However, when they insisted on leaving work before 5 p.m. each day to reach their homes in the distant surrounding hills before nightfall, I suspected they were all Hutus.

In the days that followed, my suspicion was confirmed by the receipt of written death threats warning me to stop hiring Hutus. I ignored the letters, but I was fully aware that my life was at risk. I consider myself fortunate that when I departed Burundi later that year, there had been no attempts on my life.

6. The fragments of a vehicle in the trees reminded me of the landmines that were being laid in 1997 in the streets of Bujumbura. The imposition of a 9 p.m. curfew further reminded me that I was living and working in a danger zone. In addition, soldiers had erected roadblocks

everywhere, and by 9 p.m., they were all drunk from drinking an excess of beer and, thus, trigger-happy.

7. I thought if we were able to stop the brewery from producing beer, we could make this a less violent country. I brought this point up with a local official, and he said, "That's crazy talk. The brewery is a strategic installation, and its operation around the

clock every day of the week is necessary to maintain the status quo as we know it. We violate the international boycott placed on Burundi by illegally contracting planes to fly in all the essential ingredients for making beer. Without the brewery, there would be an increase in violence."

8. My job in Burundi morphed into writing political cables for the US Embassy. It was noticed that I was one of the few Americans who could say and spell the lengthy, multi-syllable local names. I note that many of the cables I wrote received kudos from the Department of State and were included in its weekly list of best reporting cables. It referred to this list as the 'hit parade.'

This was all right with me until the USG special envoy, Howard Wolpe, for the Great Lakes Region, arrived. I was obliged to accompany him to all his official meetings, serving as notetaker and interpreter (French to English). I drafted reporting cables on his meetings for his review. He would always add stuff. I was instructed by my superior at the US Embassy, "Write all the details he indicates ... even he says he wants the colors of the curtains and walls."

9. I often went to play tennis on the clay court at the US Ambassador's residence in Bujumbura. One day, I greeted the ballboy in my rudimentary Kiswahili, and he surprised me when

he replied loudly and with much clarity in French, "Don't ever speak to me in that low-class language."

I asked my ambassador what the matter with the ballboy was. He replied forthrightly, "He fetches our tennis balls, but he's not a ballboy ... he's a former president of Burundi, Sylvestre Ntibantunganya, who has taken refuge in my residence. You would be doing me a big favor for me if you could find a house for him so the authorities could put him under house arrest. My advice for the moment is not to ask him any questions because his response to a simple question can take a long time."

I later learned that this former president was a survivor of an old genocide in Burundi when an estimated 100,000 Hutu were killed in 1972 by the ruling Tutsi ethnic group. This happened before there were international news broadcasts. Even today it's hard to find in a US newspaper any reports about what is happening in Africa.

10. One of the saddest sights for me in Africa was seeing the top of desolate hills in rural Burundi internment camps of Hutus. They were kept in these camps at night by the host government. They were all under-clothed in the freezing hilltop weather. Also, they appeared to be undernourished, although they were allowed to farm in their distant fields during the day.

11. One of the scariest moments for me was a nighttime overland drive from Kigali to Bujumbura. Our vehicle experienced mechanical problems, which caused delays and forced us to travel most of the route after dark. We were stopped several times by drunken soldiers, and I feared we might encounter even worse from roaming rebel bands. During that eerie journey, I told myself that sending four containers of office equipment and supplies from Bujumbura to Kigali was simply not worth the risk.

12. It was 1998, and I was sitting with the leader of the country at his residence on a hillside above scenic Lake Tanganyika in Bujumbura, Burundi. He said it was leaders like him who were causing all the problems, and if a plane could come at night and pick him up and about a dozen others, the people would be at peace. I asked him, "Can that plane make a few other stops in Africa?"

I also asked him, "Which ethnic group was the first to settle in Burundi?"

He did not answer, but I was ready to say the Twa, a pygmy group that has been in the territory of Burundi forever.

13. I encountered a Greek man in 1997 in Bujumbura, Burundi, who owned a shop filled with car spare parts. I went to see him

about cashing a personal check into local currency. I asked if he could do this, and he replied, "Of course—just write the check exactly as I instruct, and I'll send it to my older brother in the States."

I followed his instructions and wrote the check. Then, to my surprise, he opened a massive walk-in wall safe packed floor to ceiling with stacks of money. He counted out the local currency at the street exchange rate I had requested and placed it neatly on the counter. I thanked him.

Ever since, I've wondered where he got all that money. I was certain he couldn't have earned it just by selling car parts. I've always suspected he was involved in the lucrative gold and diamond trade from Burundi's western neighbor, the DRC.

14. This thought troubled me, but I told myself that it is often the untaxed informal economy upon which poor countries survive. It was no mystery to me that neighboring Rwanda depended greatly on the export of coltan, diamonds, and gold, but it did not produce any of these minerals ... they were all smuggled across their common but disorderly border with neighboring DRC.

I was reminded of what Rwanda's vice president said in 1994. He pointed at a map of the region and stated that Rwanda's population density demanded that it annex North Kivu, a part of eastern DRC.

15. It was 1997, and my African American colleague in Bujumbura, Burundi, was leaving the country as quickly as possible. He had had it ... because the local people had identified him as being associated with one of the two warring ethnic groups. I asked him why he could not stay, and he replied, "I'm tired of hearing, 'we have to kill you before your people kill me.' "

For him, the ethnic conflict raging in Central Africa was irresolvable, and he did not want to risk his life in a conflict that really did not involve him.

16. I have been told that it is almost impossible to survive a bullet shot to the neck because of the many veins located in this part of the human body. But I have had the pleasure of knowing two American men who survived miraculously gunshots to the neck. Both these men were armed security officials, and both were immediately evacuated for quick emergency medical care in Nairobi. One of them was in Mogadishu in 1993, and the other was in Bujumbura, Burundi in 1997.

17. I was in Kigali, Rwanda, in 1998, attending a meeting of Rwandans. The head of the meeting only spoke English, and all

the meeting participants understood only French and their local language. I found myself in the awkward position of informing the participants in French of what the meeting head had said in English.

18. My first visit to Kigali was in 1983. At that time, it was presented as an idyllic place to live and work and as a country with a bright future. There was no talk of any ethnic conflict. We took a safari up the slopes of the mountains in northwest Rwanda to see gorillas in the wild.

Later, this served as a strong lesson for me to look under the surface for potential conflicts that may burst on the scene to upset the perceived peace.

19. Anyway, this safari served to remind me of previous incursions made into Africa by fellow Kansans, Martin, and Osa Johnson, years before I was born. I enjoyed my visit to Osa's hometown of Chanute, Kansas in 1996 to visit the museum established in their honor at Chanute's old train station. Their pioneering work definitely inspired me in Africa. And I treasure my copy of Osa's bestselling 1940 book, *I Married Adventure.*

20. I often wondered why the US had an embassy in Bujumbura, Burundi. After all, it cost the USG a lot of money, and Burundi was

a former colony of Belgium. Does the US have to have an expensive embassy in every African country?

21. I am reluctant to mention Somalia again, but in 1992, the U.S. government was hesitant to engage militarily there due to what was referred to as the "Vietnam syndrome." Then, in 1994, I was deeply upset when both the UN and the U.S. failed to intervene in Rwanda to stop the mass genocide of one ethnic group by another—this time citing the "Somalia syndrome."

In my opinion, the UN or U.S. should have deployed a robust peacekeeping force, supported by attack helicopters, to halt the mass killings—brutal acts committed largely with clubs and machetes. To me, this was fundamentally different from warfare involving automatic weapons and bullets.

I strongly believe the UN should maintain a well-trained, rapidly deployable military force capable of responding to humanitarian crises anywhere in the world.

(Incidentally, I had been selected in late 1993 to serve as the new USAID representative to Rwanda, but the genocide led to the cancellation of that assignment.)

ZAMBIA

1. I was in discussion with rural Zambian farmers in 1999 and asked, "What do you like best about this project?"

One farmer immediately replied, "More money and less hunger."

This prescient phrase became the title of my review report of this activity.

2. I was impressed by the ability of farmers' groups in Zambia to speak English. It was a pleasant experience not to have to work through an interpreter.

3. In Lusaka, the capital city of Zambia, I was reading in 1999 the feature front page article of a major local newspaper about a witch who fell off her broom and was quickly burnt to death by the local population. I laughingly said, "Who would believe such stuff?"

The Zambians around me exclaimed in unison, "Everyone!"

4. I came to learn that the presence of witches and demons was a common belief in Zambia, as it is in many other African countries. One Zambian woman confided in me that demons would occupy her mother during the night and speak through her while she slept. The unsettling part was that her mother would awaken in

the morning with no memory of what had transpired. Because of this, the daughter was tasked with sitting by her mother's bedside at night to transcribe the words of the demons. A serious responsibility indeed.

5. Later, in 1998, in Lusaka, Zambia, I had the chance to enter for the first time into a conversation with an older Caucasian African. This poor man worked in the copper mines as a mechanic. He had been born in Zambia, but the rest of his family had moved to South Africa after Zambia gained independence in 1964.

He told me that he had not finished high school but was the one in charge of maintaining all spare part**s** of diesel engines because his bosses trusted him. I explained to him that I had been working in the field of development for a long time. His surprising reply was as follows: "Africa can never develop because the blacks are too lazy and untrustworthy."

6. This reminded me of the time an American colleague, Joe Gettier, who had previously worked in an Asian country, said, "I don't understand it. Asians work hard and get someplace. Africans work just as hard, but they don't get anywhere."

7. In Zambia, in 1998, I oversaw a food-for-work project that involved the maintenance of rural roads. We ran out of food grain

before the end of the project and we decided to give the Zambian participants cash.

When hearing this news, the female participants revolted, saying, "If you give the men money, they will use it to drink and chase loose women before they get home. At least when you gave them grain, they would bring it home for us to cook."

8. In 1999, I had a good American friend, Ron Phillips, in Lusaka, the capital city of Zambia, who, prior to managing a rural development project in Zambia, worked in the US at an alcoholic rehabilitation center. I asked him, "There is excessive drinking of alcoholic beverages in this country and across Africa. What can be done about this?"

He replied, "If all these local men were in the States, they would all be committed to alcoholic rehabilitation programs."

9. This same American friend was promoting the cultivation of a new crop—paprika—for sale to a private South African firm. When farmers saw how much money they could earn from selling high-quality paprika, they stopped planting white maize, their main food staple.

This situation became untenable for project managers, who then required participating farmers to cultivate at least one hectare of maize using conservation farming principles before becoming eligible for the paprika program. This proved to be a terrific incentive, encouraging farmers to also commit to maize cultivation. They referred to their paprika fields as "gold."

10. I rented a car in 1999 to drive from Lusaka and see, for the first time, the water being released from Lake Kariba Dam. I discovered that throngs of people had the same idea, and the road was jammed with traffic. I couldn't even get close to the dam, and after the water was released, I found myself unable to turn around and head back to Lusaka.

So, I crossed illegally into the bordering country of Zimbabwe and found that all the lodgings were full. I decided to sleep in my car before returning to Zambia.

In the middle of the night, I heard a tap on the windshield. I rolled down my window to see what the black African man wanted, and he whispered, "Follow me if you want a nice room."

I drove slowly behind him as he opened a metal gate, revealing a road leading to a new hotel that wasn't yet open. He signaled me to stop in front of a room. I got out of the car, and he showed me a well-furnished room, then said, "Pay me what you can and promise me that you'll be on your way before dawn."

11. The Kariba Dam was situated on the mighty Zambezia River. This large artificial lake was home to many animal and fish species, especially the small kapenta fish (Tanganyika sardine – Limothrisa miodon). My thoughts back then were about joining one of the fishing groups that were angling to catch the famous Tigerfish (Hydrocynus vittatus) in the Zambezia River.

12. Of course, when in Zambia, I visited its side of Victoria Falls, which was shared with neighboring Zimbabwe. I even took a motorized glider down into the deep gorge that the falls descend into. When I got back from my exciting ride on the glider, I thanked the pilot for such an exciting and wonderful ride into the Victoria Falls gorge. He replied, "You mean Mosi-Oa-Tunya." (Meaning in the local language 'the smoke that thunders.')

Evidently, he preferred the local word for Victoria Falls instead of the name given to it by the missionary explorer David Livingston, who named the falls after the Queen of England when he first came upon it in 1855.

13. There were many financial banks in Lusaka, Zambia, in the late 1990s. I asked one African colleague about this, and he replied, "Those banks launder the money that flows illicitly into Zambia. You should know that more money goes out of Africa annually than donor countries provide."

I was dumbfounded by his assertion and started to object that it was not as bad as he said, but I bit my lip. The level of corruption was high in Africa and it was likely that more money flowed out than in.

14. In Zambia, new foreign businesses found a convenient way to get around this country's draconian labor laws and the employee benefits they provided. These businesses would hire new local employees for only ninety days, as benefits would not start to kick in until after ninety days.

I inquired about this to a recently dismissed local employee and she replied, "It's okay. We understand their position, and ninety days is enough to work in one place. This work experience will help me find another job at a different place."

15. I was driving from Mozambique to Zambia in 2004. The crossing of South Africa went smoothly. In Zimbabwe, the main problem I faced was the car fuel shortage. My car tank was empty, and when I arrived in Harare (Zimbabwe's capital city), I found all the gas stations to be empty. I finally ended up at the UN compound and begged for the fuel I needed to get to Zambia.

I got to the Zimbabwe side of the border, but I did not count on being held up on the Zambia side by security agents because they thought I had stolen the car I was driving. One of the agents said, "If you give twenty US dollars, this entire matter can be settled."

I refused to give a bribe, and thus, I sat there the whole day in the hot sun. As the sun was setting, I finally gave up and handed the agent a $20 bill. All road barricades were quickly lifted, and I saw a lot of smiles on the faces of the agents manning these barricades as I went on my way into Zambia.

16. I visited all the flour mills in Zambia in 1998 and found they were all managed by Greeks. I learned that Greeks had monopolized for decades the production of flour from imported wheat grain. I asked a Greek flour mill manager why this was so, and he replied, "This is what we do in this country ... somebody has to do it. If we leave, probably the Lebanese will replace us."

17. Somehow, this made me think of what I heard had happened with US wheat grain in the DRC. The US provided much wheat as food aid, so the local people would be hooked on bread and thus would have a high demand for wheat in the future.

MALAWI

1. I was staying in 2011 in a lodge in Lilongwe, Malawi, and there I met a British gentleman, Stephen Carr, who had worked for years in South Sudan. He revealed to me that he had published a book in 2004 about his time in South Sudan that was entitled, *'Surprised by Laughter.'* He gave me a copy of his book and said, "No matter how hard the times were for the Sudanese, they would always laugh."

2. I was in Malawi in 2004, visiting rural farmers. Major concerns were the thievery of their ripe crops and livestock. They took the extreme option of keeping their livestock in their houses at night. I asked, "Why don't you call the police?"

The response I got was, "They're useless or dead."

I asked why you would say that, and a woman replied, "All the police have died from AIDS, leaving us to fend for ourselves."

Later, I visited some large estate plantations and was told, "Around 20 percent of our annual budget is for security, but we still continue to lose a large portion of our ripe crops to thieves."

3. I was told by the British aid representative that southern Malawi was expanding each year by five kilometers into Mozambique.

Evidently, many Malawian farmers would cultivate fields on the Mozambique side of the nearby border and return to their homes in Malawi at night. It appeared there was no way to halt the flow of the Malawian population into northern Mozambique, particularly since Malawi was heavily populated and this area of Mozambique was sparsely populated.

This same British man said that his agency had just doubled the aid it gives to Malawi.

When I asked him why, he responded, "Because Malawi is too poor."

4. I marveled over the fact that the neighboring country of Zambia had over five times the land area of Malawi and about the same population of Malawi. The population density in Malawi was nine times greater than in Zambia.

5. I was in the capital city of Lilongwe, Malawi, in 1999, expressing satisfaction with the decision of the new government (which followed the iron-fist rule of a long-term, 30-year dictator) to allow small farmers to grow tobacco. This was a real breakthrough, giving thousands of small farmers access—for the first time—to this lucrative export cash crop.

An association was organized for the small growers of this crop. With US backing, progress was being made in the adoption of tobacco cultivation by poor smallholders.

Then, suddenly, the US withdrew its support because it violated a US law designed to protect American tobacco farmers from foreign competition. I was to learn that this Congressional act also covered other crops. I concluded from this action that the US was not a reliable partner. It prioritized protecting its own interests, even if it meant reducing assistance to one of the poorest countries on Earth.

SENEGAL

1. In Dakar, Senegal, in late 2010, I had the opportunity to once again observe the artistic work of the North Koreans. They showcased their handiwork by constructing a massive new 52-meter-tall bronze statue on a hilltop on the outskirts of Dakar. This controversial statue, called the African Renaissance Monument, was erected to commemorate Senegal's 50th year of independence.

The enormous statue depicted an African man and woman holding an infant, but their facial features appeared more Asian than African. Many Senegalese protested both the construction of the statue and, after its opening, the fact that part of the entrance fee revenue was allegedly being collected by their national president.

2. I was walking through a traditional African market in Dakar, Senegal, in 1998 when a hand entered into my back pants pocket. Instinctively, I turned around and slugged my pickpocket in the face. He fell down, and all the shopkeepers came out from behind their stalls.

My first thought was that I was in big trouble with them for hitting one of their compatriots. I was ready to apologize to them when they all applauded me, and one of them said, "Good. That thief deserved being hit."

3. A Senegalese colleague in Dakar informed me, "You'll have to work out of your hotel room because our office building has been declared a high-security risk."

I replied, "Okay, but what's the risk?"

"There's a filling station located next to our building, and it represents a hazard. Our security chief has instructed us to find another office building."

4. I was treated in 1998 by my Dioula family hosts in Ziguinchor, Casamance, Senegal, in a royal fashion to a delightful dinner. The master of the house said, "In your honor, we are eating rice that we have stored for five years."

The same host was a lively conversationalist and said, "We refuse to be absorbed and exploited by a larger and predominant ethnic group, Wolof, in Senegal. We must maintain our own language and customs and instruct our children accordingly. We must avoid 'Wolofization' at all costs. "

5. A Guinean family invited me to lunch in their house in Dakar. In the customary fashion, the family gathered around a large basin to eat with their right hands a delicious pile of seasoned rice. I

followed suit and started to dig in with my right hand when an elderly woman slapped my hand and wagged her finger, saying, "You are a special guest, so you do not feed yourself."

Before I could reply, a beautiful young African woman was seated next to me and scooped out some of the rice to place into my mouth. This culinary experience was unforgettable.

6. In 1986, I traveled from Conakry, Guinea to attend a conference in Dakar, Senegal on the topic of democracy in West Africa. At the time, Senegal was widely regarded as the only functioning democracy in the region.

The U.S. Ambassador, Lannon Walker, was one of the keynote speakers at the conference. During a break in the proceedings, I approached the front of the auditorium to congratulate him on his speech and to commend Senegal's democratic status.

He chuckled lightly and replied, "Yes, Senegal is democratic about five minutes each year."

7. The joke in Senegal was that you could not be the country's president if you were not married to a white French woman (Senegal's first three presidents were married to such women. It was only its fourth president who had a Senegalese spouse.)

8. I enjoyed taking long walks around central Dakar, but inevitably, there would always be a young Senegalese guy who wanted to accompany me. I tried to explain that I wanted to take a walk alone, but that was beyond the comprehension of any of the guys who wanted to escort me.

9. I was happy to see in 1995 in the US, a celebration of an African American Christmas called Kwanzaa. But I was confused by its use of the Kiswahili language, which is prevalent in East Africa, whereas African Americans in the US trace their origins to multilingual West Africa.

NIGER

1. While living in Niamey in late 1999, I had a Tuareg man guarding my house at night with his big traditional sword. He said he wanted to return to his homeland, where there were no trees. I commiserated with him by saying, "I appreciated the open spaces provided by the desert. No wonder that many of the great religions originated in the desert."

He was worried about losing his job and not finding another one and said, "I've never been to school, and now those who have some education are being hired as houseguards (askaris). What will illiterate people like me do? I've a family which depends on me."

2. It was 2000, and I was with my African driver traveling at a good clip on one of Niger's laterite rural roads, trying to keep the dust of our four-wheeled vehicle behind us, when we came up behind a big truck. My driver pressed his hand against the front windshield and I asked him. "Why are you doing that?"

He replied, "I do this to cut down on the vibrations of any rocks tossed up by the truck we're trailing. In other words, by reducing vibrations, we keep the windshield from breaking."

Anytime I am driving behind another vehicle on a gravel road in any country, I place my hand on the inside of the windshield exactly like my Nigerien driver did years ago.

3. I traveled from Niger in 2000 to participate in a conference in Cairo, Egypt. in 2000. A shopkeeper in Cairo told me that as an infidel, I should not use the common Muslim greeting, "Salam alekoum," that I always used in Niger. He also said, "You can never understand Islam until you can read the holy Quran in the saintly language of Arabic."

4. There was a strange smell in 2000 in the Niamey, Niger neighborhood next to the new stadium that the Chinese built. Nigerien investigators went into the adjoining empty houses that the Chinese had occupied and found the origin of the foul smell. They covered their noses while they pried up the plywood ceiling boards to find stacks of rotting dog bones. One of the Nigerien team members said, "I wondered where all the stray dogs had gone. Now I know."

5. On an upcountry trip in 2000, my Nigerien colleague and I stopped to visit a village. To our surprise, the place seemed deserted—only the elderly and people with disabilities remained. My colleague asked an elderly woman in the local language where everyone had gone. She replied, "They are all at the cemetery,

attending the burial of one of the village's migrant laborers who returned home gravely ill after falling under the charms of a coastal commercial sex worker."

My colleague followed up, asking, "What sickness did he have?"

She responded in Hausa, and I didn't understand, so I turned to my colleague and asked, "What did she say?"

He replied, "AIDS. Around here, we call it 'Welcome to the cemetery'—kabari salamou aliekoum."

6. In Niger, also in 2000, I became aware of a large number of women who suffered from obstetrical fistula. These women were warehoused in the back of the national hospital in Niamey. They had been shunned by their husbands and ostracized by their villages. (I thought that ostracization from your community was the worst punishment that could befall Africa.)

There was only one surgeon for hundreds of these women who knew how to perform the delicate operation they needed. I asked a Nigerien nurse about the hiring of another surgeon, and she replied, "The surgeon we have is on loan from a clinic in northern Nigeria where they also have a surplus of fistula women."

7. Getting pregnant as a young teenager was the cause of fistula for most of these women. Also, female genital mutilation (FGM)

played a part in this fistula problem that caused a smelly rupture in the internal reproductive organs of these young women.

Women experiencing fistula would be prevented from going to their home villages, and their husbands divorced them. (Years later, I met an African woman who had gained asylum in the States because she did not want to undergo FGM in her home country.)

8. In 2000, I had a close Nigerian friend in Niamey. He ran a shop to sell printer ink. He was a faithful Christian and went to the Catholic Mass every day. I trusted him enough that I recommended my office to buy its printer ink from him.

My office thus bought a large quantity of printer ink from him. The original sealed boxes arrived in perfect condition, but when they were opened, and the printer cartridges were visible, it was evident that they were all counterfeit. For sure, I had egg on my face, especially as my good friend had absconded to his home country of Nigeria. I now saw why many Nigerians had a reputation for being con artists and I got another lesson in corrupt acts.

9. This incident reminded me of one that happened years ago to a good Togolese friend who had worked at the US Embassy in Niger for twenty years. An investigation found that he had been

skimming off the official purchases for years. I visited him when he was in jail, and I asked him, "Why did you do this? Surely, you knew they would catch up with you sooner or later."

He replied straightforwardly, "What I did was wrong, but the money gained set my family on the path to prosperity for life. There was no other way for me but to pursue this corrupt path."

This reminded me that, generally, in Africa, family came first, and there was no true sense of nationhood. It appeared that family came first then came your ethnic group and region. The nation Africans lived in was an artificial construct usually inherited from their colonizers. Of course, most African countries have been independent for a fourth of the time the US has been independent.

10. My driver in Niger was a Fulani. On one of our long trips overland upcountry, he expressed himself by saying, "Whatever happened to my people? A couple of centuries ago, we ruled over all this land, and now we are relegated to the lowest rung of society. What happened to the days of Usman dan Fodio?"
I sat quietly. I did not want to upset him further by trying to reply to his unanswerable question. I was thinking that life was not fair, particularly for the downtrodden.

11. I was often asked what that big rock was on my work desk. My response was that rock was a reminder to not be in the wrong place at the wrong time and to never let your guard down.

In fact, the rock had been thrown through the back window of my car by a protestor in a spontaneous demonstration outside the University of Niger in Niamey. Evidently, they were protesting the closure of the university and their forced transport back to their respective villages.

12. In 1991, I was exceptionally honored to be selected for a year-long enrollment at the National War College (NWC). During my time there, I was not permitted to take any courses on Africa, as they said I already knew enough about the continent. Instead, I was assigned to a group focused on Asia.

Nonetheless, I managed to develop a special presentation with my teammate, Colonel Charles Swannack of the U.S. Army, on the insurgency movement in Angola—a country to which I was later assigned after graduating from NWC in 1992. Our presentation was well received by interested groups in Washington, D.C., and it helped secure a high grade in my insurgency course.

I also vividly recall a discussion group at NWC focused on the bloody decimation of Liberia by the maniacal rebels led by the infamous Samuel Doe. I was particularly interested in this group because, during my 1983–1987 posting in Conakry, Guinea, I had been privy to all the reporting cables coming out of Monrovia that described the utter mayhem unfolding in Liberia.

I will never forget what a crusty Marine colonel said during one of these discussions: "We could have done more than take candy bars to the embassy." He had been serving on the Marine Expeditionary Force (MEF), stationed offshore Liberia aboard U.S. Navy ships for six months. At any time, these Marines and their attack helicopters could have intervened to stop the chaos and killing, but they never received the order.

It was hard for me to believe at the time that we would sit idly by while some of the U.S.'s major assets in that beleaguered country were destroyed.

13. On February 2, 2000, in Niamey, at a local clinic, my second son was born. The physician did not show up, so I assisted the very capable Nigerien midwife, who demonstrated her expertise by unwrapping without hesitation the umbilical cord which was bound tightly around the newborn's neck. Years later, my son and I stopped by the clinic to greet the midwife, and we were told that she had emigrated to the US.

14. In the last month of 1999, I began working for non-governmental organizations (NGOs). Part of my reasoning for going to work for three NGOs for ten years was that I was thinking that they held their ground through thick and thin with their assistance work. However, I found that NGOs were dependent upon funds provided by donors, and when the money ran out, many of their activities ended. I was also disturbed by the use of some of these NGOs to raise funds by using the plight of poor children.

15. I was pleased when national governments began adopting laws that allowed for the creation of local NGOs. With the passage of these laws, hundreds of local NGOs sprang up almost overnight. Many of them were what we referred to as "suitcase NGOs," as they didn't even have offices.

Unfortunately, most of these organizations also lacked proper accounting systems, making it impossible to provide them with external funding. And the few we were able to fund eventually became entangled in fraudulent schemes. It was a classic case of "damned if we do, and damned if we don't."

16. In all the African countries, there were always some emergencies to which to respond. At the same time, there was much touting of disaster prevention activities. But there was

plenty of money for emergency responses but almost nothing for disaster prevention.

PART IV: THE FOURTH DECADE (2000 – 2010)

Mozambique – Niger – Burkina Faso – South Africa

1. It was communicated to me that one village in 2001 in northern Mozambique was losing all of its chickens to Newcastle disease, and its pigs were dying of swine fever. I went to the village and told them there were vaccines available for both of these diseases.

All of a sudden, a young woman participating in the meeting stood up and complained loudly, "We get foreign people like you all the time coming to our village to tell us why our animals are dying, but you all leave, and we never get the help promised."

2. I always wondered why all the interior commercial flights I took while I was in Mozambique in the 2001-2006 period had so many Pakistani passengers who obviously came from their villages in Pakistan. They did not speak a word of Portuguese or any of the local languages used in Mozambique. While I am still puzzled by the bizarreness of this view, perhaps my early morning intrusion into a room in Nampula in northern Mozambique gave me some answers.

I was staying in a hotel and got up early for breakfast. The kitchen was empty, so I looked into other rooms. I opened one room to find a group of Pakistanis in their home-country attire sitting cross-legged on the floor, counting huge piles of local currency. I could only surmise that they were counting the money for laundering in local banks and that, possibly, this money came from the sale of illegal drugs.

3. Mozambique continues to cope with the legacy of 500 years of Portuguese colonization. Along with Portugal's three four other African colonies, Mozambique gained independence in 1975. However, its post-independence period was marked by violent, protracted internal conflict that undermined its newfound sovereignty. The country embraced socialist policies and revered global figures who had struggled against imperialism.

Nowhere is this more evident than in the renaming of streets in the capital city, Maputo, following independence. For example, the British High Commission sits near the intersection of Vladimir Lenin and Patrice Lumumba Streets, not far from Karl Marx and Ho Chi Minh Boulevards. I've always hoped these names might one day be updated to reflect a broader national identity.

Even more, I've long wished Mozambique would reconsider its national flag. To my knowledge, it remains the only country in the world to feature a gun, specifically, an AK-47—on its flag, which it still proudly displays today.

4. I was surprised during a 2001 visit to some of the popular neighborhoods (bairros) in Maputo to see street signs written in French rather than the usual Portuguese. I asked a passerby about it, and he explained, "They filmed part of the international movie, Ali, here and changed the signs to French to make the area look like somewhere in Congo. The residents asked that the signs be left in place as proof that part of this famous movie was filmed here."

Later, I learned that Mozambique's capital city was frequently used as a filming location for international productions. I also came across an old book from the 1940s that stated the two most beautiful cities in the world were Cape Town, South Africa, and Maputo—then known as Lourenço Marques.

5. I visited the Mozal bauxite smelting plant near Mozambique's capital city of Maputo. This South African-operated plant was built to take advantage of the electrical power generated by the Cahora Bassa Dam completed in 1974 by Portuguese colonists and transported over transmission lines for about 1,000 kilometers southward to the Mozal plant. The bauxite was imported from Australia and smelted into aluminum ingots for export.

6. In Moz in 2005, there was a huge shipment of food aid at the Maputo port, but the new Minister of Agriculture would not allow it out of the port because of the fear that this US maize would introduce Genetically Modified Organisms (GMO) into the local maize crop. The minister insisted that this imported shipment of maize be ground into flour before being distributed.

The only choice was to grind the maize into flour, but the cost of doing this and the problems associated with distributing flour instead of whole grain maize ensured that this kind of food aid shipment would never be undertaken again.

7. In Maputo, the capital city of Moz, I had a problem with a rat living in my car. My dog and I tried every way to get this rat to leave my car, but without success. All the papers in my glove apartment were chewed up. Finally, the rat died in my car, and its rotting body permeated the inside of the car with an awful smell.

To get the awful smell out of my car, I had to take my car to Nelspruit, South Africa, to have it dismantled and fumigated. After it was put back together, I was advised to leave an electric lightbulb burning all night under an opened hood. I did this and had no more problems with rats infesting my car.

8. All of a sudden, the cable TV in my house stopped working. I checked the TV and its remote control. As everything I checked was working properly, I went outside to check the external cable.

My five-year old daughter followed me around the house and pointed out proudly how she had sheared the grass around the house. We arrived at the spot where the TV cable entered our house. My daughter exclaimed with pride, "I cut the cable too."

9. I frequented the famous seafood restaurant in Maputo located along the seacoast. This old Portuguese restaurant, Costa da Sol, offered many seafood delicacies. Of course, I could go to the fish market, which was near my house and pick out my fish and have it prepared in one of the many restaurants adjoining the fish market.

10. In Maputo, one of my American colleagues, Martha Newsome, told me of her terrible incident with local bandits who raided her house at gunpoint. Their house guard was held roughly with a pistol pointed to her head while the bandits backed up their truck and loaded all the household items they could.

After the bandits left, the police were called, but they did not have transport. So, my colleague took her car and went to transport the police. They arrived at the house, but she was reluctant to allow them entry to her home because she was afraid they would help themselves to some of the remaining household items.

11. The saddest moment for me in Maputo was the unexpected death of a delightful toddler, a boy child of an American friend. He died in his crib while taking a nap. He was asphyxiated by aspirating his own vomit. I gave a heartfelt eulogy at his funeral and suffered heavily as I observed his small body crudely burnt at the Hindu cremation center in Maputo.

NIGER

1. Everybody supported Niger's democratic decentralization process in 2007 that gave localities the freedom to elect their own leaders for the first time. In one meeting, a woman in a village in northern Niger asked to be heard and said, "We really like being able to elect our leaders, but we have no money. It's like being given a flashlight without batteries."

2. This incident led to the commissioning of a lengthy paper entitled "Democracy and Islam in Niger" by a European specialist, Deborah Taylor, who had been a long-term resident of Niger. The reading of this paper made me think deeply about the compatibility of democracy with Islam. In Niger, how can you separate the culture from the religion or the secular from Islamic scripture?

3. I cannot help but think about the time in Niger in 2007 when Islamic radicals ransacked a Christian church. My Nigerien colleague said authoritatively, "It is wrong to violate the place of worship of an earlier revelation."

4. I complained to a young Nigerien colleague in 2007 that he was missing too many workdays because of sickness. His response

was, "You need to understand that the younger generation is not as healthy as the older one."

5. In 2008, I ended my meeting with the governor of the Agadez Region in Niger more quickly than I wanted because he had been sitting at his desk with two unexploded landmines. He explained that there was an active smuggling network of the mines from Niger's eastern neighboring country of Chad. I asked myself if he was not aware of the danger he faced by keeping these mines on his desk as conversational pieces.

6. In 2007, my Nigerien colleague was worried about how he would feed a large group of his extended family who decided to travel from their village upcountry to visit him in Niamey. Although it was natural for family members to render visits to their Niamey-based relatives, times were tough, and food items were scarce and, hence, expensive. He grumbled about feeding all the family members but finally concluded his worrying spell by saying, "We'll just add more water to the soup."

7. Through a translator, I spoke in 2007 to an elderly man who was the owner of a store and a member of Niger's national parliament, asking him if he liked democracy. He replied, "Democracy is a wonderful thing because with a small investment,

I can get elected to the national assembly, and then I can get profitable government contracts to provide goods."

I followed up by asking him whether he believed members of parliament should be literate. He replied, "No. I've never been to school, and I manage just fine speaking a local language in parliament."

I reminded him that his government was trying to increase school enrollment by hiring contract teachers. He scoffed at the idea. "What kind of quality teaching can they provide? Their students still won't be able to write a letter in French, and most of them will fail the national exam."

I had clearly opened a big topic, but I wanted to add one more thought. "Maybe they should adopt English as the language of instruction—after all, Niger shares a long border of 1,500 kilometers with Nigeria, which might now be more relevant than France."

He paused and said, "I never thought about that. But you're right—if they were going to do that, it should've been done years ago, back when we had very few high school graduates. All our leaders are still products of the French system."

8. Along Niger's long southern border with Nigeria lies its commercial capital, Maradi, situated near the center of the border. As an Islamic country, Niger has many deeply religious communities, and in Maradi, many women refused to shake hands with an infidel like me.

Curious about this, I asked a Nigerien Islamic scholar who was riding in the car with me. He replied, "Don't worry. Although they act that way and are covered head-to-toe in black Islamic dress, nothing about their clothing or behavior in public tells you anything about the strength of their convictions, especially behind the walls of their home compounds."

9. We met with the head Iman for Maradi to ask him how he was dealing with a new Islamic sect from nearby Nigeria that was making inroads in his town, and he said, "I'm not going to argue over whether or not they keep their arms at their sides and the length of their pants."

10. We were going to stay overnight in what I considered the best hotel in Maradi. I was surprised to find the hotel incredibly rundown, so I asked the receptionist why the hotel was in such a shabby state. She replied, "The owner died." This reminded me that many African businesses collapsed after their founders died.

A similar situation carried over to government officials. Directors of an office would not tell their deputies all they knew. I concluded that this must be a carryover from traditional culture, which frowned on sharing knowledge with subordinates. I asked myself, "How can the institutions Africa sorely needs function if this attitude prevails?"

11. The next day in Maradi, I told my driver I wanted to go to a bookstore I knew decades ago to buy some books that taught me some Hausa, the lingua franca for this part of Africa. Normally, this bookstore had many books in Hausa that would come from Nigeria across the border.

We finally found in 2008 the bookstore I had frequented in the late 1970s. It was in a rundown condition. I asked the clerk to see Hausa books. To my surprise, he said, "Sorry. It has been years since we carried any Hausa books."

Of course, I asked, "Why?"

He replied to the unknown white foreigner by saying, "Nobody wants to learn Hausa anymore."

12. I headed north into the wide expanse of the Sahara Desert in search of a hot springs site. About 260 kilometers west of Agadez, I found it—an isolated place called Tafadeck, located deep in the

heart of the desert. Groups of people were camped around a few old buildings that housed the curative hot springs, with separate structures designated for men and women.

Visitors had come from as far as Algeria and Nigeria. I spoke with one highly educated Nigerian man who told me he visited the site once a year to benefit from the healing properties of the hot waters. He also mentioned that these springs were referenced in the Holy Quran, suggesting that this was a site of great antiquity and spiritual significance.

13. In 2005, the harvest of millet in Niger was poor because of a severe drought and swarms of locusts (grasshoppers). I said to one of the Nigerien farmers who had lost his harvest. "At least you can eat the locusts."

He muttered, "No, we can't eat them because they are the yellow ones, and we only eat the red ones."

14. I was told in Niger in 2008 that its landlocked status raised the prices of imported goods from the coast across the board by at least twenty percent. Again, Niger was also dependent on Lebanese businessmen for almost everything.

15. I had hoped the Lebanese community in Niamey would serve all by getting into the trash collection business so the mounds of

garbage piling up on almost every street corner in Niamey would be regularly picked up and disposed of. I asked a Lebanese man who ran a local popular restaurant why the Lebanese did not get into the trash collection business, and he said, "It's simple ... there's no money in doing that. Most of the household waste consists of dirt swept daily from housing compounds."

16. In 2008, I visited another Sultan in the old section of Zinder, Niger, known as Damagaram. Before meeting him, I stopped at the remains of the old earthen wall of Fort Zinder. From that vantage point, I expected to look out over the vast pastureland where I had once seen herds of grazing cattle back in 1976. Instead, I was met with the sight of hundreds of houses tightly packed together.

I recalled being told years earlier that building on this land was prohibited, as it was designated for communal grazing. So when I met the Sultan, one of the first things I asked was, "I thought it was prohibited to build on the adjoining pastureland. What happened?"

He replied with noticeable hesitation, "Times have changed, and people need a place to build their houses."

I accepted his explanation at face value, but I couldn't help suspecting that he had profited significantly from the sale of that land.

17. There was a goat leather worker in Zinder who made bags and sandals for all the PCVs. I searched for him because I wanted to get the same items as the PCVs. I found him and he said, "You are a rare non-PCV person who I've sold these items to."

18. In 2008, I was in Niamey, the capital city of Niger, where I often took local taxis. One day, I took a taxi, and the driver said, "You don't remember me. Years ago, I was a PCV."

This African American ex-PCV, Willie Russell, talked to me in English for a while to jog my memory of him. I started to see that he had been a PCV who had decided to fade into the local environment. I could not believe his story, but there was no denying it. He had made a life choice that few would make.

Not long after this encounter, his grown children came to the US Embassy in Niamey where at the time I worked. The consular officer called me to say that my name had been given as a reference for him. I confirmed that I knew him. The consular officer had difficulty processing his children as American citizens because some of his children were older than the required age limit of eighteen years of age.

19. I was in a village north of Niamey and spotted a boy with a T-shirt with a picture lauding Osama bin Laden and depicting the Twin Trade Towers in flames. I proclaimed that Osama was a terrorist and questioned him about his shirt. He meekly replied, "This is just a shirt. I've no idea about what it depicts."

20. In 2009, I was again up north in Niger, near Agadez, when we stopped at an isolated small earthen shop chock full of goods for sale. On the shop wall, there was a big poster extolling Osama bin Laden. I bargained with the shopkeeper to buy it. I think it is in storage in my Texas home attic.

21. On this same trip, I was taken by my Tuareg companion to Mano Dayak's grave ... which, in the typical way, was marked by a big pile of stones near his home village of Tiden. I shamefully admitted, "I didn't know he was dead, and I didn't know he was the head of a rebel movement. I knew him in the mid-1970s when he had come from France to try to set up a tourist agency for travel to the Agadez area. His French wife worked for the US Embassy."

My companion, who had also spent some time in France, said, "He was a great man. They named the Agadez International Airport after him. He died in 1995 in a mysterious plane crash. He was a true scholar of Tuareg culture."

22. I am careful about repeating this story because most Nigeriens represent other ethnic groups who live in the southern part of Niger, and they are tired of this foreign idolatry of the Tuaregs.

23. This made me think of the southern Nigerien soldiers who were gleefully fighting against the Tuareg rebels. One of the soldiers told me, "We like fighting against Tuaregs. We get combat pay, and we get to kill Tuaregs."

They did not like the peace treaty signed with the Tuareg rebels because they earned less, and some of the leaders of the Tuareg rebellion were made ministers in their national government.

24. My many travels cris-crossing the desert in Niger earned me the nickname 'camel' because I would go all day without drinking any water. I was asked how I did this, and I responded, "By not opening my mouth to talk."

25. 1999 was a rough year in Niger. The sitting president had been assassinated and was replaced by a lower-ranking military officer. This new leader quickly emptied the national treasury, and there was no cement to be found in Niamey because he had shipped it all to his hometown to build an oversized villa.

Conditions deteriorated rapidly under this military dictator. Civil servants went unpaid for six months, and the police resorted to stopping drivers for made-up infractions just to solicit money they desperately needed. I remember being pulled over for allegedly using my turn signal too early or too late. Another "offense" was failing to stop at a stop sign they had already removed.

My Nigerien colleague lamented the government's failure to pay its civil servants but pointed out that soldiers were always paid on time and in full. I asked him why the military was prioritized. He replied, "They know what the soldiers will do if they're not paid. Niger is a hostage to the military—they can seize control of the country at any time."

26. Site visits to observe trees reminded me of an earlier time, between 1977 and 1981, when we promoted the planting of the slow-growing indigenous Gao tree (Faidherbia albida) in this western part of Niger. Widely considered the cornerstone of the agro-pastoral zone in the Sahel, this remarkable tree grows its leaves and seeds in reverse season, providing shade in the dry season and shedding leaves during the rains, which benefits crop cultivation. Yields were often higher under the canopy of these

trees, which also offered shade for cattle and roosting places for birds.

We encouraged farmers to plant them at six-meter intervals across their fields. However, their slow growth rate and the need to water the seedlings throughout the long dry season discouraged many. Perhaps the greatest challenge was protecting the trees from marauding goats. This required either costly barbed wire or constant repairs to thorn bush enclosures.

I recall a Senegalese friend telling me in 2005 that a rural African could make a living from 100 mature Gao trees. He even proposed that primary schools establish tree plantations, an idea I thought held real promise.

27. I discovered in Niger that one person could own a tree and another its leaves. This was particularly true for the leaves of the baobab tree (Adansonia digitata), which were collected for human consumption. (Much as were pumpkin and other green leaves.)

Baobab trees, particularly old ones, were considered sacred, and their wood was so spongy and fibrous that they were spared felling. And removing a baobab tree would require the performance of indigenous religious ceremonies and an increase of offerings at the base of this sacred tree.

I did enjoy several times in Africa sauces made with baobab leaves and a drink made from its fruits. This majestic tree is native to Africa and, for me, symbolizes much of the Sub-Saharan African continent.

While on the subject of local drinks, I will note that my favorite drink was the red beverage made from hibiscus flowers and kinkeliba tea made from the leaves of an indigenous African shrub (combretum micranthum).

It is sad for me to read that ancient baobab trees are dying across Africa for reasons that are not clear. It was also sad for me to read that the historic and old (estimated age is 400 years) Cotton Tree (Kapok) in Freetown, Sierra Leone (Salone), had fallen to the ground in 2022 during a fierce rainstorm. The remaining large old trees in Africa deserve to be protected and cared for.

28. As previously mentioned, a severe drought in Niger in 2005 led to widespread famine. Locally, people referred to it as the "Buhari Drought" because Muhammadu Buhari, the Nigerian military strongman at the time, had closed Niger's 1,500-kilometer southern border with Nigeria.

The consequences were devastating. Many people—particularly young children, the elderly, and those already ill—were dying from hunger. I visited several child rehabilitation centers and witnessed heart-wrenching scenes: five-year-old children with matchstick-thin bodies, barely clinging to life despite the care being provided. The smell of death hung heavy in the air.

Most of these children came from impoverished families, but to my surprise, some arrived in chauffeur-driven Mercedes-Benz sedans. This made it painfully clear that the crisis wasn't always due to a lack of food. In some cases, it was a lack of knowledge—wealthy mothers, too, did not know how to properly nourish their children with the foods needed for survival and health.

29. My Nigerien colleague came to work with his face covered in bruises and cuts. I asked, "What happened to you?"

He replied with a tint of anger in his voice, "I was walking peacefully along the road last night when a military pickup full of unruly government soldiers stopped beside me and roughly threw me in their pickup bed. They took me to their camp, where they tossed me out of their pickup and proceeded to kick me and pummel me with their fists. One of them yelled out, "This is how we treat dirty Tuaregs!"

He said he managed to say, "I'm not a Tuareg ... I'm a Fulani."

30. Many years later, I thought that maybe he would not be so quick to announce his ethnic affinity. Sadly, rural Fulani are suspected of supporting violent extremist groups that are making their presence felt across the Sahel Region of Africa.

Fulani groups usually lived separately from other ethnic groups but typically were in symbiosis with them. They were already discriminated against and looked upon as a lower caste. It was easy for other ethnic groups to pick on the rural Fulani, who usually lived in their separate communities (this is an exceedingly difficult and sensitive subject to address).

For me, Fulani are beautiful people who played a useful role as herders of cattle across a swath of West Africa's pastoral zone. They lived with their livestock and treated them like family. Many Fulani believe all cattle belong to them. (I found in East Africa that the Maasai believed the same thing.) One Fulani told me that his people had originated many centuries ago from Yemen.

31. In Niger, I became a specialist in waiting. Anytime I was scheduled to see a top Nigerien government official, I went with something to read as the wait for your appointment would usually be lengthy. Sometimes, I thought they purposely made me wait a long time because they hoped I would leave without seeing them.

32. As already noted, I worry about farming in Africa. Many youths no longer want to farm and out-migrate to the cities or abroad. Thus, the average age of the African farmer is increasing.

Also, the impact of national research institutions is diminishing as the number of African agriculture research staff decreases. And agricultural extension programs have, for the most part, ceased to operate.

I visited with the African agricultural research management team in Niamey, Niger, in 2008, and they concluded our lively exchange by saying, "We don't have any budget to do needed crop research, and all of us will retire soon as the official retirement age is 55."

33. I was asked in 2008 by the US military attaché at the embassy in Niger what should be done to win the 'hearts and minds' of the people, and I replied, "Build another bridge across the Niger River."

I explained, "The single bridge across the river is the Kennedy Bridge that the US built-in 1970. Since then, the population of Niamey has more than tripled, and another bridge is needed."

Unfortunately, the US did not build bridges anymore. (When I visited Niamey in 2014, the Chinese had built two more bridges across the river.)

34. The pastoral zone was not overlooked, as it represented a significant portion of Niger's national wealth. Its promise prompted the deployment of a team of specialists from arid land universities in the southwestern United States. The team spent several months studying Niger's pastoral zone, and there was widespread anticipation surrounding the release of their findings.

In the end, the conclusion was blunt: "The pastoral zone is overgrazed, and all people and animals must be removed for ten years to allow it to recover."

Of course, such a recommendation was impossible to implement. Thirty years later, I attended a meeting at Niger's Ministry of Livestock, and the same concerns were still being discussed—namely, the chronic overgrazing of the pastoral zone and the need to shift herders' mentalities. Officials emphasized the importance of encouraging herders to adopt a more commercial mindset, rather than treating their cattle as family. Ironically, a herd might be worth a small fortune, while its owner remained penniless. There was even discussion about introducing modern ranching practices.

35. Shortly after the US study of the pastoral zone, we received from the US one of the first satellite photos of the zone and we

were intrigued by a flaky spot of green that appeared in this photo. A team was sent to investigate this green spot in the middle of the desert and found it was the former French ranch that existed in the colonial past. It still had most of its barbed wire fence standing; therefore, this part of the zone was not being grazed.

No matter what transpired in the pastoral zone ... Nigeria will always consider Niger as its ranch.

36. An interesting fact about Niger is that even in its far northern desert, there is a vast quantity of water deep underground. So far, the cost of bringing this water to the surface has been prohibitive. One of the much talked about ideas was pumping this water to the surface for the irrigation of fields of vegetables, which could be harvested and sent by plane to Europe via the international airport in the not-too-distant Agadez.

37. I will never forget the time in 2007 when the President of Libya, Muammar Gaddafi, came to Niamey overland for an official visit. He spread his Bedouin tent on the grounds of the Libyan embassy, and the diplomatic community was invited to an outdoor reception in his honor. I was one of the invitees who was obliged to listen to his long-winded, twisted speech.

He talked at length in Arabic, which another man translated into French. I felt sorry for the interpreter who was challenged to put into French words the incoherent mishmash of the president of Libya's extemporaneous speech. One thing I recall from his speech is that he said, "The Nigerien Constitution was only a piece of paper ... the will of people is more important."

Of course, he said this in support of the Nigerien president's desire to amend the constitution so he could run for another term.

During his travel overland through the desert from Tripoli to Niamey, he stopped at population centers and handed to the people who lined the roads prayer rugs and money. This generosity reminded me of the historic crossing of the Sahara by the fabulously wealthy Mansa Musa, ruler of the Mali Empire in West Africa, in the 14th century as he and his large entourage and a huge supply of gold bars made their way on a lengthy pilgrimage to Mecca.

38. While he was alive, Muammar Gaddafi spread his wealth across Africa. For example, the new part of Ouagadougou, Burkina Faso, Ouaga 2000, was funded by him. His death in 2011 represented a financial loss for many countries in Africa and upset the balance of power in the countries bordering the Sahara Desert.

39. In 2007, the so-called uranium road in Niger was in a pitiful state. Heavy trucks from uranium mines in the far northern desert transported ore all the way south to the coastal port of Cotonou, Benin. The roads used by these trucks were in constant need of repair and rebuilding.

Unfortunately, road construction in Niger rarely seemed to meet proper standards. I asked my Nigerien driver why this was the case, and he responded with a single word: "Corruption."

As we passed a stretch of road under repair, he pointed and said, "Look—they're just pouring a thin coat of tar when the budget calls for a thick coat with gravel."

I commented, "I've driven on the highway in northern Benin and it seems strong and durable."

He replied, "Yes, that road was built according to standards by an American company."

Indeed, poor road conditions and high transport costs remain major development constraints across Africa.

40. This talk about Africa's major roads made me think about how the high cost of road transport in Africa was a major constraint to development. I also thought that a super coastal highway from Lagos, Nigeria, and Abidjan, Côte d'Ivoire (829 kilometers), without any country border checks, would be a positive measure.

The ideal for me would be to eliminate the custom agents and external donors could better apply their funds to cover the gap in any funding lost to the abolition of custom taxes. A common phrase among the African people is. "You never see a skinny customs agent."

41. The President of Niger, Mamadou Tandja, was overthrown by the military in 2008 because he was trying to run for a third term. He said he needed a third five-year term to complete all his projects. He coined a local language word, "Tazarché (continuation), for this official extension of his presidency.

42. I was stopped at the Niger-Burkina Faso border in 2008 on my way to the annual softball SOFANWAT (Softball Fanatics of West Africa Tournament) in Ouagadougou when the Nigerien guards told me that the border was closed because there was fighting between the army and police in Ouagadougou, the capital city of Burkina Faso. I asked, "What are they fighting over?"

A Nigerien border guard replied, "Over their roles."

I note there was a softball tournament in numerous West African countries every time there was a three-day American holiday weekend.

43. In 2012, I was at the same border completing all the information required in an old ledger book and commented that this was the same book I had written in twenty years ago.

The border agent near me interpreted my comment as indicating that I wanted to introduce computers to keep track of the border crossings. He immediately demanded that I follow him to see his boss in his office in an adjoining building.

When I stood in front of his boss, who was seated behind his desk, I thought I was in big trouble for criticizing how they continued to keep records by hand. His boss spoke the following words, "I hear you want to modernize our record system. We welcome that."

I apologized for any confusion I caused, but there was no way I could assist them in upgrading their system. But I would keep an eye out and not fail to mention that this was another need for Niger.

He thanked me and sent me on my way. I have always wondered if they are still using the same ledger book to register the handwritten crossings at the border.

44. In Niger in 2008, I was told by a Nigerien from far eastern Niger that his family would light every evening a cooking fire so their neighbors would think they were cooking food, but the truth was that they had no food to cook. (This is an example of the 'false pride' which I believe contributes to holding forward progress back in Africa.)

45. I was arriving on a plane at Niamey's airport. There were some Togolese seated next to me. It was their first time to come to Niger. They looked out the plane's windows and exclaimed. "It all looks like a bombed dry soccer field."

My thought at that time was, "Maybe all the coastal people should be brought to Niger so they could appreciate more where they reside."

46. I regularly attended the Catholic Cathedral in Niamey, Niger in 2008-2010. I discovered most of the priests were Igbos from southeast Nigeria. I inquired with one of the priests about this to get more details. He told me, "Yes, we have a surplus of priests in my hometown of Onitsha, so we come to this arid

Islamic country where there is a shortage of priests. We sign a ten-year contract, and we are obliged to learn French. After a few years here, we can give the Mass in French."

47. I was puzzled by the many young Muslim boys who crowded outside of the exit of this Christian church, begging for money. This reminded me of a time in Somalia years earlier when I visited a village that was busy praying. I asked them what they were praying about, and one of the elders replied, "We are giving thanks to the Christian nations for helping us. Our Muslim brethren in Islamic countries have failed to come to our aid in our time of need.

48. Usually, farmers who tilled the soil and pastoralists who raised livestock belonged to separate ethnic groups. Perhaps the biggest divide in Africa is between these two groups. Sadly, this glaring fault line is the basis for many conflicts.

49. Being cognizant of this divide, we helped several villages to lay out 'passage corridors' that pastoralists could use when they embarked on their annual descent during the dry season into the southern regions in search of pasture for their herds. This effort prevented many conflicts.

It also demonstrated to us the importance of each village having a map devised by its leaders to show the use of the land under its authority.

50. Maybe I am retrogressing a bit again, but I believe as long as there are different ethnic groups in Africa, there will be conflict. It is kind of like a Tuareg told me in 2009 in Niger after the Tuareg rebellion had ended. When I asked him if all was calm, he replied, "All is quiet now that the war is over. Things are back to the normal thievery of livestock and factional disputes with our neighbors."

51. I oversaw a primary school construction activity in Niger in 2009. The Ministry of Education had determined the locations of the construction sites. Much to my surprise, some of the carefully selected locations were belatedly changed by the President of Niger.

I was upset over this decision by the president to change the locations of some of our sites. This prompted me to see the president with my ambassador, Bernadette Allen. The president was adamant. Either we do it his way or the highway. I was ready to take the highway and close the project but the ambassador overruled me and said, "We must keep the best interests of the Nigerien people in the forefront of our minds."

52. In the 2006 – 2009 period that I was working in Niger, this same president refused the conclusions of the UN Development Program's HDI annual report because he did not believe Niger should be ranked so low. He also had torn down any NGO signs that they were working to stop hunger and stopped all food for work activities. In addition, he stopped work on all erosion control activities and others designed to conserve water runoff on farmers' fields.

53. I was driving through Niamey, the capital city of Niger, with a naturalized African-American colleague who was born and raised in a West African country. We stopped at a busy intersection that had its usual clutter of signs on every corner indicating the location of the offices of international NGOs. He commented the following: "When those signs are gone, we'll know Niger has made substantial development progress."

I replied, "When I first came to Africa in 1970, there were not any international NGOs. Since then, they have been implanted and multiplied with the availability of donor funds.

54. In 2008, I traveled along a dusty road northwest of Niamey to visit a farmer who had been deeply involved in the comprehensive integrated rural development project I had co-managed with a Nigerien colleague thirty years earlier. He was still living in his

earthen courtyard with his large family. As I arrived, he greeted me with a single word in French: "Tranquillité."

That word said everything. It told me his granary was full, and his household was at peace. We launched into an animated conversation, and I remarked, "If your granary is full, then all your needs are met."

He immediately corrected me. "That's no longer the case. Let me show you."

He gave instructions in Hausa to his sons, who went to the granary and returned with five bundles (bottes) of millet grain heads. Laying them before us in a line, he said, "This is what we used to need—to eat, pay debts, and cover the cost of ceremonies back when you were here."

Then, he sent them back to the granary to fetch ten more bundles. Placing them next to the first five, he continued, "Now you see fifteen bundles. That's what we need these days to do what we once did with just five." He gestured to the many family members gathered around and added, "And I've got all these mouths to feed."

The message was clear, and it saddened me deeply. My sorrow grew as I reflected on the eight-year project we had once been so proud of, staffed with the best minds and blessed with generous funding. Now, I could find no trace of that highly acclaimed effort. I asked myself whether all we had done back then had ultimately been for naught.

This conversation also reminded me how mounting household debt remains a persistent challenge across Africa, worsened by the predatory practices of local moneylenders.

Sustainable change was—and is—difficult to achieve in a country where development funding is tied to annual US congressional appropriations and shifts with every new administration's changing priorities. I was coming to terms with a hard truth: that US assistance, however well-intentioned, is often fickle and ultimately driven by foreign policy interests.

55. It also saddened me to see how deeply indebted many countries in Africa were. Evidently, in spite of having all their debts forgiven by external donors in exchange for promises to exercise greater fiscal responsibility, they could not stay on a good financial management track.

56. I tripped over second base in 2008 on Niamey's softball field, stubbing my big toe on my right foot. A few days later, I went to see a local physician because my big toe was aching. He had my toe X-rayed and drew a blood vial to analyze in his laboratory.

He came up to me and said, "You got gout. We get a lot of gout in Niger because we eat too much meat. I'm going to prescribe a medication for you that you have to take for the rest of your life." (I continue to take this medication twice daily.)

57. In 2008, I was taken by a Nigerien colleague, Ari Malla, to Niamey to see his house. He was the top civil servant in Niger's government. He showed me a modest house that had been under construction for over ten years and still was not ready for the building of its roof. My highly respected colleague said, "I wanted you to see the house of an honest man."

I interpreted this as meaning that all the mansions and large houses I saw in Niamey were built with illicit funds.

BURKINA FASO

1. My female office assistant in Ouagadougou, Burkina Faso, in 2011 was always reluctant to talk, but I encouraged her, and she said, "You have to know that it's tough to plan ahead in Africa because there are too many 'unpredictables.'"

2. I was visiting an African friend in Ouagadougou, Burkina Faso, in 2013. This friend was a pastor and the head of a civil society organization. He said, "If the government says something, the people will do the opposite of what the government wants."

3. My Burkinabé driver, who ran over in the street an errant dog, which he could have easily avoided, said, "That'll teach him." (That was in Ouagadougou in 2012.)

4. This same driver complained when I lowered my car window to give a Tuareg child some money. This child had walked with his family south over 500 miles. He said, "Why did you do that? The boy and his family eat more meat than I do."

5. Most of the time in Africa, I enjoyed talking with my drivers. I learned a lot from them. In 2014, I had my Burkinabé driver navigate through jam-packed traffic that was populated with the usual melee of motorbikes to find a scarce parking place.

When we were stuck in this dense traffic, I said "Where are all these people going, expending money on fuel and emitting much pollution."

He quipped, "They got to eat, don't they?"

6. I asked my Burkinabé driver in 2013 if he could make a large sum of money by driving a truck full of guns to a neighboring country. Would he do it? He replied, "When do I go?"

7. These thoughts were on my mind when I paid a courtesy visit to the Minister of Education of Burkina Faso at her office in Ouagadougou in 2013. She was an impressive Muslim woman from a small village upcountry. Exceptionally, her father had sold some of his cattle to send her to school.

We spoke at length about the generally poor quality of education in public elementary schools. I told her that everyone in my office was working in the private sector so they could earn enough money to send their children to private schools where they could at least get a quality education.

She acknowledged the shortcomings of the public school system and described the various reforms she was pursuing to address the situation. But then she shifted the focus of our conversation to me.

She referred to me as the baobab, a nod to my deep knowledge of Africa.

Our discussion was videotaped, and parts of the video were broadcast on national television that evening. Afterward, I quickly became known in Burkina Faso as "the Baobab" and was later given the title Naaba Toéga (Chief Baobab) in the local language, Mooré.

8. I had another experience in 2012 with the drinking of local sorghum beer, dolo, in western Burkina Faso. Again, you could not get any of the men to work in the afternoon because they were soused by drinking dolo, a beer made by women from sorghum grain. My thought was how could this part of the country advance if all the men were inebriated in the afternoon.

I wanted to start a campaign against the excessive drinking of dolo, but as making it was a female enterprise, I dropped this idea. I did tell the women who made dolo that they are using scarce water and causing much environmental damage by cutting the trees down for firewood to make dolo.

9. In this part of western Burkina Faso, there was a school built and operated along European lines by its German founder. There

was a large clamor to attend this school with its modern curriculum. Unbiased enrollment was by lottery.

When the chief's son in the adjoining village did not gain entry by this annual lottery, there was a boycott by the local population of the school. I never learned about how the school resolved this serious conflict with the local authority.

10. Before I saw the school, I was taken into the vast African bush to see the World Heritage Site of Loropéni. I was impressed to see this thousand-year-old earthen structure still stand. Its high walls were testimony to what had once been an important center for participating in the gold trade. I was given a souvenir walking cane in honor of my visit.

11. All the supermarkets in which I shopped in landlocked Ouagadougou, Burkina Faso, were owned and operated by Lebanese. They also owned wholesale stores that supplied products to other stores managed by local people. They had connections with their numerous Lebanese family members who resided on the coast at Abidjan, Côte d'Ivoire. I asked a man from Burkina Faso what would happen without the Lebanese, and he replied, "We would die."

12. In May 2010, I was working in Ouagadougou, the chaotic capital city of Burkina Faso, when I was diagnosed with a kidney stone. I was told this was a common medical problem in Africa due to excessive perspiration in the intense heat. I received my first morphine shots from the Chilean nurse at the U.S. Embassy, which allowed me to take a commercial flight to London for treatment.

(Sadly, this nurse and her French husband were later among those killed when their passenger plane crashed in a violent storm over the Sahara Desert.)

Upon arrival in London, I went directly to St. John's Hospital, where I felt momentarily transported back to Africa. The attending physician was Nigerian, and all the nurses were from Zambia and Zimbabwe. They provided excellent care, and just a few days later, I was on my way back to Burkina Faso.

Seeing so many skilled African professionals working in London reminded me of the serious brain drain that continues to affect the continent. It echoed what I had once heard about Benin—that more Beninese physicians live and work in France than in Benin itself.

13. While working and living in Burkina Faso in the 2011-15 period, I had the pleasure of participating in the construction of primary schools in a way that would attract more girls to attend school. We encouraged girls to attend school by offering each month a kilo of grain for good attendance and the creation of childcare centers and separate latrines.

This activity was a success as the classrooms evolved in a way that the majority of students and graduates were female. This feminization of the classroom prompted one male student to blurt aloud, "What about us boys?"

14. During this time in Burkina Faso, I became committed to the idea of a healthy and good head start in life. I was convinced that healthy children who attended preschool would go on to be top students in higher grades and become productive citizens. I saw this job had to start at conception with the mother and required the establishment of pre-schools. We were limited by funding to only work in a relatively small geographic area.

I was impressed by the brilliance of the children in our first preschool class and told the teacher so. She responded to my enthusiasm by saying, "Yes, many of these children are brilliant and should go a long way in life, but they will end up like all other students and will not find jobs that pay a decent wage. There are no good work opportunities in our country."

15. Her words reminded me of the time I saw in Ouagadougou the national stadium filled to the brim with thousands of candidates who were taking the civil service test. Only a handful of candidates would actually be hired. Working for the government was considered the best option for these candidates.

My African driver said, "Almost all of them will be back next year to try their luck again. Each year, the number of applicants taking the test grows, so the stadium will soon become too small."

16. While I was living and working in Ouagadougou, I had a docile large dog who played nicely with my children. One day, this very friendly dog bit the watchman. I was astounded by this and could not stop asking myself the question, "Why would this dog, who never bit anybody, bite the security guard?"

An investigation of this dog-biting incident was conducted. The head of the security guard force came to my house to interrogate the watchman who claimed to have been bitten by my dog. This security chief had only one question to ask the watchman, "Do you eat dog meat?"

The watchman unashamedly answered, "Yes, that is my custom."

17. Incidentally, I mixed the nutritious leaves of the moringa (moringa oleifera) tree into the food I fed this dog, a golden Labrador retriever. I was pleased to see this drought-resistant tree from India's sub-continent flourish across the arid parts of Africa.)

18. One day, the electrical generator at my house in Ouagadougou broke down. My private electrician came to inspect the issue and informed me that the problem wasn't with the generator itself, but rather with the electrical pole in front of my house, which made it the responsibility of the local electric company.

I contacted the company, but their workers never came. When I told my private electrician, he simply said, "You have to pay a small bribe to get them to show up."

I followed his advice, and sure enough, the problem was promptly fixed.

19. My very able Beninese electrician expounded on how the possession and operation of a washing machine should be a key development indicator. He supported his statement by saying, "First, you have to be able to buy a washing machine if you can find one to buy. And then you have to hire somebody to install it. You have to have a good supply of reliable electricity and water

(cold and hot) with good pressure for it to work. If you have all those things, you have truly reached a high stage of advanced development.

20. I would often sit on a roadside bench with Burkinabé men to pass the time by making small talk and watching vehicles and pedestrians pass by. One day, we somehow began discussing politics and I tried to drive home to them that they had rights guaranteed by their constitution. My comments gave them a hearty laugh, and then one of them said, "You got to understand that it's the man with the biggest gun who rules. The constitution is only a piece of paper."

I continued, "Well, you got elections to make your voices heard."

My words elicited another big laugh from the African group, and one of them said, "Listen, we've had the same president for decades. Elections cost a lot of money and don't change anything because they're not free and fair, and they are held mostly to satisfy Western countries. They also cost large sums of money. It would be better to spend this money on public works that improve the lives of the people and give them hope for a better future."

21. I was in a donor meeting with Burkina Faso's Prime Minister (PM) in 2010, where we discussed all the pressing country's

development issues of the day. After the meeting was adjourned, I greeted the PM and asked him, "What development model is your country going to follow?"

He replied, "Our own model."

22. The elderly Burkinabé woman had worked as a cashier at the US Embassy in Ouagadougou for twenty years and, therefore, was qualified for a special invitational visa to the US for her and her family. She said, "I don't want to go to the States, but I'm doing this for the future of my children."

23. The Malian refugee camp in northern Burkina Faso in 2013 was an eye-opener. The camp was full of noble-class Tuaregs, and one of their main complaints was that their large huts were too close together. They were used to living at least a kilometer apart from one another.

I reminded them of the obvious: "This is a refugee camp—it's not designed to offer all the amenities you're accustomed to. We've already separated the Arab population from your group."

At the same time, the local African staff working with my organization were growing frustrated by the continued enforcement of the caste system within the camp. The 'black' caste (the Bouzou) had been assigned all the menial tasks. The staff wanted to intervene and correct this age-old hierarchy immediately. I cautioned them, "A refugee camp is not the place to dismantle a centuries-old system."

I had several long and insightful palavers with the refugee leadership group, which included representatives from the many factions present. Interestingly, they were united on one front: they feared the Malian army more than the advancing rebels.

Months later, I visited a Tuareg refugee camp in northwest Niger. When I brought up the camp I had visited in Burkina Faso, the response was cold. They didn't want to hear anything about it. As far as they were concerned, they wanted nothing to do with that particular class of Tuaregs in Burkina Faso.

24. Almost everywhere in Africa, I would see innumerable women vendors of tomatoes installed alongside the roadsides. I could not possibly see how any of them would make any money. I asked one of them if she had made a profit, and she replied, "We usually don't make any money, but this activity gives us an identity."

25. In Burkina Faso in the 2011 – 2015 period, I had the opportunity to visit many primary school classrooms and meet some very bright and articulate students. It depressed me that the

future of these high-achieving students was bleak. Also, they did not have any good role models to emulate. I asked myself, "Where are their good role models?"

26. There were some months during this period that I was residing in Burkina Faso's capital city of Ouagadougou when I was trying to raise three of my children alone. During this time, some local women would knock on the front gate of my residence and state, "My house was in need of a feminine presence."

This reminded me of when I first arrived in Africa in 1970, when women would wanted to cook for me because I was too shiny.

SOUTH AFRICA

1. To be open and transparent, I have to admit that in early 2011, in Pretoria (Tshwane), South Africa, I got a tattoo on my upper right shoulder that depicts an outline of the African continent and the outline of a heart traced in the middle of this outline. This tattoo was to commemorate 40 years in Africa.

2. I was in South Africa in 2011, visiting a huge game reserve, Kruger Park, with an American friend, Richard Feutz. The park ranger warned us not to provoke the elephants. While we were parked to observe at a safe distance some elephants frolicking in a river, a bush near where we parked the car began shaking violently.

We thought that an elephant was hidden in the bush and about to attack our car. We rushed in a panic to get in our car and drive it off. As we were leaving, a small monkey was spotted coming out of the bush. We had a hearty laugh over our frightful foolishness.

We told the story to black South Africans working at our lodge and they also laughed heartily. One of them said, "Just like life. We feel sometimes that an elephant is storming into our lives when it is only a small monkey."

Another South African said, "Like the billboard at the entrance to the park says, "The mosquito is the most dangerous animal in the park."

This same African man asked me, "Did you roll up your car windows and lock your car?"

I replied, "No."

He said, "Can I have your car keys to lock it up well so the baboons don't destroy the interior of your car?"

3. We also visited the 40-room Victorian mansion and large flower garden near Pretoria that was left in tack by a wealthy Jewish businessman, Samuel Marks, many years ago. I learned much about the role the Jewish community played in South Africa's history.

There were two World Heritage sites we visited. This included going down into a deep cave where early human remains were discovered in a place that is called the Cradle of Humankind. Also, we saw one of the largest craters on Earth, caused millions of years ago by a meteor that slammed into the Earth at a place called Vredefort.

4. I enjoyed in 2011 my long walks in the old city parks of beautiful Pretoria (Tshwane), South Africa. I was puzzled about how they

were void of people. I asked some hotel staff why this was, and the reply I got was, "Since the legal end of apartheid in 1992, nobody goes to the parks except the drunks and a few crazy people."

5. The word "apartheid" was well known to me and forced me to recall the first time I went to South Africa in 1991 when the "apartheid" system was still practiced. The white immigration officer at the airport warned me that if he stamped my passport, I could not travel to other African countries because none of them accepted passports with apartheid South Africa stamps in them. I thanked him and spent the rest of the day in the transit lounge of the airport.

6. I saw one thing in 2005 in Durban, South Africa that I never before had seen before in Africa. I could not believe that I was seeing white street beggars. I commented on this to my black South African colleague, and he said, "The whites have been here a long time, and it's not unusual that the more uneducated and unemployed ones end up in the streets in this post-apartheid era."

I asked this same colleague, "Why is the infrastructure in South Africa so well developed?"

His answer to my question was simple but perplexing. He replied, "Because we have whites here."

7. In 2011, I was working on the design of a Southern Africa agriculture project, so I was making the rounds of the local agriculture research institutions. My main question concerned how to raise crop yields. One white South African researcher told me that the answer to my question was simple but fraught with complications. He said, "If all the countries in Southern Africa could raise their average crop yields so they were about equal to those of South Africa, there would be no hunger, and Southern Africa would be a major exporter of food crops."

8. While a PCV in Togo, I took on trying to domesticate the rat-like agouti (genus Dasyprocta) ... the favorite meat of the local population. After three years, I had to depart, so I turned this activity over to a local Togolese farmer.

Thirty years later, I was sitting next to a Nigerian colleague in a meeting in South Africa and I mentioned this agouti story to him. He became excited and said, "I work in Ghana, and they trace the first domesticated agouti to where you worked in neighboring Togo. It's a big business now."

I exclaimed, "After 30 years, I finally learn of my success."

9. In 2011, I also enjoyed the well-stocked modern shopping malls in South Africa but was perplexed by their early closing at 5 p.m. I

asked one shopkeeper about this, and she replied, "We have to get home before dark so we don't expose ourselves to criminal elements."

I got what she meant when I observed the armed SWAT (Special Weapons and Tactics) team making their regular rounds inside the mall.

10. Once, in 1998, I took the two-day 'Pride of Africa' Rovo's two-day train ride from Pretoria/Johannesburg to Cape Town. For most of the time, I stayed in my luxurious room looking out the huge window to watch the endless Karoo pass by and reading a book. When I finally ventured out of my room, the white South African hostess greeted me and said, "You really know how to enjoy this long train ride."

11. In late October 2010, while attending a meeting in Accra, Ghana, I suffered a severe heart attack. I was admitted to a local hospital, which managed to keep me alive for three days until I could be put on an emergency medevac flight to Johannesburg, South Africa.

A white South African cardiologist, Dr. J. Badenhorst, and his team met me at the airport and stabilized me before performing a procedure the next day to remove the blockage in one of the arteries leading to my heart.

I was placed in a ward with other white South African men who had experienced similar medical issues. I had arrived with nothing but a hospital gown. In an unexpected act of kindness, my fellow patients took up a collection, and one of their wives bought me a set of new clothes.

When I was able to speak again, I told them, "I'm forever thankful for the generosity you've shown me."

12. For me, there was only one place in Pretoria, South Africa, in 2011 that seemed well integrated, and that was the wonderful zoo. All races saw the animals and many roasted meat on their braais (barbecue grill) ... a South African custom that was shared by all races.

I was told that South African whites suffered from the highest incidence of skin cancer of any country in the world because they spent so much time outdoors, mainly to tend to their braais.

13. Another place South Africans were well integrated was at rugby matches. When there was a rugby game at the nearby stadium in Pretoria, cars were parked everywhere ... even on well-manicured

lawns, and the stadium was jam-packed. All races had their rugby fanatics.

South Africa is a beautiful country with many scenic sites, and it is one of the most advanced countries in Africa. Lamentably, I found it suffered from endemic racism. It also suffered from a high crime rate, particularly with regard to sexual violence and vehicle hijackings.

14. I noted that all South Africans ate their white maize mush (pape), and I concluded that this food is a common denominator across much of Africa. In the southern, eastern, and western regions of the continent, the main staple is this same white maize mush, served with a spicy sauce. Most Africans—both black and white—eat some version of it daily, though it goes by different local names.

Ethiopia stands out as the exception. There, the staple is injera, a fermented flatbread made from teff flour. In fact, in Ethiopia, there's a saying: if you haven't eaten injera, then you haven't eaten at all.

In South Africa, I observed that people purchased refined white maize flour in packaged bags at local supermarkets. In contrast, in

West Africa, it's more common to take your white maize to a local grain mill to have it ground into flour.

Even during times when there was a shortage of white maize on the international market, I found it nearly impossible to convince Africans to consume the more nutritious and widely available yellow maize. The preference for white maize was deeply ingrained. Even in the US, my African friends would seek out farina masa, a finely refined white maize flour used for making tortillas, because it most closely resembled what they were accustomed to back home.

15. I went to a physician in Joburg in 2001 to have the larva that Putzie (Cordylobia anthrophaga) flies had laid deeply under my skin along my waistline removed. It took minor surgery for the doctor to remove the worms. As he bandaged the holes in my body from which he had dug out the worms with a surgical knife, he said firmly, "Always have any clothes that have been hung outside to be ironed ... even your underwear. Putzie flies lay their eggs in your clothes, and they hatch on your body."

16. I discovered in South Africa that one of their favorite foods is mopane (colophospermum) worms (caterpillars), which mainly live, of course, in mopane trees. These worms are an important

source of protein. I was told that it was Nelson Mandela's favorite food. I ate these worms at a fancy restaurant in Johannesburg that I am told that Nelson Mandela frequented.

17. I was surprised to see in the modern shopping mall in Nelspruit, South Africa, many white South Africans barefooted and grown men dressed in the shortest of shorts. I was told that these were rural Boer farming families.

They reminded me of the big land issue in South Africa, where most of the agricultural land was controlled by white farmers, and the political thrust was to give more land to black South Africans. A major catch in doing this was keeping the land productive and not going the disastrous way of Zimbabwe, which confiscated the land by force from white farmers. For sure, farmland distribution is a big issue in South Africa.

18. This browsing in South Africa's modern shopping malls reminded me of the days you would drive from Zambia to Zimbabwe to shop at the South African malls. These days, it is the reverse, and you drive north from Zimbabwe to Zambia to shop at the new South African malls.

19. I was in Johannesburg (Joburg), South Africa, in 2005, taking a taxi tour of the old and new parts of this large city. Within the

confines of the city, I observed huge man-made hills almost everywhere I looked. I asked the African driver about this, and he said, "Those are slag hills built with decades of diggings from the rich underground gold mines. In our own language, we call Joburg 'Egoli.' The economy of our country depends on the international market value of gold and diamonds."

20. On the way back from Zambia to Mozambique in 2005, I wanted to be sure to stay in the same hotel in South Africa that I did when going to Zambia two weeks prior. As I was driving along the modern highway in northern South Africa, I was watchful of the road signs, looking for the one that announced we had arrived at Pietersburg.

Later, I learned from some people standing near the edge of the highway that the road sign for Pietersburg had been changed to Polokwane. I had forgotten the new national government had proposed changing all the place names in South Africa to indigenous ones since the installation of democracy in 1994.

Later, in 2011, I was living and working in Pretoria, South Africa, and learned that the name of this capital city had been changed to Tshwane.

21. I was visiting Soweto, South Africa, in 1995 with a group of American colleagues, and I said, "I can see many poor households, but anyone in West Africa who possessed what the average person here does, he or she would be considered wealthy."

My American colleague replied, "Poverty is relative."

This made me think of the ways used to define poverty in West African villages. In my PCV village in Togo, an impoverished family was one that did not possess a chicken. A real poor person was one who had to borrow embers from a neighbor because they could not afford the matches needed to start a cooking fire. In other parts of Togo, a poor family did not own a tree or its leaves. These days, a poor household is one that does not regularly receive remittances from a family member living abroad.

22. I was always addressed as "maneer" when I went to one of the numerous restaurants in Pretoria, South Africa, in 2011. I finally asked one of the Zimbabwean waiters what this word meant. He said, "It's the word in Afrikaans for 'sir.'

I replied, "You do not have to use that word for me. I'm American."

The reader may be wondering why the waiter was from Zimbabwe. I can only say that the economic conditions in Zimbabwe were so bad that thousands of Zimbabweans have fled to South Africa in search of employment that paid a decent wage.

23. I did a six-month stint with USAID's regional office in Pretoria, South Africa, in 2011. Part of my job description was to monitor new US employees. As I got ready to leave this assignment, I apologized to several new employees for not giving them enough attention. One of them replied, "No matter. You did your job in this regard by "stealth."

PART V: THE FIFTH DECADE (2010 – 2020)

Multiple African Countries

(Burkina Faso - Ghana- Mali - Angola – Guinea)

This past decade has presented a particular challenge in offering new highlights from my five-decade-long African journey. After the first twenty years or so, there wasn't much left that felt new. I was often told, "You've been there and done that," implying that I had little left to see or comment on.

In June 2015, I moved my family to Lubbock, Texas. It wasn't until 2016 that I returned to work in Accra, Ghana. That same spring, Texas Tech University's academic committee approved my syllabus to teach an honors course in international development. The course focused on the world's lowest-ranked countries on the UN Development Program's Human Development Index (HDI)—countries that, notably, have remained largely the same since the HDI's inception in 1990.

Since nearly all of these countries are in Africa, my students and I explored the factors that could help move them higher on the HDI scale. Our class was held in the Philosophy Building, which I felt was fitting. I told my students that the central question of our course was philosophical in nature: To help or not to help? Should aid always be given? Or, in cases of uncertainty, might non-intervention be the wiser path toward sustainable development?

To illustrate this dilemma, I told the story of a film I once watched, in which thousands of starfish had washed ashore. I asked my students: how many could we realistically save by tossing them back into the sea? The point was clear—you cannot help everyone. Likewise, it is impossible to aid every vulnerable population in need of assistance. This led to deeper questions about resource prioritization. Should U.S. taxpayer funds be used to help struggling communities abroad when so many Americans are also in need? As one U.S. Senator cynically remarked, "Foreign aid is like pounding sand down a rat hole." And indeed, despite decades of development work, the number of poor people in Africa today is higher than ever before.

While based in Ghana, I also made trips to Togo, Benin, and Burkina Faso. In 2017, I visited Bamako, Mali, and in 2018 I took on a six-month work assignment in Angola. During that time, I joined my wife and daughter for a two-week visit to their home country of Ethiopia. To maintain my Angolan visa, I also made several brief trips to Namibia.

In 2021, I was scheduled to travel to Guinea to assist with the design of a health systems project. However, the COVID-19 pandemic intervened, and I ended up completing the assignment remotely. I did manage to visit Accra again in 2019 before continuing on to Ouagadougou, Burkina Faso, where I worked for six weeks.

What follows is a short compilation of moments from my final decade on the African continent—a hodgepodge of memory fragments, reflections, and impressions from across various countries. I've also included some anecdotes from my travels beyond the workplace and thoughts on how I've tracked my interactions with all 54 African nations.

- - - - - - - - - - -

1. Before I left my job at the U.S. Embassy in Ouagadougou at the end of 2010, a new local female embassy driver greeted me in the parking lot and said, "I heard you were leaving. Too bad, as you were the only American who spoke our language."

I quickly contradicted her by saying, "I don't speak any of your local African languages, and there are plenty of Americans in the embassy who speak French."

She responded, "No, I don't mean African languages. You're the only American in the embassy who speaks French like we do."

I note that I learned to speak French in Francophone Africa. My French friends referred to my accent as being 'Atlantique.'

2. It was big news in Ouagadougou, Burkina Faso, that the international school was going to adopt the 'journée continue' (continuous workday). This would mean that it would do like many other institutions had already done and have its employees, and in this case, its students, travel to and from school or work only once during a workday, thus saving fuel and time.

My satisfaction with this decision came to an abrupt halt when it was reversed. Evidently, the influential Lebanese community objected. It wanted to keep things the way they were. They liked the long lunch hour and the option to take a nap and avoid the hottest part of the day.

3. In my Texas home, I have on display something from all the African countries I have lived in or visited. I am proud of every item, but special to me are the Adinkra symbols, which have been used for centuries in Ghana. I have framed two of these bronze symbols --- 'Nye wo ho nhye" which means 'imperishability of self' and "Ese ne tekerema" which means 'improve and advance.' My

youngest son has tattooed on his upper right shoulder' Gye nyame,' which means the omnipotence and immortality of God.

4. In Mali in 2017, I wanted to travel north out of the capital city to visit the irrigation infrastructure constructed with USG funds, but for security reasons, I could not go. Violent extremists posed a real threat in a region where they often killed or kidnapped foreigners.

5. It is with much sadness that I see today that violent extremists control large swaths of territory in the Sahel part of Africa and now threaten coastal West Africa. Their incursions have prompted, in recent years, military coups in Burkina Faso, Guinea, Mali, and Niger, allowing for the inroads of Russian groups. I have spent 20 years of my life in these countries. For me, these countries and others in Africa are taking steps backward.

6. I accompanied several Burkinabé colleagues to visit Niamey, Niger, a neighboring country that I knew well. We were sitting on the back terrace of our hotel, enjoying cold beers and mini brochettes, when one of them suggested, "Let's go out on the town and see all the hotspots."

After laughing, I said, "This is the main hotspot. In other words, this is it."

7. I marveled at the donkey cart that came by my house in Ouagadougou, Burkina Faso, to collect my household trash. For a small payment to the elderly female cart driver, my trash was picked up and disposed of once every week.

I was curious about the location of the city's dump yard, so one day, I followed the woman and her loaded cart. I drove my car far behind her cart. I was surprised that she dumped all the refuse in the cart only a few blocks away from my house in a vacant lot behind the city's most luxurious hotel.

I found there were many empty lots in the city, and they were filled with trash, squatters, or used as a toilet by the latter.

8. In Ouagadougou, Burkina Faso, I was surprised to see in the early morning offerings of food grains in the middle of traffic intersections. I asked a colleague about this, and he replied, "Our country is 60 percent Christian and 40 percent Muslim, but it's 100 percent animist."

9. In 2018, I was in Windhoek, Namibia, looking for a unisex salon where I could get a manicure and pedicure. After some searching, I finally found one and stepped inside. I was warmly welcomed by two African women working in the shop. I told them what I wanted, and they politely asked me to take a seat.

As one of the women began working on my toes, I asked her, "Do you often give pedicures to white people?"

She smiled and replied, "No, you're the first, but you must be a foreigner."

"Yes," I said, "I'm not from your country. By the way, I took a little walk around your city earlier and noticed a statue of your founding president and a street named after him. Did he pass away?"

She looked up and said, "No, he's not dead. Why—must he be dead before we honor him?"

I responded, "No, not necessarily. But in my country, we usually wait until our great leaders have passed away before honoring them in that way."

10. For the most part, everywhere I worked in Africa, I kept two publications on my desk. One was Alan Mosher's 1965 book, *Getting Agriculture Moving in Africa*, and the other was Carl Eicher's 1982 article in the Foreign Affairs Journal entitled, "Facing Up to Africa's Coming Food Crisis."

Of course, there were other books I kept close by. Those books included an early French version of the *Mémento de l'Agronome* and Earl M. Kulp's books printed in 1970 and 1977, with titles on how to design, plan and manage rural development projects. I also kept near me Robert Chambers's timeless book, *"Rural Development: Putting the Last First,"* published in 1983.

Of course, I keep at my side copies of my 12 published books and 48 professional articles. I hope this will be my 13th published book. It was not until after I had my heart attack in October 2010 that I started writing in earnest. (See Annex E for a complete list of my main written works.)

11. While riding in a taxi in Accra, Ghana in 2016, I found myself enjoying the US Country Western music playing on the car radio. Curious, I asked the driver if this genre was popular in Ghana. He replied enthusiastically, "It's extremely popular. We enjoy it so much because it tells stories about life."

That sparked a lively conversation. I asked him where his car had been manufactured, and he answered, "South Korea."

I responded in a way that caught him off guard: "You know, back when Ghana gained independence in 1957, your country and South Korea were at the same level of economic development. By now, you should be manufacturing your own cars."

12. Almost everywhere in Africa, farmers set their fields on fire during the dry season—a practice commonly referred to as "slash and burn." I spoke with many farmers about this method, and they explained that it was the only effective and labor-saving way to eliminate heavy top brush. They also noted that burning helped kill snakes, added potash to the soil, and aided local hunters by driving animals ahead of the flames.

I tried to explain that this burn-off practice had long-term negative effects on the already fragile African soils and contributed to air pollution. But my warnings were largely ignored. The farmers pointed out that they simply didn't have the labor required to clear the land by hand. As one farmer put it, "We know the soil will get tired in a few years, and when that happens, we just move our fields to another place."

I replied, "That age-old approach may work for now, but once the population becomes too dense over 100 people per square kilometer—you'll be forced to abandon swidden, extensive cultivation and adopt more intensive farming methods. Population density changes everything."

13. This discussion reminded me of my talk in Accra with an elderly white British agricultural officer who had worked when

Ghana was the colonial Gold Coast. He was clear on the subject of burning off farmers' fields, "Burn-off is bad for the soil. African soils do not usually contain the same level of organic matter as soils elsewhere in the world. Without a rise in soil fertility, there cannot be a rise in the general level of development, especially in an agrarian society."

14. This reminded me of trying to obtain funding for disaster prevention activities. All the donor agencies touted disaster prevention by often saying, "An ounce of disaster prevention is worth a pound of disaster response."

But there was plenty of funding for disaster response and little to none for disaster prevention. I guess this is a case of not putting your money where your mouth is.

15. There was no doubt that African farmers' soils needed enrichment with organic matter. To address this, we encouraged the tethering or penning of livestock so that manure could be collected and later spread on fields. This recommendation stemmed from the observation that crop yields were noticeably higher near farmers' dwellings, where manure naturally accumulated.

We also promoted the use of compost pits. However, these efforts faced several challenges. Spreading manure and compost required additional labor—labor that was often unavailable during the long dry season when household labor resources were already stretched thin. Furthermore, much of the organic matter spread on the fields would volatilize under the intense heat of the sun, reducing its effectiveness.

Another obstacle was behavioral: many farmers were not accustomed to working during the dry season. Instead, they often migrated seasonally in search of paying jobs. Those who remained behind typically placed a higher value on rest and social life. One of the key lessons I took from this experience was that cultural and social values are deeply embedded and slow to change, making it difficult to introduce, let alone enforce, new practices that reflect external value systems.

16. I often heard the phrase "Green Revolution (GR)" used in the context of Africa. I once believed that a GR was truly possible in Mali, particularly because the bend in the Niger River offered year-round water availability. With the right irrigation infrastructure and sound water management, this region had the potential to become a highly productive agricultural zone.

The French had recognized this potential as far back as the 1930s during their colonial administration. With the arrival of democracy in 1990, I hoped that this region of independent Mali would emerge as the breadbasket of West Africa. However, subsequent events proved me wrong and underscored a critical lesson: peace and political stability are essential prerequisites for meaningful progress. Without them, even the most promising agricultural opportunities remain unrealized.

This experience led me to conclude that, for the foreseeable future, farmers in West Africa would remain reliant on seasonal rainfall and a traditional agricultural system that offers little room for trade-offs or innovation. One of my Malian colleagues once remarked that Africa was littered with networks of irrigation canals, many of them abandoned and in disrepair. He argued that donor efforts should focus first on rehabilitating and managing these existing systems before attempting to build new ones.

17. Yes, I often didn't notice mosquito bites, but as mentioned earlier, I was hospitalized four times with malaria during my fifty years in Africa. When I first arrived in Togo in 1970 as a Peace Corps Volunteer, I was issued a generous supply of Aralen (chloroquine phosphate) and instructed to take two 500 mg

tablets each week. I followed the instructions faithfully, yet I still contracted malaria.

When I had young children, I would crush the appropriate dose of these pills into a fine powder and mix it with chocolate syrup to ensure they took their weekly antimalarial dose. I was also careful to keep them indoors after 6 p.m. since dusk was the prime feeding time for mosquitoes.

Years later, I asked a pharmacist for advice on a reliable antimalarial medication. He said simply, "There are no longer any drugs that can truly prevent malaria. If you experience symptoms, the best course is to get a blood test immediately. If treated within 48 hours, malaria is manageable." In the early years, I noticed the French often fared better by taking a small 100 mg Nivaquine tablet daily. Regardless, all of these regimens eventually lost their efficacy as the female Anopheles mosquito adapted.

Malaria remains the leading killer of young children in Africa and is the most common reason for medical consultations at clinics. Its eradication—or even significant reduction—would ease the burden on health services and improve productivity by reducing the number of sick days. Africa still accounts for 90% of the world's malaria cases.

Despite decades of effort, the Anopheles mosquito continues to evolve in its feeding habits and behavior. The development of an effective child malaria vaccine brings hope, although I remain skeptical that such progress would have taken so long had malaria been a significant problem in the United States. The investment might have come sooner if wealthier nations had been directly affected.

I have always advocated for eliminating mosquito breeding grounds, but large-scale vector control projects are rarely carried out. While in Ouagadougou, Burkina Faso in 2013, I read a report estimating that eliminating all mosquito breeding sites in the city would cost over a billion U.S. dollars. Yet every night, crowds would gather to drink beer and enjoy grilled "poulet télévisé" or "poulet bicyclette" next to open drainage ditches—prime mosquito breeding grounds. (These French terms refer to chickens transported across the city strapped to bicycles and later displayed behind glass while being grilled.)

Personally, I did little to prevent malaria aside from carrying medication wherever I traveled—even to countries not considered malaria zones. I rarely used mosquito nets or burned coils. But I campaigned vigorously against malaria nonetheless.

As a word of caution to others spending long periods in Africa: I also never wore sunglasses or used sunscreen. While my eyes are still in good condition, my skin has thinned and aged from decades of tropical sun exposure. I now regret not using lotion or taking better precautions.

18. I had a Fulani friend in Mali who told me in Bamako in 2017 that "When the extremists come to where you live and ask you to join them and offer you some money, a rifle, and a new motorbike, it is easy to say yes, especially when they tell you if you say 'no,' they will kill your family. What do you want done under those circumstances?"

19. I now struggle to recognize the African cities and towns I once knew so well more than 30 years ago. The pace of population growth across the continent has been staggering. When I began my African journey in Togo in 1970, the country had a population just over two million. Today, that same small nation—once dubbed the "Switzerland of West Africa" and seen as a future

regional trading hub—has a population exceeding nine million. Nearly half its citizens are under the age of 19, and the national population density has soared to 166 people per square kilometer. Togo is just one example among Africa's 54 nations experiencing similar demographic shifts.

Perhaps one reason I find myself less drawn to many places in Africa today compared to decades past is this rapid demographic transformation, especially the surge in urbanization. I've been told that some cities are expanding at rates as high as ten percent annually.

Back in 1990, I discussed these trends with a Togolese colleague who observed, "Yes, and this growing population strain is causing problems in every sector. The economy can't generate enough decent-paying jobs for all these people. And as rural residents move to the cities, fewer remain to grow food, which increases hunger. On top of that, urban poverty is fueling crime—people steal just to survive. The outlook for the next generation is grim, and now we have climate change compounding these already difficult challenges."

20. Castelli, a historic Italian restaurant in Addis Ababa, Ethiopia, traces its roots back to the period of Italian occupation from 1935 to 1941. Known for serving some of the finest Italian cuisine in the country, the family-run establishment remains a culinary landmark. I dined there both in 1985 and again in 2018. During my most recent visit, I mentioned to the waiter that I remembered a beautiful aquarium once adorning the dining room. He replied, "Oh, that was removed years ago because all the fish died, and no replacements could be found."

After our excellent meal, we concluded the evening with a traditional Ethiopian coffee ceremony. As we lifted the small porcelain cups to our lips, I was reminded that arabica coffee—now beloved around the world—originated in the Ethiopian highlands and remains a cherished part of the nation's culture.

I was not alone in 2018. Dining with me were my Ethiopian wife and our daughter. (My first wife, from Togo, I divorced in 1995. She sadly passed away in 2023. I met my current wife in Addis Ababa in 2011.)

21. I visited with my wife in 2018 the many museums in Addis Ababa, Ethiopia. I saw where the last emperor lived and was strangled to death in his bed by soldiers in 1975, thus ending a

royal dynasty that had lasted over 1,000 years. I also saw in one museum the skeletal remains of Lucy, one of the earliest humans that had been found in 1974 in the Awash Valley of eastern Ethiopia.

22. In 2011, I attended a meeting at Africa Hall in Addis Ababa, Ethiopia—the headquarters of the African Union (AU), which has convened leaders from across the continent for over fifty years. Lining the ceiling of the main auditorium are sculpted busts of the AU's founding fathers. I recall being tempted, half-jokingly, to sneak in at night and chisel out a few of them. It was a mischievous thought, but it reflected my genuine belief that some of those leaders did not deserve such honor.

Over the years, I have rarely been satisfied with the AU. Too often, it has appointed some of the continent's most controversial or ineffective presidents as its annual chairperson. This, along with several questionable decisions or glaring inaction, has eroded my confidence in the AU as an institution meant to drive meaningful progress for Africa.

23. In Accra, Ghana, there were practically no motorbikes on the streets. In neighboring Togo, the streets were gorged with motorbikes. I asked a Ghanaian why there were no motorbikes,

and he said, "The people here prefer taking a vehicle with four wheels and frown on using a two-wheeler. Often, they prefer to go by foot than take a motorbike."

24. In Luanda, Angola, in 2018, I looked out the window of my 14th-floor temporary apartment and eyed several glamorous skyscrapers in my neighborhood. But I did not understand why these skyscrapers and others in Luanda stood finished but empty. I asked one of my Angolan colleagues why these Chinese-constructed buildings were empty. She smiled and said, "There's money to be made in their building but not in their occupancy."

25. A few words about the Chinese ... they are everywhere in Africa now, but when I first came to Africa in 1970, there were no Chinese. Now, besides building skyscrapers all over Africa, everywhere you look in Africa, you can see Chinese-built dams, railroads, roads, bridges, airports, conference centers, and stadiums. I do not know how African countries will ever pay off their opaque Chinese loans for these infrastructure projects.

26. In 2018, while in Angola, I traveled to Dundo in the far northeast, near the border with the Democratic Republic of Congo, to visit some Angolan colleagues. Before departing from

the capital, Luanda, I phoned one of them to ask if he needed anything. His response was unexpected: "Bring me a shovel."

I did as he asked, though I was curious about the unusual request. When I arrived and handed him the shovel, I asked, "What's it for?"

He explained, "Everyone here digs for diamonds in the streambeds during their spare time. Some have even struck it rich."

That's when I learned just how diamond-rich this region is. Nearby was a large industrial diamond mine reportedly owned by the former president's daughter—a woman of Angolan and Russian descent who was said to be the richest woman in Africa. Her father, José Eduardo dos Santos, served as president of Angola for 38 years and was widely believed to be the largest landowner in Brazil.

27. This same woman had used her immense fortune to build a huge modern shopping mall in Luanda, the capital city of Angola. The mall was multi-storied, thus requiring the installation of long escalators. At each escalator, there were attendants standing at the tops and bottoms of them to instruct local people on how to use

the escalator. I noted that even with the placement of these attendants, many people's fear of the escalators made them take the stairs.

28. It was pleasant traveling overland in northeast Angola with my Angolan colleagues. We spoke in French instead of the national language, Portuguese, because, like many Angolans, their families had fled to the DRC during Angola's protracted civil war.

29. There were two Dundos ... the old and the new. The Chinese helped build the new Dundo, which was about a kilometer from the old Dundo. We visited a new, well-equipped hospital, but no patients and few health staff. I spied one Asian person working and asked what he was doing. The reply I got was that Angola has had for years an agreement with North Korea to provide physicians.

30. I went to a barbershop in Luanda to get a haircut from a barber who spoke French. While he was working on my hair, the man in the chair next to mine got into a heated argument with his barber. Suddenly, he stood up and left in frustration.

Curious, I asked my barber what the argument was about. He replied, "They were arguing about Angola's recent history. It's a difficult subject—no one really knows the full truth because the government keeps it hidden from us."

31. When I was in Accra, Ghana, in 2016, I noticed the unusual sight of young Ghanaian men wearing shorts. In the past, the only place you would see men wearing shorts was when doing cultivation work on their farms, on sports fields, or at a worksite. Traditionally, in spite of the hot climate, nobody wore shorts.

I asked someone who the men with shorts were, and the reply I got was, "Those are Ghanaians who have lived abroad. They are part of our large diaspora population."

32. In 2016, I would frequently sit in the shopping mall built by the South Africans in Accra, Ghana, and ask myself how Africans looked different from thirty or forty years ago. Sure, many had their cell phones, helping fill the large digital gap Africa has with the rest of the world.

I noted that one of the most significant changes for me was their dress. Gone, for the most part, were the colorful wrap-around skirts worn by women in the past. It used to be the custom for a woman to buy a yard or more of the colorful, decorated Dutch-wax print cloth than she needed to make a skirt and blouse for herself so she could also make a matching shirt for her husband. It was said if a woman really loved her husband, she would do this.

But there was something else that I had trouble pinpointing, and that was they were all educated. At that moment, I thought that the best any black African country could wish for was to be like Ghana. The majority of Ghanaians had been to school and knew how to read and write, and that made a huge difference.

33. In 2005, I rented a car and driver to drive me across Zimbabwe to see its second-largest city, the historic Bulawayo. This city is the regional capital of Matabeleland and was the center of a competing ethnic group, the Ndebele.

The Shona ethnic group, under the direction of Robert Mugabe, used Zimbabwean troops trained by the North Korean Army to massacre up to 20,000 Ndebele living in and around Bulawayo in the 1980s. For me, this terrible stain on the early years of Zimbabwean independence in 1980 is too often overlooked and is a forgotten genocidal pogrom.

34. I heard that the President of Zimbabwe, Robert Mugabe, recommended to other African presidents that to keep the people happy and quiet. They had to keep the price of mealie meal (white

maize flour) low. As this was the main food staple, this was understandable, but its underlying truth was painful.

35. I was impressed by how fast they built the AU conference center in Maputo, Mozambique, so I asked a Mozambiquan colleague how it was done so rapidly. His reply was simple, "Chinese prison laborers worked around the clock to build this center."

36. The center was completed in time for the annual AU summit. I attended the opening ceremonies. There was a delay in starting because they waited for one president who was running late. Then, all of a sudden, the President of Zimbabwe entered the large auditorium, and without apparent shame, he was given a standing ovation. I have always wondered how such a despicable person who had run his country into the ground could be honored in such a way. This incident made me think there was something I was missing in the African psyche.

37. In 1998, I spent six weeks at the historic and luxurious Hotel Meikles in central Harare, Zimbabwe (Zim), while leading a study on the potential impact of USAID's withdrawal from the country. Our team concluded that it was ill-advised to exit when the ship was sinking, especially since USAID was the sole supplier of birth

control pills at the time. Fortunately, Washington ultimately permitted USAID to continue its operations in Zimbabwe.

I remember a local physician on our team who also ran an AIDS prevention program. At the time, Zimbabwe was near the epicenter of the HIV/AIDS pandemic. He told me grimly, "There are too many deaths now. I only go back to my village for a funeral after there have been at least ten." He had conducted a survey among the highest-risk group—young people aged 18 to 22—and found that while they were well-informed about HIV/AIDS, their behavior remained unchanged. A common response was, "You have to die of something."

I replied, "I've encountered this kind of fatalism everywhere in Africa."

38. A white American woman was the head of Mozambique's national HIV/AIDS commission. She had been the spouse of the leader, Eduardo Mondlane, one of Mozambique's independence movements who had been killed many years earlier. She was celebrated as the 'Mother of Mozambique.'

I attended one of the regular meetings of her commission and she said loud and clear, "That the reason for Mozambique's high HIV adult prevalency rate was the high level of promiscuity."

39. I was heavily involved with HIV/AIDS at the onset of the pandemic when there was no medicine available for treating this deadly disease. I noted that people working in AIDS clinics did not last long because they got tired of seeing their patients shrivel up and die.

40. In the early years of Mugabe's administration, I saw in my Harare hotel an unforgettable TV broadcast in black and white. It was a live broadcast of the opening of Zim's new parliament. This TV program displayed Mugabe and the white leader of the opposition debating in a civil manner. I could not wait to get back to my post in West Africa to tell everyone that peace between blacks and whites was possible in Zim.

Analysts say that while Mugabe's first Ghanaian wife, Sally, was alive, she was able to suppress his more radical tendencies. With her death in 1992, he became increasingly radical, corrupt, and against white Zimbabweans.

41. In Maputo, Mozambique, I did like I had done in all the African countries and played tennis on the courts in the middle of the day when they were usually unoccupied. It was a scorching hot time of the day to play tennis, but I did not care as long as one of the ball boys wanted to play.

I recall one time in Maputo that it was so hot that even the red-headed rock agama lizards which dared darting out on the surface of the court died. I pointed this out to the ballboy, and he said in Portuguese, "If nothing else, that should tell us not to play at this time.

42. At the Sommerschield Clinic in Maputo, my youngest son was born on August 1, 2004. The clinic required that I pay a 1,000 USD cash advance. This baby was too large (10 pounds, 14 ounces) for normal delivery and had to be extracted by emergency cesarean surgery in the middle of the night. The clinic doubled its cost, and I had to get a cash advance from my office.

43. In the southern Casamance region of Senegal, the fight over the trade in cashews evolved into the traffic of illegal drugs from South America. It is believed that its southern neighboring country of Guinea-Bissau had become a narco-state.

44. I visited Nouakchott, Mauritania, in 2007, and I was taken aback by the discrimination displayed by Moors against Haratin. Another thing that became embedded in my memory is how they would fatten up young women so they would be more desirable for marriage. Evidently, corpulent women were in high demand for

marriage. These overweight women demanded a higher bride price from the groom's family.

45. I visited Lilongwe, Malawi, several times in the 1998 – 2003 period. As there was really no place to go at night in northern Lilongwe, I went to one bright spot in southern Lilongwe, which was a kilometer away. This was a restaurant owned and operated by an Italian man. I asked him why he was in Malawi, and he replied, "I came here to train Malawians in hotel management, but all my students died of AIDS, so I started this business."

One of the things his restaurant did was to make wooden signs portraying your carved name to hang on the wall. I paid the amount required for the sign and was pleased to see it still hanging on the wall of his restaurant when I visited there in 2011. I wonder if it is still hanging now on the wall (if this restaurant still exists).

46. In 2011, I rented a car to drive north of Lilongwe. After driving for a while, I observed a huge billboard with the words "24 Hour Coffin Service."

I turned around and spotted a small carpentry shop making simple coffins. I noted that the billboard took more lumber to build than the building of the shop did. I asked a man working in the cramped shop how his business was going, and he replied, "Never been better. AIDS has given us more than enough work."

47. I was told that the elderly first president of Côte d'Ivoire, Félix Houphouët-Boigny, did not know his exact age, though most accounts placed him in his nineties. He had lived to see the completion of the grand Catholic basilica in his hometown, Yamoussoukro—a project he regarded as the capstone of his life and reportedly felt ready to die afterward. As he wished, the basilica was constructed just slightly larger than St. Peter's Basilica in the Vatican. It has since been noted as the largest indoor air-conditioned space in Africa.

By the time of his death in 1993, Houphouët-Boigny was so frail that his hand had to be physically guided to sign official documents. He had served as president for an extraordinary 33 years.

This anecdote is just one of many I picked up during my more than thirty visits to my regional West Africa office in the picturesque capital city of Côte d'Ivoire.

48. A man could display his status by penning or tethering a highly regarded hoofed animal in front of his dwelling. In South Africa,

this was a bull. In Burkina Faso, it was a stallion. In their respective cultures, these were prestigious animals.

49. I have often been called an Afro-pessimist by those who can be classed in the Afro-optimist category. I always reply that I prefer to be tagged as an Afro-realist. I believed that there was no sense in sugar-coating Africa's development predicament.

50. I was satisfied with the assistance I gave to an initiative to introduce into western Niger donkey carts by borrowing technology from its southern neighboring country, Burkina Faso. The initial users of donkey carts to provide transport services found the carts very profitable.

After a few years, almost every household owned a donkey cart, and nobody made a profit from the donkey transport business.

51. I was in Burkina Faso in late 2016 to evaluate a cotton project that was taking place in this country, as well as Benin and Mali. I learned this project was the US' attempt to attenuate complaints from these countries received by the World Trade Organization (WTO) about the unfair trade practices caused by subsidies on US cotton. This reminded me of all the subsidies applied by the USG on American farm products.

I was also reminded of the hue and cry of many for more trade and not aid. I asked myself at the time, if a country had nothing to trade, does that mean it will not get aid? I remain skeptical of those demanding 'trade, not aid.'

52. In Burkina Faso, we developed an outstanding child nutrition proposal in 2014. It focused on a district known for consistently producing a crop surplus, yet children under five years old (U-5) in the area continued to suffer from malnutrition. This clearly indicated that the root cause was not a lack of food availability but rather a lack of knowledge about appropriate child feeding practices.

All the donors agreed that the proposal was excellent and that something needed to be done to tackle this critical issue. However, after more than a year of discussions, expressions of support, and promised funding, the initiative remained unfunded. The proposal was quietly added to the growing stack of unfulfilled good intentions. I ultimately attributed this disappointing outcome to what I call "donor fatigue."

53. I accept that sustainable progress requires strong national institutions. However, international institutions also have an important role to play. In my view, there are both strong and weak

entities within the UN system. Among the strongest humanitarian agencies, I would rank UNICEF (United Nations International Children's Emergency Fund) and the World Food Programme (WFP) at the top. As for the rest, I believe there is a compelling need to streamline and consolidate UN operations in developing countries to enhance efficiency and impact.

Perhaps one exception to this general proposition should be noted. If UN-led military forces are to continue playing a meaningful role in resolving violent conflicts, the UN should consider establishing a permanent standing force. This would be a significant improvement over the current system of negotiating troop contributions from member states for each peacekeeping or peacemaking mission.

54. Many Africans have reminded me that my reasoning is influenced because my 'context' is different than theirs. I was a white foreigner from a developed country, and they were black Africans from a poor country. I could go home anytime while their homes were in the poor countries where they were born. If I got sick, my government would take care of me, etc. Yes. My 'context' was very different, no matter how poor I lived. There was always a better exit for me, and in that, I was permanently separated from Africans.

55. I was walking at night from a restaurant to our hotel in Harare, Zimbabwe, with a group of expatriate colleagues in 2005. Suddenly, a young local man ran past us, snatching the purse of one of my colleagues. Without thinking, I ran after the thief, and he dropped the purse just as I was catching up with him. I walked back to my group and handed the purse to its owner, saying, "You may not be so lucky next time."

56. In my younger days, I was something of a free spirit and a daredevil. After almost drowning in an ocean riptide off the northern coast of Puerto Rico during my first Peace Corps Honduras training program, I was summoned by the training camp director. I thought for sure that I was going to be terminated and sent home.

He gave me a strong talking to, but he did not terminate me. He said in his judgment, "You are high risk but high gain."

Many years later, I was obliged to take the Meyers-Briggs personality test and was classed as an INFP. I asked myself if that was the personality of a 'high-risk, high-gain' individual.

57. I would often get American visitors in Africa. I noticed that these visitors had a hard time understanding what development in African countries entailed. I would frequently tell them that

they should visit an American Indian reservation in the US and figure out what needed to be done to improve the quality of life of people living on this reservation. I would say, "If we can't develop these reservations in one of the richest countries in the world, how are we going to improve living conditions for Africans?

58. In Niger in the early 1970s, all the so-called intellectuals and top professors at the national university belonged to a lowly regarded ethnic group, Bella. The Bella were the former slaves of the ruling ethnic group. I asked why this was so, and the answer I got was as follows:

"When the French colonists wanted every village chief's oldest son to be educated, the chiefs gave them one of their male slaves and said they were their biological offspring. Thus, the Bella came to represent Niger's first wave of educated people."

59. In Niger, the women's rotating credit and savings program proved to be a remarkable success. What began as small groups of women in rural villages quickly grew into a nationwide movement. For the first time, women on motorcycles were actively mobilizing their peers across remote areas. This initiative came to be known in the local Hausa language as Mata Musa Dubara (MMD)— loosely translated as "Women on the Move."

During my visits to many of these groups, I witnessed firsthand a troubling pattern: in some households, male heads began withdrawing their financial support for household expenses upon realizing their wives were earning income. As a result, the additional income generated by the women did not lead to greater financial autonomy or benefit within the household. This unintended consequence left both the women and program facilitators at a loss for a clear solution.

This experience reinforced two important lessons for me. First, one must always remain alert to unforeseen outcomes that can undermine even the most well-intentioned initiatives. Second, changing circumstances within the host country can complicate implementation and make it difficult to control or predict the outcomes of development activities.

60. My experience with MMD brought back memories of my first Peace Corps training program in 1976 in a local girls' secondary school, Lycée Kasai, in Niamey. The woman who ran this school told me that she was the first woman in Niamey to ride a bicycle.

I observed during my last visit to Niamey in 2014 that it was still rare to see a Nigerien woman on a two-wheeler. Usually, if you saw a woman driving a motorbike in Niger, she was from Burkina Faso.

61. I am still tormented by the premium placed on 'responsiveness' as a value. This value prompted me to react immediately to the extent possible to any development need or related bureaucratic need. It is only advanced age that has reduced the energy needed to address this value. But still, there is no time to lose in addressing human misery.

62. In 2014, I was attending a regional meeting in Conakry, Guinea, and staying at a modest motel run by a Lebanese family. Though the power was out and there was no air-conditioning—a comfort I rarely used—I managed to sleep fitfully. The next morning, as I prepared to join my colleagues for breakfast, a motel staff member informed me that the rest of my group had left during the night. The motel's generator had broken down, cutting off electricity and air-conditioning, prompting them to relocate to another hotel in Conakry where the meeting would now be held.

I soon realized I was the only member of the group who had remained. With help from the motel's front office, I was transferred to the new hotel. Initially, everything proceeded smoothly—until news broke that the hotel cook had died of Ebola.

Panic spread instantly among the attendees, and the meeting was abruptly canceled. There was a chaotic scramble to reach the airport as everyone rushed to return to their home countries.

I recalled this experience upon returning to the United States, when someone asked where I had spent most of my professional life. I replied simply, "Africa." Their immediate response was, "Oh, Ebola." It struck me how limited many Americans' understanding of Africa was—framed almost entirely by headlines about disease outbreaks. I tried to explain that Ebola had affected only a small portion of the continent. Still, I couldn't help but worry. Just as HIV/AIDS had once ravaged parts of Africa and shaped its global perception, I feared Ebola would not be the last deadly disease to emerge from the continent.

63. I learned about generational curses from a South African pastor who was visiting my house on Maputo in 2004. He noted that the walls of my living room displayed a number of African masks and said, "You should remove and destroy all those masks because they harbor evil spirits that can be passed on for generations, and the curse of one family member can be inherited by another."

I politely replied that we would consider what he said, but I had no intention of destroying my collection of African masks. His words did make me think of something I had heard a carver of masks say: "Our job is to release the spirit occupying the wood."

64. The biggest adjustment for me when moving to the US was America's gun culture. Also, the custom of giving and taking anything with your right hand in Africa was not applied in the US. At first, I was in a panic in fast-food drive-in eateries because you had to give your money and take your food with your left hand.

Annex A

Summary of Views on African Agriculture

In the preceding sections, I have shared observations on African agriculture—not only because of its critical role in the continent's development but also due to my own long-standing engagement in this vital sector. The magnitude of what must be done to improve agriculture on a broad scale is daunting. Perhaps one of the most pressing questions facing Africa's future is this: how can African agriculture be mobilized—and kept mobilized—to realize its immense potential?

Let there be no ambiguity about where I stand. Every proven method to restore and sustain soil health on the average African farm must be implemented to increase crop yields. However, even the most committed efforts to preserve and enhance soil fertility may not be sufficient to feed Africa's rapidly growing and youthful population. Multiple complex factors are involved, but one truth looms large: "A rising standard of living cannot be built on a falling level of soil fertility."

After fifty years of working closely with African agriculture, I have come to a sobering conclusion: reversing the widespread decline in soil fertility across the continent may be beyond reach. African soils are, in general, more fragile and more difficult to amend than those found elsewhere in the world. Moreover, the extent of land degradation is often underreported, despite being severe and far-reaching.

Population growth and rising population densities demand a shift from extensive to intensive agricultural systems. Yet this transition is frequently blocked by a range of persistent challenges: the aging of the farming population, limited labor availability, insecure land tenure that discourages long-term investment, and lack of access to irrigation or water control infrastructure. Cultural norms that prioritize leisure time or alternative work opportunities further complicate the adoption of intensive farming methods.

The price of key food staples and cash crops in African markets often fails to provide sufficient incentive for farmers to increase production. Without the appropriate, affordable, and timely delivery of chemical fertilizers, food crop yields in Africa will continue to lag far behind those in other regions of the world.

Unlike other continents, Africa has yet to experience a true agricultural productivity transition.

After half a century working with agriculture in Africa, I cannot claim to have all the answers needed to resolve these persistent and critical challenges. What I do know is that, on paper, Africa holds the potential not only to feed its own population but also to contribute meaningfully to the global food supply.

Many African economies rely heavily on the export of cash crops or mineral resources to international markets. This raises pressing questions: How long can these countries sustain such dependence? How should the revenues generated from these exports be strategically invested to prepare for a future in which such income may decline or disappear altogether? And perhaps most urgently—has the opportunity already passed to craft a long-term investment strategy that addresses these realities while also supporting increased food crop yields?

The development path for a primarily agrarian society is especially difficult when much of the rural population remains engaged in subsistence farming and levels of literacy remain low. On top of this, the average family farm must contend with a high burden of disease and widespread nutritional deficiencies—both of which limit the productivity of the available labor force.

Climate change is compounding these issues, contributing to more frequent and severe droughts and floods, and accelerating the spread of crop pests. These troubling developments are steadily undermining the productivity of family-run farms across the continent and encouraging rural laborers to migrate to urban centers or seek opportunities abroad.

Africa's rural landscape is undergoing a profound and unsettling transformation. The future awaiting the next rural generation must be anticipated with accuracy, and clear, pragmatic approaches must be developed now to begin addressing the agricultural challenges that lie ahead.

ANNEX B

POINTS TO CONSIDER WHEN ELABORATING A

FOOD, AGRICULTURE AND NUTRITIoN STRATEGY FOR AFRICA

Based on over fifty years of first-hand, relevant experience in Africa, I offer for consideration forty points that should be taken into account when developing a Food, Agriculture, and Nutrition (FAN) strategy for Sub-Saharan African countries. I believe any such strategy must encompass at least five broad, yet interrelated, components:

(a) agricultural productivity and nutrition;

(b) trade and markets;

(c) the natural resource environment;

(d) humanitarian and development food aid; and

(e) policy and advocacy.

Elaborating on these components requires grappling with a complex web of interconnected issues while also keeping pace with an ever-changing global landscape. In an effort to stimulate meaningful discussion on this multifaceted topic, I present what I call forty statements on the hard "realities" of making sustainable agriculture work in Africa.

I welcome your review of these forty statements. If you feel I have strayed from the truth, I encourage you to say so. It may also be worth reflecting on which African countries currently measure up when viewed through the lens of these pointed and, at times, provocative observations. Please feel free to add to or subtract from this list. Constructive disagreement is both expected and encouraged.

Without a doubt, there is much more to consider than what is captured in these forty points. Nonetheless, I hope the lessons and reflections I share here will offer food for thought and spark lively and productive dialogue.

After all these years on the continent, I continue to search for answers. My sincere hope is that this presentation contributes to a deeper understanding of what it truly takes to get agriculture moving—and to keep it moving forward—in Africa.

FORTY STATEMENTS FOR CONSIDERATION

1. You cannot build a rising standard of living on a falling level of soil fertility.

2. For poverty reduction to be durable, it has to be market-driven. (Household resiliency depends on a durable reduction in poverty.)

3. Without good governance, the conditions needed for the development process to succeed and sustain itself are absent.

4. Inadequate nutritional levels render null many other development efforts.

5. Sound environmental and conservation practices are needed now to preserve soils and the livelihoods of future generations.

6. Climate change is a fact, and we need to come to grips with how this affects current and future food security scenarios.

7. Changing demographics, especially rapid urbanization, the youthful structure of Africa's population, high fertility rates, and changing dependency ratios, require that we seek new food security models for Africa of the future.

8. If Africa is to close the food gap, it must take full and quick advantage of the latest scientific and technological advances.

9. Communities hard hit by Ebola and HIV/AIDS will need to adopt new types of farming systems and community care mechanisms.

10. The largest and best-untapped investment in Africa is related to doing very basic things that raise crop yields and fully employing the resources provided by women.

11. One of the best ways to increase crop production in Africa is to increase the amount of land under irrigation.

12. Crop yields in Africa will remain much lower than in other regions as long as the use of essential inputs remains much lower. Africa is still waiting for a productivity transition to higher yields experienced by other regions in the world.

13. It is hard to accept the fact that for some areas and countries, there are not any viable development models available that are capable of creating wealth.

14. Africa continues to fail by a large measure to satisfy the essential development litmus test of creating enough jobs that pay a livable wage.

15. Much of Africa has been left out of 'globalization' and, therefore, local factors will often remain more important in Africa than international ones.

16. Increased crop diversification and exports are key food security elements that are far from being achieved in Africa.

17. Eight out of ten African farmers are women; therefore, as long as women are not able to get ahead, it is hard to move agriculture ahead.

18. Africa's special soil, water resources, and climate limitations, as well as its environmental fragility, need to be taken fully into account when trying to achieve a Green Revolution on the continent.

19. Weak governance, excessive corruption, low institutional capacities, and low literacy levels in many African countries compromise the achievement of sustainable rural livelihoods.

20. Poor and worsening health conditions in Africa undermine agricultural productivity.

21. The land tenure mess and the predominant reliance on hand tools to cultivate in Africa make modern agricultural development impossible.

22. Experience indicates that people will usually only move from extensive to intensive agriculture when population densities reach a point where they have no other choice.

23. Many populations in Africa are already dependent on food aid, and reducing this dependency will be a monumental challenge.

24. With constant increases in world food market prices and crises, there will be an increased need for food aid, especially if more attention is not paid to increasing local food production.

25. Declining food production in the rural areas of Africa contributes heavily to outmigration to towns and cities, thereby contributing to rapid urbanization.

26. As long as there is not a rise in the percentage of low birth weights (less than 2.5 kilograms), it will be hard to break the vicious 'recycling of poverty' paradigm."

27. Subtract at least 20 percent from annual productivity levels as long as malaria continues infecting and killing as many people as it does.

28. Add 20 to 30 percent to investment costs because of rising crime and insecurity in many areas of Africa.

29. Poor infrastructure and the landlocked position of many African countries add 30 percent to investment costs.

30. Without electric power, it is much harder to move agriculture forward and engage in agribusinesses.

31. You cannot talk about sustainable development as long as households are without safety nets.

32. The advance of globalization in Africa will mean that African smallholder farmers will have to become much more competitive in the marketplace.

33. Without increases in agricultural productivity and household incomes, poverty will continue to persist and rise in Africa.

34. Pursuing agricultural development in fragile, failing, or failed states is something akin to mission impossible.

35. Consistent low investment (less than 10 to 15 percent) of the national budget in agriculture by national governments increases the failure of agriculture over the longer term, especially as most African countries depend on rainfed agriculture and there is only one planting season a year.

36. Saving the livelihoods of Africa's small-holder farmers is dependent on raising crop yields, and this requires preventing soil and environmental degradation.

37. More robust and drought-resistant crop varieties are needed in Africa to reverse the 40-year decline in per capita food production.

38. While all-natural means to improve soil fertility and structure should be consistently employed, only the increased use of chemical fertilizer will result in the kind of food production increases that Africa needs.

39. Careful orchestration of progressive land redistribution and resettlement programs, as well as the division of land use between pastoralists and farmers, will be needed in many areas of Africa to raise food production levels and prevent conflict.

40. Similarly, good planning of access to and control over water resources for irrigation purposes will be needed to prevent conflict and to achieve increased crop production.

ANNEX C

THREE POEMS DEDICATED TO AFRICA

Ode to Fufu

I eat fufu. Do you eat fufu?

No, I like my yams soft-boiled, and you?

I like my yams fried crispy. What about you?

I like my yams pounded into fufu

Do you eat fufu like I always do?

No, I cannot pound yams every day like you

You need a mortar, pestle, and wife

Indeed, I need a wife in my life

So I can eat much fufu like you

My Love is Gone

My love, wait for me here, I will not be long

Please stay here; I need your sweet song

I found the man I had to meet in a shop

He was eating some greasy chop

He told me to sit down while he ate a rack

Much later, he finished his juicy stack

I told him of my love and gave him my sweet smile

He pointed to bills on the shiny floor tile

I grabbed the sum and ran to my girl in town

Woe is me, she was not around

Everyone I asked said she had gone away

My love broke her promise to stay

I cried as I looked for her all the long day

Africa Home

Why go to USA? Why go to France?

When Africa is the best place to dance

You are happy and with family here

Here you were born, and we love when you're near

Please stay with us. Why go so far away?

Life is fine, and your family begs you to stay

Why leave us and go live where no one cares?

Why be a stranger and get many stares?

Please do not break up now our jolly band

Nowhere is better than your African land

Do not make us shed even a single tear

Make us happy by seeing you always here

ANNEX D

SYLLABUS

INTRODUCTORY COURSE

INTERNATIONAL DEVELOPMENT

Instructor: Mark G. Wentling

Date: July 10, 2015

COURSE GOAL: Provide a solid understanding of international development concepts, challenges, trends, policies, and practices, as well as a good grasp of the effectiveness of foreign aid in achieving poverty reduction.

COURSE OVERVIEW: This course contributes to satisfying Texas Tech University's core curriculum requirement in the Humanities. The objective of requiring Humanities in a core curriculum is to expand and enrich the student's knowledge of the human quality of life conditions and cultural values that impinge on developmental progress.

428

Pursuing this objective also entails giving serious consideration to how behaviors, ideas, imagination, and thoughts influence the development process and the human condition. A multi-disciplinary course of study in a broad range of key areas will enable students to increase their engagement in critical thinking about the state of world development.

A keen appreciation of the Humanities is fundamental to the well-being and advancement of any society. All students graduating from Texas Tech University need to be able to think critically and demonstrate a good understanding of multiple interpretations of similar situations. They must also be able to readily grasp differences of opinion caused by varying cultural contexts, belief systems, and values.

EXPECTED LEARNING OUTCOMES: This course is designed to provide students with a solid foundation in understanding the key elements that influence the social and economic development of countries. Through an in-depth examination, students will explore why some nations have reached advanced stages of development while others have not.

The course will analyze the critical factors that distinguish high-income countries from low-income ones. Pursuing the course objectives will involve studying the processes of poverty alleviation and the promotion of sustainable economic and social growth.

Students who successfully complete this course will gain a comprehensive and coherent understanding of both historical and contemporary economic, political, and social dimensions of development practice.

The knowledge acquired in this course will be particularly valuable to students interested in careers in international development, global business, diplomacy, intelligence, or further studies in international affairs.

Upon completion of the course, students will be able to:

- Express a firm understanding of the pre-conditions of development
- Explain why some countries have advanced and others haven't
- Articulate a clear awareness of key development issues

- Describe key factors that promote and impede the 'development process'
- Demonstrate a specialized knowledge of one or more developing countries and what is required to enable them to achieve a higher stage of development.

The student will also have a good appreciation of the specific development challenges facing low-income countries and the role of external aid from high-income countries and multi-lateral organizations in assisting with the acceleration of the development process, as well as the role of local organizations. Also addressed will be the role of private foreign investment, Non-Governmental (international and local), and charitable organizations in supporting the development process. The student will also be able to distinguish between humanitarian and development assistance.

METHODS FOR ASSESSING EXPECTED LEARNING OUTCOMES:

Student performance will be based on class participation, a special project paper as described below, a research paper on a selected development topic (combined with its class presentation); and a comprehensive final exam.

COURSE CONTENT AND OBJECTIVES: Most people are unaware of the complexities and interconnections that define the fields of international development and poverty reduction. The stark contrast between life in the United States and in many other parts of the world is often difficult to comprehend. For instance, an amenity as basic as a washing machine—taken for granted by most Americans—may be unimaginable for individuals in developing countries who struggle daily to meet their basic needs. At the same time, even in one of the world's wealthiest nations, inequality persists, and the gap between rich and poor remains significant.

This course aims to examine why some countries have successfully improved the quality of life for their citizens while others have fallen behind. The central objective is to explore the root causes behind these differing outcomes and to assess the types of interventions and policies that can support developmental progress in countries that are not yet reaching their full potential.

A number of important and diverse factors underpinning the development process will be covered. These include:

Peace And Stability Natural Resource Endowment

Geographical Location   Nutritional Levels

Demographic Factors Health And Sanitation Conditions

National Leadership And Managerial Competence Educational Attainment

Natural Disasters   Environmental Impacts/Climate Change

Historical Legacies and Level Of Social Cohesion Gender Equity

Infrastructure Constraints   Cultural Values And Religious Beliefs

Governance, Corruption, And Human Rights   World Market Access

Food Security

New Technologies And Information

CORE CURRICULUM REQUIREMENTS: This course fulfills the "Multicultural" and "Social and Behavioral Sciences" core curriculum requirements. As outlined in Texas Tech University's educational objectives, students are expected to think critically, consider multiple interpretations of similar issues, and articulate differences shaped by diverse cultural contexts and values. The instructional approach emphasizes real-world development practice and the application of contemporary knowledge about global development assistance trends. By examining the complex social, economic, and political challenges faced by countries across

433

the globe, the course provides an inherently multicultural learning experience that deepens students' understanding of international development dynamics.

COURSE EXPECTATIONS AND GRADING: Most learning will occur during the demanding class discussions on key international development topics; therefore, consistent attendance and active participation are essential.

IMPORTANCE OF ACTIVE CLASS PARTICIPATION: Students are required to attend all class sessions, arrive on time, and have read all items on the reading list for that day. Given that there are only fourteen or fifteen class sessions, any absences will be detrimental to your grade. If you miss three or more classes, you will not earn an "A" (unless exceptional circumstances can be documented). Class attendance will be closely monitored. Participating constructively in each class will boost your final grade. Participation will be judged by quality, not quantity; an insightful comment or question based on the readings will count more than numerous ill-informed comments. Key topics to be presented and discussed in each class will be announced in advance.

FINAL EXAM: The main aim of the final exam is to test the student's understanding of the key points stressed in the readings and the lectures. This exam will contain a series of questions that require the student to respond by writing succinct, accurate, and complete responses.

PROJECT PAPER: A list of the 42 least developed countries (37 in Africa) will be provided to you during the first class session. You will be asked to select one country for in-depth study. Your project paper will involve elaborating in 20 pages (single-spaced) or less a development plan for your selected country. A basic outline to follow in drafting your paper will be provided. For discussion purposes, a selection of papers will be presented to the class. (Note. You cannot choose a country in which you have lived or worked.)

RESEARCH PAPER: Identify key development assistance issues and write up to 10 pages (single-spaced) describing the pros and cons of this issue. This should be an issue of keen interest to you. Part of this exercise will involve giving a 10-minute presentation of the issue you have researched. Each presentation will be followed by a brief classroom discussion.

REQUIRED TEXTS:

Why Nations Fail: The Origins of Power, Prosperity and Poverty by Damon Acemoglu and James A. Robinson (2012)

African Development: Making Sense of the Issues and Actors by Todd J. Moss (2012)

Dead Aid: Why Aid is Not Working and How there is Another Way for Africa by Dambisa Moyo (2009)

USEFUL SECONDARY REFERENCES

The Idealist: Jeffrey Sachs and the Quest to End Poverty by Nina Munk (2013)

The Bottom Billion: Why the Poorest Countries are Failing and What Can Be Done about It by Paul Collins (2007)

The White Man's Burden: Why the West's Efforts to Aid the Rest Have Done So Much Harm and So Little Good, by William Easterly (2006)

The End of Poverty by Jeffrey Sachs (2005)

Collapse: How Societies Choose to Fail or Succeed, by Jared Diamond (2005)

Culture Matters: How Values Shape Human Progress by Lawrence E. Harrison and Samuel P. Hutchinson (1999)

The Greening of Africa - Breaking Through the Battle for Land and Food by Paul Harrison (1988)

Dissent in Development by Peter Bauer (1972)

Reports and Information Sources:

In addition to the sources noted below, a regular reading of pertinent articles in the New York Times, Washington Post, The Financial Times, The Wall Street Journal, and The Economist will be useful. Consulting regularly in the following can also be rewarding.

World Bank Annual Development Reports

IMF Annual Reports

UNDP Annual Human Development Reports

World Food Program (WFP) Annual Reports

Food and Agriculture Organization (FAO) Annual Reports

UNICEF Annual Report on the State of Children

UN Millennium Development Goals – Progress Reports

Organization for Economic Co-Operation Reports

Economist Intelligence Unit Country Reports

Department of State and USAID Country Strategy Papers

U.S. Department of State and USAID Annual Performance Reports

U.S. Department of State Bilateral Relations Fact Sheets

CIA World Fact Book

U.S. Foreign Assistance Annual Funding Requests: Congressional Budget Justifications

OXFAM International Position Papers: Freedom House, Annual World Freedom Reports

Transparency International Annual Corruption Perception Reports

World Bank Annual Doing Business Reports

Annual Fragile State Index

Index of Economic Freedom

Freedom House Indicators

World Bank Governance and Doing Business Indicators

World Economic Forum Global Business Report

Instructor's Papers and Books, as appropriate

<u>Useful Websites:</u>

Global Center for Development — Economist
Magazine

American Diplomacy — Foreign
Affairs

Foreign Policy — Chris
Blattman Blog

William Easterly Blog — Duncan

Green Blog: Power and Poverty

International Crisis Group

International Jobs Alert

RECOMMENDED ADDITIONAL READING LIST

China's Second Continent: How a Million Migrants are Building a New Empire in Africa by Howard French (2015)

Tyranny of Experts: Economists, Dictators, and the Forgotten Rights of the Poor by William Easterly (2014)

Nigeria: Dancing on the Brink by John Campbell (2013)

Dancing in the Glory of Monsters: The Collapse of the Congo and the Great War in Africa by Jason Stearns (2012)

More than Good Intentions: Improving the Ways the World's Poor Borrow, Save, Farm. Learn and Stay Healthy by Dean Karlan and Jacob Appel (2012)

The Modernity Bluff: Crime, Consumption and Citizenship in Cote d'Ivoire by Sasha Newell (2012)

Poor Economics: A Radical Rethinking of the Way to Fight Global Poverty by A.V. Banerjee and Ester Duflo (2011)

Famine and Foreigners: Ethiopia Since Live Aid by Peter Gill (2010)

The Shackled Continent: Power, Corruption and African Lives by Robert Guest (2010)

It's Our Time to Eat: The Story of a Kenyan Whistleblower by Michela Wrong (2010)

A Farewell to Alms: A Brief Economic History of the World by Gregory Clark (2009)

Poisonwood Bible by Barbara Kingsolver (2008)

Central Liberal Truth: How Politics Can Change a Culture and Save It by Lawrence E, Harrison (2006)

The Fortune at the Bottom of the Pyramid: Eradicating Poverty Through Profits by P.K. Prahalad (2006)

Confessions of an Economic Hitman by John Perkins (2005)

The Elusive Quest for Growth: Economists' Adventures and Misadventures in the Tropics by William Easterly (2002)

Another Day of Life by Ryszard Kapuscinki and William R. Brand (2001)

Wealth and Poverty of Nations: Why Some are So Poor and Some So Rich by David S. Landes (1999)

King Leopold's Ghost: A Story of Greed, Terror and Heroism in Colonial Africa by Adam Hochschild (1999)

Africa in Chaos by George B.N. Ayittey (1999)

The Hot Zone: The Terrifying True Story About the Origins of the Ebola Virus by Richard Preston (1995)

Good Man in Africa by William Boyd (1981). Movie: 1994

The Rich Nations and Poor Nations by Barbara Ward (1962)

Mr. Johnson by Joyce Cary (1951). Movie: 1991

ANNEX E

ARTICLES & BOOKS PUBLISHED
by the AUTHOR

Articles Published in the Monthly Foreign Service Journal:

"Losing Hope for Africa," September 1, 2022.

"Redesigning U.S. Assistance to Africa," March 2020.

"Slaughter South of the Sahara: No Scope for Business as Usual," November 2020.

"Notes to the New Administration," December 2020.

"Remembering 1989: Berlin Wall Stories," November 2019.

"Africa Hunger: Up-Close and Personal," January 2018.

"Making Aid Work by Building Strong Institutions," January-February 2017.

"*The Great Surge: The Ascent of the Developing World*," Review of book by Steven Radelet, July-August 2016.

"Africa's Great Hunger Handicap," September 2016.

"Assisting Refugees in Africa," March 2013.

"Togo Today and in 1970," October 2013.

"Born in Kansas, Made in Africa," January 2012.

"The Grand Syli's Funeral," February 2011.

"My 40 Years in Africa: Still Searching for Answers," May 2012.

"First Christmas in Africa," September 2004.

"My 30 Years in Africa: Still Searching for Answers," May 2002.

Articles Published in the American Diplomacy Online Quarterly Journal;

"Labor Migration, Remittances and Development Assistance," August 1, 2024.

"Tough Love and the Diplomacy of Foreign Assistance," May 1, 2024.

"Coming to Grips with Poverty in Africa, May 1, 2023.

"Restructuring our Assistance in Least Developed Countries, August 1, 2022

"Democracy in Africa is Like a Flashlight without Batteries," May 1, 2022.

"Time to Rethink Development Assistance in the Sahel," May 1, 2021.

"Redesigning U.S. Assistance to Africa in the Post-Pandemic Era," November 2021.

"Trauma in Togo," February 2020.

"Grim Week in Guinea," May 2020.

"Living with Africa for a Lifetime," August 2020.

"Final Tribute to My Ambassadors," January 2016.

"Africa's Great Hunger Handicap," October 2016.

"Cacao cum Cocoa," chapter 16 from *Africa's Heart: The Journey Ends in Kansas*, March 2014.

"Reluctantly Remembering Somalia," three parts, November 2011 to January 2012.

Published in the CARE Newsletter:

"Beating Poverty in Mozambique with a Few Bags More," May 2002.

"RBA: Gender and Diversity: Moving from Theory to Practice in a Meaningful Way, May 2002.

"Coping with Climate Change on the Edge of the Sahara, A Day in Olelewa, Niger," March 2001.

"Reducing Poverty a Few Cents at a Time," May 2001.

"MMD Approach for Empowering Women," June 2001.

Other Articles Widely Disseminated:

"First PCV in Nueva Ocotepeque, Honduras, Amigos de Honduras, August 1, 2022

"Book Review of *Dead Aid* by Dambisa Moyo, February 2021.

"My Dream for Africa," May 2020.

"Lost for a Lifetime," July 2019.

"Transport and Trade Barriers to Development," April 2017.

"40 Theses, 40 Years," December 2014.

"Eight Key Reasons Why Grants Are Lost," December 2014.

"45 Years in the Making – My First Peace Corps Story," September 2011.

"Agouti – A Success 30 Years in the Making," December 2011.

"Agadez Sultan and Islam in Northern Niger," January 2007.

"A Post-Crisis Strategy for Niger, On the Edge of Survival: Searching for a Better Way Forward by Transforming Rural Households," September 2005.

"El Dorado 50th Class Reunion," July 2003.

"A Brief History of Our Mom and Her Side of the Family, September 2003.

"Central African Briar Patch: Shifting the Balance of Power Amid a Tangle of Ambitions, Interests, Fear and Hatreds," August 1997.

"A Brief History of the Ewes: 1400 – 1720," March 1988.

Note. The above does not include the dozens of papers I wrote for my employers or during academic pursuits. And, it does not include the speech I gave at my induction ceremony into Wichita State University's Fairmount College Liberal Arts and Sciences on February 4, 2025. Also, the above also does not include the articles I wrote to promote my twelve published books listed below (all available on Amazon.com.).

Books

African Trilogy: Peace Corps Writers

Africa's Embrace, September 17, 2013, ISBN 13: 978-149271243 (336 pages)

Africa's Release, The Journey Continues, May 15, 2014, ISBN 13:978193926446 (222 pages)

Africa's Heart, The Journey Ends in Kansas, February 4, 2015, ISBN 13: 978925552 (522 pages)

Dead Cow Road, Life on the Front Lines of an International Crisis, March 30, 2017, ISBN 13: 978-1-63568-496-9 (510 pages), Page Publishing

Blue Country, August 13, 2019, ISBN 13: 978-1-64544-104-5 (204 pages), Page Publishing

Africa Memoir, 50 Years, 54 Countries, One American Life, Three Volumes, Open Books

Volume I, Algeria – Liberia, August 24, 2020, ISBN 13: 978-194859385 (232 pages)

Volume II, Libya - Senegal, November 5, 2020, ISBN 13: 978-194859392 (238 pages)

Volume III, Seychelles – Zimbabwe, and Epilogue, December 17, 2020, ISBN:

13:          978-1948598408   (251   pages)

Kansas Kaleidoscope, August 10, 2022, ISBN 13:978-1957864297, (186 pages), Wild Lark Books, Lubbock, Texas

Jackleg Boys, August 29, 2024. ISBN 9781837942374, (506 pages), Pegasus Publishers – Vanguard Press, London, United Kingdom

Falling Seven Times, August 30, 2014. ISBN 9781665763219 (305 pages), Archway Publishing, Bloomington. Indiana

Born in Kansas but Made in Africa, to be published in June by Amazon KDP

Breaks from Reality, full manuscript completed, May 2025

www.ingramcontent.com/pod-product-compliance
Lightning Source LLC
Chambersburg PA
CBHW051129120626
46547CB00012B/730